Organizational Creative Capabilities

Organizational Creativity Set

coordinated by
Guy Parmentier

Volume 1

Organizational Creative Capabilities

Management Factors, Processes and Devices

Edited by

Guy Parmentier

iSTE

WILEY

First published 2024 in Great Britain and the United States by ISTE Ltd and John Wiley & Sons, Inc.

ISTE Ltd
27-37 St George's Road
London SW19 4EU
UK

www.iste.co.uk

John Wiley & Sons, Inc.
111 River Street
Hoboken, NJ 07030
USA

www.wiley.com

Library of Congress Control Number: 2023947062

British Library Cataloguing-in-Publication Data
A CIP record for this book is available from the British Library
ISBN 978-1-78630-812-2

Contents

Foreword

Creativity management has become a priority for companies today. Since the 1990s, work in the field of management has recognized the collective nature of creativity and the importance of the organization of new ideas conceived as complex socio-cognitive processes that must be managed. Progressively, companies have equipped themselves with tools and methods to support the ideation process, from the emergence phase of new ideas to the "landing" phases within the organizational structures of ideas that have reached the stage of maturation. However, as the introductory chapter to this book clearly points out, research on organizational creativity has so far developed in parallel and without any precise link to fundamental reflections on strategic management and organizational business models.

Hence, the originality and the major contribution of this collective work concerns the consideration of organizational creativity as located at the heart of the strategic management of organizations. By considering that organizational creative capability is "the ability, using processes and routines, to generate, select and integrate new, appropriate, and useful ideas and solutions to improve, change and renew an organization's processes and outputs, as well as the organization itself", this book contributes to filling an important gap in the management literature. Taking a clear stand against the view of Napier and Nilsson (2006), who equate creative capabilities with dynamic capabilities of an organization, the book convincingly argues that creative and dynamic capabilities are two distinct types of organizational capabilities. More specifically, in the first chapter of this book, Guy Parmentier argues that creative and dynamic capabilities can be complementary, and that creative capability could form part of dynamic capabilities by providing the ideas necessary for organizational evolution and renewal. This point is essential, because in the now classic conception of dynamic capabilities given by Teece (2007), each of the firm's dynamic capabilities (sensing, seizing or reconfiguring) refers to the notion of ideas: sensing refers to the firm's ability to capture external ideas in order to create value; seizing translates the firm's ability to select and develop ideas that are aligned with the organization's common vision; as for reconfiguring, it refers to the company's ability to reconfigure the company's tangible and intangible assets according to the ideas it receives. Creative and dynamic capabilities thus appear to be closely complementary, confirming one of the major contributions of the book.

The different chapters of this book offer the opportunity to analyze in depth the organizational processes of creative capabilities and the organizational factors that act at all levels of the organization to foster the development of creative processes.

The analysis of the organizational routines of creative capabilities (the opening of the boundaries of the organization to nourish the process of creativity, the possibility of leaving "creative slack", the arrangement of spaces favorable to the deployment of creativity, the implementation of systems for evaluating ideas, etc.), which is presented in several chapters of this book, underlines the complexity and richness of the creative process. This analysis also shows that the phase concerning the emergence of ideas, on which many managers focus (through the use of many tools to generate creative ideas), is a necessary, yet insufficient condition for the development of a creative process. Idea management is a long, complex and highly strategic process. After the creative "spark" (the generation of the idea), the path to follow aims to mature, question, enrich and validate the ideas. Cummings et al. (2015) designate this path by the term creativitying (the creativity integrated into the action corresponding to the sequence of actions going beyond the generation of the idea). This conversion of the idea requires an investment of time, resources and effort, in order to clearly identify, actualize and extract the potential value of the idea. Mastering this conversion phase gives the organization a significant competitive advantage. As several of the contributions in this book point out, this control, which is an essential strategic capacity of the organization, is based on internal procedures and specific leadership, and cannot be delegated to external partners.

In these organizational routines of creativity, many of the authors of the book emphasize the active and central role of various "knowledge communities". These communities share, question and assemble elements of knowledge around a common object of interest, whether it is a practice, an emerging paradigm or the construction of a new framework of understanding in a creative field. They are one of the main cogs in the socialization process within the company. As Boland and Tenkasi remind us:

> Organizations are characterized by a process of distributed cognition in which multiple communities of specialized knowledge workers, each dealing with a part of an overall organizational problem, interact to create the patterns of sense making and behavior displayed by the organization as a whole (Boland and Tenkasi 1995, p. 351).

These communities act as an active repository of cognitive and practical resources that fuel not only the exploration capabilities of the company, but also its exploitation activities. The members of these communities often have both one foot in the cognitive construction of new ideas and the other in the company's innovative projects. They are then in the best possible position to trace the (exploratory) ideation processes with the elements of knowledge acquired in the (operational) processes of the projects. These communities also compensate for the possible local limitation of resources by connecting to other external knowledge communities from where they can import relevant elements to enrich their creative explorations and conversion of ideas. They represent much more than just a passive repository of knowledge. Rather, they act as an active device for exploring, exploiting and renewing the "creative slack" that influences the organization's strategic innovation pathways.

Another important contribution of this book is the careful examination of the organizational factors that favor the development of creative processes. These different factors (organizational climate, autonomy, organizational structure, encouragement and incentives, shared vision, etc.) constitute the "fertile ground" that allows creative processes to take shape and develop. In this line of argument, the book highlights the importance of an "organic structure" of the firm, which is based on continuous interactions between the formal structures of the firm and the informal structures (communities) that allow the circulation and enrichment of ideas. According to Burn and Stalker (2011), such an organic form is appropriate for changing conditions, which constantly give rise to new problems and unforeseen requirements for action that cannot be decomposed or distributed automatically from the functional roles defined in a hierarchical structure. In such an organic form of the firm, the implementation of devices, allowing for the enrichment of ideas as they circulate between the informal structures of the firm and the formal structures, is akin to the design of an internal middleground (Cohendet et al. 2010), composed of places that encourage exchanges, projects that allow communities to interact, events (such as hackathons, ideation days, etc.) that allow new creative ideas to be revealed, and the staging of a common vision (cognitive space).

By placing organizational creativity at the heart of the strategic management of organizations, and analyzing in depth both the organizational processes of creative capabilities and the organizational factors that promote the development of creative processes, this book makes a valuable contribution to the theory and practice of organizations, and provides essential insights for the development and enhancement of creative ideas in innovation processes.

Patrick COHENDET
Professor at HEC Montréal

References

Boland, R.J., Jr., and Tenkasi, R.V. (1995). Perspective making and perspective taking in communities of knowing. *Organization Science*, 6(4), 350–372.

Cohendet, P., Grandadam, D., Simon, L. (2010). The anatomy of the creative city. *Industry and Innovation*, 17(1), 91–111.

Napier, N.K. and Nilsson, M. (2006). The development of creative capabilities in and out of creative organizations: Three case studies. *Creativity and Innovation Management*, 15(3), 268–278.

Teece, D.J. (2007). Explicating dynamic capabilities: The nature and microfoundations of (sustainable) enterprise performance. *Strategic Management Journal*, 28(13), 1319–1350.

Author Biographies

Florence Jeannot is a marketing professor at INSEEC/CERAG Grande École, France. She is a graduate of ESCP and has a doctorate in management science. Her research focuses on the contribution of marketing during the development, pre-test and launch phases of new products, three key stages of the innovation process. It is based on a hypothetical-deductive approach and mainly uses experimental methods and causal modeling via structural equations. These works refer to theories from research in cognitive and social psychology, which have been published in peer-reviewed journals such as *Journal of Business Research*, *Journal of Marketing Management*, *Recherche et applications en marketing*, *Revue française de gestion*, *Systèmes d'information et management*, etc.

Séverine Le Loarne-Lemaire is a professor at Grenoble École de Management, France, where she teaches strategic management and the place of innovation in the formation of corporate strategy to a wide range of audiences (in France, and also in Asia and North America, in initial and continuing education programs). Her research focuses on gender identity and social identity of the creative person: their posture and ability to put forward their creative ideas and to exploit them in an intrapreneurial or entrepreneurial process. Her work has been published in multiple research journals (*Journal of Business Research*, *Technological Forecasting and Social Change*, *Journal of Knowledge Management*, *Entrepreneurship and Small businesses*, etc.). She is also the author of pedagogical manuals on innovation, including a comic book (*Histoires d'innovation*, Pearson).

Maxime Mellard is an assistant professor at the IAE Lille University School of Management of Université de Lille, France. He mainly teaches strategic management and innovation management, with a particular focus on creativity management and idea management. His research focuses on these same topics applied to creative industries such as video games, fashion and zythology, using qualitative and mainly QCA methodologies. He has published in the *Journal of Innovation Economics & Management* and the book *Research in the Sociology of Organizations*.

Guy Parmentier is a professor at Université Grenoble Alpes and a researcher at CERAG, France. His research interests include the management of innovation and creativity. He has edited the collective work *The Practical Guide to Communities* (Éditions d'innovation) and co-wrote the book *Stratégies et business model à l'ère digitale* (De Boeck Supérieur). His work has also been published in journals such as *Management International*, *Technological Forecasting and Social Change*, *Creativity and Innovation Management*, *Revue française de gestion*, etc. He has also been a project manager in the publishing industry and directed, for eight years, the video game production studio Galilea in Grenoble and Montreal.

Romain Rampa is an assistant professor at the École Polytechnique de Paris in the Management of Innovation and Entrepreneurship department, France. He is also a researcher at the CRG and the Institut interdisciplinaire de l'innovation de Paris (I3). His research focuses on the management of innovation and creativity, as well as on the management of ideas in organizations. During his studies, his research projects led him to work in the gaming industry (Ubisoft), the aerospace industry (Bombardier), the health sector (Sainte-Justine university hospital), as well as with large companies in the field of energy and sustainable mobility (IREQ, Michelin, Canmet Énergie). His work has been published in several journals, including *Creativity and Innovation Management*, *Revue française de gestion* and *Management International*.

Émilie Ruiz is an associate professor of innovation management at the Université Savoie Mont Blanc and a research fellow at the Institut de recherche en gestion et économie (IREGE), France. Her research, published in journals such as *Revue française de gestion*, *Management International*, *R&D Management*, *Technovation* and *European Management Journal*, deals with open innovation, in particular with communities of innovation, and organizational creativity as well as cultural and creative industries.

Zeinab Sheet is a young doctoral student in management sciences at the Université Grenoble Alpes/CERAG, France. Her research focuses on the management of creativity and innovation. She specializes in statistics applied to social sciences, particularly in the modeling of structural equations and the construction of measurement scales. During her studies, her research projects led her to interact with creative organizations such as Walt Disney, Dream Works and Ubisoft. Her research work also focuses on open innovation practices in innovative companies.

Bérangère L. Szostak is a professor at the ISM-IAE of Versailles Saint-Quentin-en-Yvelines, Université Paris-Saclay, France. She is the director of the Research Center LAREQUOI. She specializes in the strategic management of innovation and organizational creativity in various organizations (SMEs, cultural and creative industries, social economy organizations, hospitals, etc.). Her contributions concern the development of creativity, particularly through design thinking. Her work has been published in journals such as *M@n@gement*, *Revue française de gestion*, *Revue internationale de la PME*, *Revue d'économie industrielle*, *Journal of Innovation Economics & Management* and *European Journal of Innovation Management*. She is the author, along with C. Gay, of *Innovation and Creativity in SMEs* (ISTE-Wiley, 2019).

Introduction

In the last decade, business leaders have realized that creativity has become a major challenge in the organizations who seek to make profound changes within, in order to achieve their strategic goals (IBM CEO study 2010[1]). Just as in the economic field, Nobel laureate in economics Edmund Strother Phelps argues that modern economic growth is a direct result of human initiative and creativity (Phelps 2013). Creativity has thus become an issue for the development of organizations and society in a globalized world, in which ideas and people circulate rapidly, technological change is extremely rapid, competition is increasingly exacerbated, and environmental issues are becoming increasingly prevalent (Parmentier et al. 2017). Thus, organizations must find and implement creative ideas to survive this era; they must constantly reinvent themselves.

After a long history of being confined to the fields of art or great inventions and being the prerogative of exceptional individuals (Kris 1952), creativity is now perceived as a fundamental human capacity (Lubart 2003). Progressively, during the 20th century, work on the processes, methods and cognitive foundations of creativity made it possible to understand how this capacity is activated and developed in the individual. The term creativity itself is a recent one, appearing in the latter part of the 20th century in the work of Baron, "in the narrow sense, creativity refers to the abilities that are most characteristic of creative people" (Baron 1951, p. 444), and Stein, "creative work is a novel work that is accepted as tenable or useful or satisfying by a group in some point in time" (Stein 1953). Previously,

Introduction written by Guy PARMENTIER.

1 IBM 2010 Global CEO Study: Creativity Selected as Most Crucial Factor for Future Success.

authors used the terms "invention" (Poincaré 1908) or "creative thinking" (Wallas 1926; Hutchinson 1931). More recently, Amabile's much-quoted definition, "creativity is the production of novel and useful ideas by an individual or small group of individuals working together" (Amabile 1988a, p. 126), has illustrated this dual dimension of novelty and usefulness, in which "to be creative, an idea must also be appropriate, useful and actionable" (Amabile 1998b, p. 78). This can be summarized as follows: creativity is the activity of producing new, appropriate and actionable ideas, conceived by an individual or a small group of individuals working together.

At the collective and organizational level, research on creativity dates back to the 1990s. The research aimed to describe the individual factors (character traits, emotions, qualities of the person) and contextual factors that are favorable or unfavorable to the expression of creativity (Sarooghi et al. 2015). Thus, since the work of Amabile (1988a, 1988b), who was the first to address the individual and collective levels of creativity in organizations, many works have been developed on the topic of organizational creativity. Amabile has developed a componential approach that identifies three essential composites for creativity: motivation (intrinsic and extrinsic), skills specific to the individual's domain (expertise and knowledge) and skills specific to creativity. She translates this model to the organizational level to qualify innovation. Other works, such as the interactionist approach of Woodman et al. (1993), have emphasized that the performance of an organization in terms of organizational creativity depends on the interactions between individual factors, creative behaviors and creative outcomes (Woodman et al. 1993). Ford's evolutionary approach more specifically identifies the factors that intentionally lead the individual to undertake creative action, i.e. what constrains and facilitates creative action at both the individual and collective levels (Ford 1996). At a more empirical level, the creative environment approach, based on extensive field research, has attempted to identify the organizational factors that create a favorable environment for creative action (Amabile et al. 1996; Ekvall 1996).

Progressively, it is therefore a multilevel approach that has been developed to explain the phenomena of organizational creativity and take into account the intertwining of the individual, group and organizational components. However, organizational approaches to creativity are limited in explaining creativity in organizations. Amabile's componential model establishes a process of group creativity, individual and organizational components of creativity, but it focuses, at the organizational level, more on innovation than on creativity. The interactionist model of Woodman and his team tries to link organizational creativity to individual, group and organizational characteristics, but creative processes and the creative act are absent from their model. Ford's evolutionary model proposes a social process of selecting the creative act at the individual level, which, however, is not linked to the process of individual and organizational creativity. The organizational climate approach shows that managers can have a strong influence on organizational creativity with management styles that integrate the KEYS and SOQ[2] (Amabile et al. 1996; Ekvall 1996).

Previous research on organizational creativity has therefore mainly focused on creativity in organizations or with the organization. It has been hampered by the complexity of the "organization" object, with a lack of links with strategic management and business models. At the same time as this literature was being developed, a new understanding of the strategic capabilities of an organization was being constructed through the notion of organizational capabilities, in particular to better explain the performance of an organization. The concept of organizational capabilities was developed to better explain the performance of an organization and its ability to innovate and adapt to rapidly changing environments. The organizational capabilities approach thus enriches research on organizational creativity, because it adopts the organizational and strategic level as the starting point of analysis, examining in particular the processes and routines that constitute the foundations of the organization.

The purpose of this book is to develop the concept of organizational creative capabilities and to anchor it both theoretically and empirically so that researchers can more easily apply it to their research and practitioners can integrate it into their management practices. This book is the result of the research project CCO (*Capacités créatives des organisations*, literally meaning the organizational creative capabilities) supported by the ANR (*Agence nationale de la recherche*, French Research Agency). The project regularly brought together a dozen researchers, who debated with passion and method the interest, the foundation and the constituents of the concept of organizational creative capability. They went into the field to identify the existence of these capabilities and deployed large-scale surveys among

---

2 The KEYS and SOQ are tools for measuring an organizational climate for creativity in organizations.

managers of small and large companies around the world to build tools for measuring creative capabilities.

The book consists of eight chapters.

The first chapter establishes the value of a capabilities approach to organizational creativity and explores the concept of organizational capabilities. In this chapter, Guy Parmentier identifies the routines that make up these capabilities and the factors that promote their proper functioning. He proposes a model whose components will be developed in part in the following chapters.

The second chapter develops the link between openness and organizational creative capability. Émilie Ruiz and Guy Parmentier present the origin of the concept of open innovation, the different modalities of openness that support the organizational and key role of absorptive capacities for this openness to be transformed into creative capabilities.

The third chapter explores the critical role of equipment in developing the creativity of individuals and teams. Romain Rampa and Guy Parmentier identify the effects and limitations of equipment on creative abilities. They document methods and present concrete examples of innovative spaces and tools that have been implemented by various companies.

The fourth chapter clarifies the different conceptions of slack and its role in organizational creative capability. Romain Rampa and Guy Parmentier point out that the pool of creative resources and ideas is one of the main levers on which organizations can rely to introduce novelty and support creative capabilities. They give concrete examples of organizational arrangements that enable the deployment of a slack that is favorable to organizational creativity.

The fifth chapter analyzes the effect of agile methods on organizational creativity in video games. Florence Jeannot, Maxime Mellard and Guy Parmentier build and test a model where the agile method has a direct effect on the perceived originality of a video game and an indirect effect via organizational creative capability. The study validates the direct effect of the use of agile methods on the creativity of video games, as well as the mediating effect of creative capabilities between agile methods and the creativity of these video games.

The sixth chapter details the journey of an idea and the formal and informal approaches to managing this journey in an organization. Guy Parmentier, Séverine Le Loarne-Lemaire and Romain Rampa discuss the different challenges of idea management that need to be addressed in order for organizational creativity to become a full-fledged capability.

The seventh chapter provides a scale for measuring organizational creative capability. Zeinab Sheet, Florence Jeannot and Guy Parmentier propose a five-dimensional scale (socialization of ideas, room to maneuver, creative equipment, idea management, openness and organizational agility) that affect the creative outcome. The scale is a second-order reflexive scale, with four control variables: psychological safety, work atmosphere, project team diversity and social desirability.

The eighth chapter presents a general framework for analyzing creative performance. Bérangère L. Szostak proposes a creativity ladder to help managers position their organization with respect to creativity and to guide them in choosing measurement indicators to assess their performance. She lists indicators for the marketing, strategic, process and financial dimensions.

Finally, the conclusion proposes to return to the contributions of each chapter and to the understanding of creative capabilities. It also opens up research perspectives for further studies on the constituents and effects of organizational creative capability.

References

Amabile, T.M. (1988a). A model of creativity and innovation in organizations. *Research in Organizational Behavior*, 10, 123–167.

Amabile, T.M. (1998b). How to kill creativity. *Harvard Business Review*, 76(5), 76.

Amabile, T.M., Conti, R., Coon, H., Lazenby, J., Herron, M. (1996). Assessing the work environment for creativity. *Academy of Management Journal*, 39(5), 1154–1184.

Baron, F. (1951). The disposition towards originality. *Journal of Abnormal and Social Psychology*, 51, 478–485.

Ekvall, G. (1996). Organizational climate for creativity and innovation. *European Journal of Work & Organizational Psychology*, 5(1), 105.

Ford, C.M. (1996). A theory of individual creative action in multiple social domains. *Academy of Management Review*, 21(4), 1112–1142.

Hutchinson, E.D. (1931). Materials for the study of creative thinking. *Psychological Bulletin*, 33, 309–329.

Kris, E. (1952). *Psychoanalytic Exploration in Art*. International Universities Press, New York.

Lubart, T. (2003). *Psychologie de la créativité*. Armand Colin, Paris.

Parmentier, G., Szostak, B.L., Rüling, C.C. (2017). Créativité organisationnelle : quels enjeux en management stratégique dans un contexte mondialisé ? *Management International*, 22(1), 12–18.

Phelps, E. (2013). *Mass Flourishing How Grassroots Innovation Created Jobs, Challenge, and Change*. Princeton University Press, Princeton.

Poincaré H. (1908). L'invention mathématique. *Bulletin de l'Institut Général Psychologique*, 8(3), 2–15.

Sarooghi, H., Libaers, D., Burkemper, A. (2015). Examining the relationship between creativity and innovation: A meta-analysis of organizational, cultural, and environmental factors. *Journal of Business Venturing*, 30(5), 714–731.

Stein, M.I. (1953). Creativity and culture. *Journal of Psychology: Interdisciplinary and Applied*, 36, 311–322.

Wallas G. (1926). *The Art of Thought*. Harcourt Brace, New York.

Woodman, R.W., Sawyer, J.E., Griffin, R.W. (1993). Toward a theory of organizational creativity. *Academy of Management Review*, 18(2), 293–321.

1

The Foundations of Organizational Creative Capabilities

Originating from the RBV (resource-based view) theory, the concept of organizational capability is of great interest when studying organizational creativity. Currently, organizational capability is the source of strategic advantage, and the organization is considered as a combination of resources, skills, processes and routines. Thus, anchoring organizational creativity in an RBV approach, centered on capabilities, makes it possible to adopt a level of analysis that is both organizational and strategic, and to identify the factors, processes and routines that make creativity a true organizational capability that can be maintained and evolve according to the constraints of the strategic environment. We therefore propose to consider organizational creativity as an organizational capability. Firstly, we will specify the notion of organizational capability in order to determine its different components and to draw lessons for defining organizational creative capabilities. Secondly, we will identify the factors likely to promote the development of creative capabilities. In the third part, we will lay the foundations of the routines that constitute organizational creative capabilities.

1.1. Organizational capabilities

The concept of organizational capability stems from the emergence of the strategic analysis paradigm, the resource-based view (RBV), which takes into account not only the economic environment of companies, but also its

---

Chapter written by Guy PARMENTIER.

resources and skills. In RBV theory, the firm is considered as a set of resources (Grant 1991), giving it a competitive advantage when these resources are valuable, rare, inimitable and non-substitutable (Barney 1991). However, it is not the mere possession of such resources that can explain the differences in performance between firms (Grant 1991), but rather the ability to deploy and coordinate these resources in order to achieve the firm's objectives (Amit and Schoemaker 1993). Organizational capability, derived from RBV theory, thus describes a capability, located at the level of the organization, that efficiently exploits its resources and skills to transform input factors into products and services, and that allows it to possess a unique market position with a competitive advantage (Collis 1994). While resources can be acquired in the market, capability is an organizational construct of its own that is difficult to duplicate in other organizations.

In the literature on organizational capability, the words "ability", "aptitude", "capacity" and "competence" are often used in English as synonyms, but they have different Latin origins and meanings. Before going any further, it is worthwhile to examine their meaning and to describe their differences. Derived from the Latin *aptus*, meaning "attached to something", an aptitude is a natural or acquired disposition of someone to do something[1]. It is fundamentally integrated by its essence or learning into an entity. An ability, whose Latin origin is *habilitas*, meaning "to make fit", is a quality concerning capability[2]. Note that the terms "ability" and "aptitude" have very similar definitions in English and are used interchangeably in the sense of "being able to do something". It is also used in English to refer to a level of ability. The Latin origin instead gives it an enabling quality, thus giving an aptitude, which would be the prerequisite to the revelation of the aptitude. An ability is the capacity of someone in such and such field or their power within a certain field. The Latin origin, *capax*, meaning "which can contain", associates it with the quality of a container to integrate a particular disposition[3]. A competence is a recognized capacity in a given matter due to the knowledge possessed and which gives a person the right to judge it. Derived from the Latin *competentia*, meaning "right relationship", competence adds the notion of external evaluation to its possessor. The English definition

1 Aptitude: "Natural ability or skill at doing something" (*Oxford English Dictionary*).

2 Ability: "The fact that someone/something is able to do something or a level of skill or intelligence" (*Oxford English Dictionary*).

3 Capacity: "The ability to understand or to do something" (*Oxford English Dictionary*).

adds to it the meaning of efficiency[4]. According to these multiple definitions, a capacity is an aptitude transformed into skill, i.e. a disposition of someone to do something efficiently after learning in a particular field.

At the organizational level, this disposition is the ability for a set of resources to accomplish a task or activity (Grant 1991, p. 119). For Collis (1994), it is socially complex routines that determine the efficiency with which firms physically transform inputs into outputs (p. 145). For Amit and Schoemaker (1993), it refers to the ability of a firm to deploy a combination of resources, using organizational processes, to achieve a desired end (p. 35). These three definitions indicate that, at the organizational level, a capacity is a unique combination of resources (tangible or intangible), routines and processes for transforming incoming inputs into intermediate or final products and services. They can take the form of capacities to develop reliable products, repeated innovations or to develop new products extremely rapidly (Amit and Schoemaker 1993).

1.1.1. *The different organizational capabilities*

The authors distinguish with increasing complexity: functional capabilities[5], core capabilities, absorptive capacities and dynamic capabilities (Govind Menon 2008). While the former are considered uncircumventable, core capabilities are the resources and skills that are strategically important to achieve a competitive advantage. For example, Apple's success is based in part on its ability to design ergonomic digital applications, with beautiful design and strong integration between hardware and software. This core capability is a complex assembly of human resources, know-how, proprietary technology within routines unique to Apple. Other authors also mention another strategically important organizational capability that is strategically important, the absorptive capacity, which is "an ability of the firm to recognize the value of new, external information, assimilate it, and apply it to commercial ends" (Cohen and Levinthal 1990, p. 128). This ability is a dynamic ability related to learning (Noblet and Simon 2010). For example, the pharmaceutical industry sets up intelligence cells equipped with specific information tools to monitor research and acquire the best start-ups before others. These cells are partly

4 Competence: "The ability to do something well or effectively" (*Oxford English Dictionary*).

5 Ability to perform the core activities of the firm; for example, production.

responsible for their ability to integrate the latest technological innovations into their products. Dynamic capabilities mark a strong evolution in this approach, as they integrate the notion of time and the influence of the environment. Dynamic capabilities are "the firm's ability to integrate, build, and reconfigure internal and external competences to address rapidly changing environments" (Teece et al. 1997, p. 516), in order to gain competitive advantage (Teece 2007). More recently, Teece has redefined dynamic capabilities in a more strategic sense, as "the capacity to sense and shape opportunities and threats, to seize opportunities, and to maintain competitiveness through enhancing, combining, protecting, and, when necessary, reconfiguring the business enterprise's intangible and tangible assets" (Teece 2007, p. 1319). Dynamic capabilities would therefore be one of the capabilities to allow for the reconfiguration of other capabilities, in order to defend or gain a strategic advantage in an unstable environment. It is often equated with the ability to innovate, whereas in reality it affects the entire organization. The example of Ubisoft is interesting in this respect. A video game producer must develop and survive in a fundamentally unstable industry: the lifespan of creations is unpredictable, distribution media change regularly and technological change is very rapid. Yet, Ubisoft, thanks to its ability to question its design processes and routines (Cohendet and Simon 2016) and the fact that it is an organization based on both internal and external communities (Cohendet and Simon 2007), manages to renew its licenses, constantly develop new tools and adapt to new digital distribution modes.

Some capabilities are systematically evoked in the plural (core capabilities and dynamic capabilities), while others are used more often in the singular (absorptive capacity, creative capability and functional capability). The use of the plural is related to how a capability is viewed and indicates that it is the result of a set of capabilities of the same nature. On the other hand, the use of the singular places the capability as a capability in its own right, indivisible into sub-capabilities.

On the side of creativity, the concept of creative capability has not been mentioned much in the literature; it is listed as an organizational capability by Govind Menon (2008) without it being defined. To date, only one published study discusses the development of creative capabilities in creative organizations (Napier and Nilsson 2006). Napier studies the creative capabilities of three creative organizations: a theater, a football team and a software development company. He defines creative capabilities as "routines and processes that enhance organizational ability for creative actions and behaviors". He clearly equates creative capabilities with dynamic capabilities by indicating that they make it possible "to handle a changing environment by exploiting existing processes and competences, residing internally or externally" (Napier and Nilsson 2006, p. 270). This is not our approach; we believe that creative capabilities and dynamic capabilities are two different types of organizational capabilities. The whole question is to understand what creative abilities are. In their study, Napier and Nilsson identify the central role of the creative entrepreneur in establishing a structure, processes and routines of collaboration in creation favorable to organizational creativity. He is thus the main architect and developer of organizational creative capability. He also recognizes the importance of relationships external to the organization to identify potential creative resources and to develop the expertise of competitors and the market. However, the creative capabilities observed empirically are very different from one organization to another and they do not allow them to clearly identify the processes and routines of the organizational creative capabilities: for the theater, it is the capability to implement the original idea and vision of the director at all stages of production; for football, it is the routines and processes that support creative actions and behaviors during the game; for a software development company, it is the ability to constantly learn and adapt through experimentation.

Organizational capability	**Definition**
Functional capability	Ability to perform a basic activity of the firm (e.g. production).
Core capabilities	Resources and skills that are strategically important to achieve competitive advantage.
Absorptive capacity	Ability of the organization to recognize the value of new information, assimilate it and use it for business purposes.
Creative capability	Ability to generate new ideas to improve, change and renew the organization's products as well as the organization itself.
Dynamic capability	Ability of the organization to integrate, build and reconfigure internal and external competencies to respond to rapid changes in the environment.

Table 1.1. *The different organizational capabilities according to their degree of complexity*

These results deserve to be extended to reinforce the concept proposed by Napier and Nilsson (2006). It is therefore necessary to theoretically strengthen this notion of creative capabilities in order to identify its components and build the foundations of broader empirical studies that can be used in multiple industries. Based on the definition of an organizational capability, the definition of creativity, the approach of Napier and Nilsson (2006) and the examples above, organizational creative capability is thus the ability, using processes and routines, to generate, select and integrate new, appropriate, useful and feasible ideas and solutions to improve, change and renew the organization's processes and products, as well as the organization itself. We can consider that the creative capability could participate in the dynamic capabilities by bringing about the ideas necessary for the evolution and the renewal of the organization. We develop below these three approaches, processes, routines and factors, to understand the nature of organizational creative capabilities.

1.1.2. *Approaches for studying organizational capability*

The debates around dynamic capabilities are interesting for understanding the nature of an organizational capability. Depending on their definitions[6], dynamic capabilities are understood as abilities (Teece et al. 1997; Teece 2007), competences (Danneels 2008), sets of routines (Zollo and Winter 2002) or sets of processes (Eisenhardt and Martin 2000). Thus, three approaches seem to stand out when studying the constituents of a capability: the process approach (Teece et al. 1997; Eisenhardt and Martin 2000; Teece 2007); the routines approach (Zollo and Winter 2002); and the factor approach. The process approach identifies specific processes such as the detection (sense) of opportunities or threats (Teece 2007), or the creation and acquisition of new knowledge to adapt the firm to new market realities (Eisenhardt and Martin 2000). The routines approach looks for "stable configurations of collective activities through which an organization systematically generates and modifies its operational routines" (Zollo and Winter 2002, p. 340). In this view, dynamic capabilities are stable and systematic, and result in routines, i.e. habits that result from a succession of continuously repeated actions. Depending on the dynamics of the environment, simple and experimental processes with uncertain outcomes in highly unstable markets would become routines, i.e. stable processes with

6 See the Altintas synthesis presented at AIMS (Altintas 2009).

certain outcomes (Eisenhardt and Martin 2000). The routines approach, when deployed at the organizational level, is interesting for identifying the sequences of activities that guide individuals in patterns of repetitive action. At a more macro level, other studies seek to identify the factors favorable to the development of dynamic capabilities, the learning mechanisms (Zollo and Winter 2002), the role of resources (Rothaermel and Hess 2007; McKelvie and Davidsson 2009) or the role of managers (Adner and Helfat 2003; Teece 2007).

This research on dynamic capabilities indicates that an organizational capability can be characterized by the factors that favor its emergence and by the routines and processes that constitute it. These three approaches are not incompatible, yet they allow us to understand the complexity of an organizational capability that would ensure the survival of an organization in a world of rapid and permanent transformation. The factor approach will allow us to identify, at the macro-level of the organization, the organizational factors to the routinization of creative activity at the individual level. The routinization of activity in an organization is the most important form of storage of the organization's operational knowledge (Nelson and Winter 1982). Organizations remember "by doing" with individuals, who have integrated ways of doing things almost quasi-automatically. Thus, creative routines, i.e. the set of collective actions for creating new ideas and solutions, could be one of the bases of organizational creative capability. However, this routinization is often established through formalized processes, which organize the action and allow the constituents of this action to become effective routines in action (Feldman and Pentland 2003). Thus, the organizational routines approach will allow us to identify at the intermediate level of the organization the processes that support the creation of creative routines. Moreover, the organizational routines approach is essential for identifying the recurrent practices that are built from the processes and favored by the organizational factors favorable to the creativity of its members.

1.2. Organizational factors of creative capabilities

Organizational creative capabilities depend on organizational factors that will act at all levels of the organization to promote the development of creative routines. The question of linking the characteristics of an organization to the organizational elements of creativity therefore arises.

This question is not simple, because an organization can be analyzed from a structural, cultural and political point of view. The structural view describes the organization as a structure that allows the division and coordination of work, and the management of resources. The cultural point of view represents the organization as a place of socialization and construction of meaning. The political point of view describes the modes of decision and control through the interplay of actors and management practices. Based on these three approaches, an organization is thus characterized by a structure for distributing, coordinating and controlling work; resources to complete the work; a vision and missions to give meaning to action; and management methods to manage relationships and socialization in the working group.

To determine what could favor creative acts at the level of each dimension of an organization, the concept of organizational climate can provide us with some answers. Organizational climate is a series of recurring behaviors, attitudes and feelings that characterize the life of an organization (Ekvall 1991). The climate, by influencing processes at the individual and organizational levels such as communication, coordination, learning, motivation and problem solving, acts on the productivity of work teams and the creativity of individuals (Isaksen and Lauer 2002).

Nine relevant dimensions have been identified to measure the existence of an organizational climate favorable to creativity, and grouped together in the SOQ (Situational Outlook Questionnaire) after multiple empirical and theoretical works (Ekvall 1991, 1996; Lauer 1994; Isaksen et al. 2001). The organizational creative climate is thus measured with: the level of challenge and involvement; the degree of freedom; trust and openness; the time dedicated to the exploration of ideas; humor and playfulness; the level of conflict; the support of ideas; the level of debate; and risk-taking. Conflict negatively impacts team creativity, while the other eight dimensions impact it in a positive way. Antecedents to the creative climate can be leader behaviors, management practices, organizational culture, organizational processes, routines and procedures, individual skills and abilities, required tasks, resources and technologies, organizational structure and size, and organizational missions and strategies (Ekvall 1996). Among these antecedents, we find certain variables of the interactionist model of Woodman et al. (1993), without, however, knowing how these antecedents act on the creative climate. Indeed, to date, few studies have examined the effect of all of these organizational variables on the creative climate. The creative climate therefore appears as a kind of interesting proxy for characterizing the contextual variables and their effects on the creativity of the members of an organization.

With the same logic, the work of Amabile et al. (1996) led to the development of the KEYS to assess whether the work environment is conducive to creativity of work groups. The KEYS measurement scales include 87 questions along eight dimensions: four on management practices (autonomy/freedom, managerial encouragement, work group supports and challenging work); two on organizational motivations (organizational encouragement and lack of organizational impediments); and two on resources (sufficient resources and workload pressure).

The dimensions of organizational climates and work environments conducive to creativity have an impact on individual creativity in work groups. These climates foster the creation of creative routines. Thus, we hypothesize that creativity-supportive organizational climates allow creative activity to become "paradoxically" routine, thus constituting metaroutines for change in organizations.

We propose to link the dimensions of KEYS and SOQ of a creative organization to the dimensions of the organization, thus defining the image of an organization that is favorable to creativity and to the transformation of the creative act into routines.

SOQ (9 dimensions)	**KEYS (8 dimensions)**
– Level of challenge and involvement – Degree of freedom – Trust and openness – Idea support – Time to explore ideas – Level of conflict – Level of debate – Risk-taking – Playfulness and humor	– Challenging work – Autonomy and freedom – Managerial encouragement – Work group supports – Organizational encouragement – Lack of organizational impediments – Sufficient resources – Workload pressure

Table 1.2. *Dimensions of the SOQ and KEYS*

Organizational dimensions	Factors of organizational creative climates
Structure	– Autonomy and freedom (KEYS)
	– Degree of freedom (SOQ)
	– Risk-taking (SOQ)
Resources	– Organizational encouragement (KEYS)
	– Lack of organizational impediments (KEYS)
	– Sufficient resources (KEYS)
	– Workload pressure (KEYS)
	– Time dedicated to the exploration of ideas (SOQ)
Visions and missions	– Challenging work (KEYS)
	– Level of challenge and involvement (SOQ)
Management methods	– Managerial encouragement (KEYS)
	– Confidence and openness (SOQ)
	– Level of conflict (SOQ)
	– Level of debate (SOQ)
	– Humor and playfulness (SOQ)
	– Confidence and openness (SOQ)
	– Idea support (SOQ)
	– Work group support (KEYS)

Table 1.3. *Creative dimensions of organizations*

1.2.1. *Factors related to the structure of an organization*

According to Table 1.3, an organizational structure autonomy of action and risk-taking would be conducive to the creativity of individuals and teams. The opportunity for risk-taking has been identified as an antecedent of creativity in managers (Somsing and Belbaly 2017), although this relationship can be moderated by intrinsic motivation (Dewett 2007). The autonomy and freedom taking described in the SOQ and the KEYS are found in the organic form of organization described by Burns and Stalker (1961). Woodman et al. (1993) hypothesize that an organic organizational structure is more conducive to creativity than a mechanical structure. Damanpour's (1991) study shows that this type of organization acts on the adoption of innovation, but does not give any indication on the generation of ideas and the development of innovations. In reality, little research has been done on the relationship between this form of organization and creativity. However, contextual ambidexterity, which consists of conducting both exploration and exploitation activities in the same teams, contributes to the creation of an organic structure by allowing degrees of freedom and relative autonomy in the choice of activities to be carried out according to the objectives. Thus, when teams can alternate these two types of activities according to the needs and constraints of production, the organization benefits from the ideas of all collaborators and develops more innovative products (Brion et al. 2008; Parmentier and Mangematin 2009). The development of communities of practice in an organization, by creating transversalities and pockets of autonomy, could also contribute to creating an organic structure. Communities of practice in the company encourage the generation and circulation of ideas, as shown by Cohendet and Simon's (2007) work on the business communities at Ubisoft, which promote informal interactions to generate ideas that can be taken up in more formally managed projects.

In the organization and within these communities, individuals develop multiple ties that constitute social networks in relationships. The nature of these links and the position in the networks of individuals seem to influence their creativity. The creativity of an individual thus depends, in scientific activities, on the nature of the ties they deploy: the weakness of the ties they develop, and their creativity (Perry-Smith 2006). All times, in the context of high-tech companies, Zhou et al. (2009) find an inverted U-shaped curvilinear relationship between the number of weak ties and employee creativity. Employee compliance with the organization's social norms even has a moderating effect on the benefit of weak ties for individual creativity (Zhou et al. 2009). Beyond the quantity of ties, the position in networks has been recognized as a determinant of creativity. An individual at the center of a dense network with few external ties is more creative than one with many external ties. Conversely, an individual at the periphery of a network with many external ties is more creative than someone with few external ties (Perry-Smith 2006). In the same way, those who develop networks with structural holes put themselves more frequently in an intermediary position, thus more rapidly obtaining more diversified and sometimes contradictory information, likely to feed their creativity. Thus, managers in knowledge-intensive high-tech companies, who act as intermediaries between structural holes, are likely to have better ideas and have more opportunity to express and discuss these ideas with their colleagues (Burt 2004). An organization that fosters the development of weak ties and the possibility of frequent departmental and job changes for a portion of its employees could foster the creativity of its employees.

Thus, at the structural level, the development of creative capabilities would be facilitated by an organic organization that integrates communities of practice, promotes weak ties, supports network renewal and allows for risk-taking.

1.2.2. *Factors related to an organization's resources*

The organization and provision of sufficient and appropriate human resources (human, physical and temporal) could encourage creativity, and diminish and reduce the obstacles associated with it. The nature of human resources is also important, as indicated by the whole current on the cognitive foundations of creativity, which defines the cognitive styles and personality traits of creative individuals.

It is widely recognized that employee diversity fosters both organizational creativity (Amabile 1996; Han 2014; Han et al. 2014) and individual creativity (Shin et al. 2012). The generation of original ideas indeed requires us to step outside the usual frameworks of thought by drawing on new perspectives. Within a team, the diversity in knowledge and ways of thinking then promotes the cognitive mechanisms of association, dissociation and analogy that allow for the generation of new ideas. However, in order for divergent ideas to be expressed, the company must put in place a culture that values the skills, expertise and personality of each employee in a climate of trust. In addition, exposing employees to colleagues with very different backgrounds and abilities helps us to reduce the risk of rejection due to difference. However, a common culture and a common language are often necessary to avoid misunderstandings and conflicts, especially in project teams under pressure. The organization thus faces the paradox of encouraging diversity while building a cohesive team (Andriopoulos 2003). The organization must therefore develop a climate of trust so that individuals are willing to recognize their differences and share their ideas critically with a low level of conflict. In addition to diversity, the inclusion of creative resources, such as creative human resources, for example designers, also promotes organizational creativity (Szostak 2006; Parmentier and Picq 2016).

Context has been identified as having an effect on creativity, particularly by acting on the intrinsic motivation of creative individuals (Amabile 1988). Organizational constraints, external to the individual, are contextual elements that act on the individual's motivation and freedom of action to perform creative acts. Among these constraints, the lack of time and lack of material and financial resources are likely to act negatively on the creative act (Rosso 2014). According to Amabile et al. (2002), lack of temporal resources is detrimental to creativity. Thus, individuals would need time and space to be creative (Isaksen et al. 2001). Lack of material and financial resources also seems to negatively affect motivation and limit the possibilities for creative activity (Rosso 2014).

However, this relationship between lack of resources and creativity is more complex than it seems. We will see in the next few chapters that constraint is essential to creativity and that it can nurture creativity by forcing new associations. However, too many constraints kill creativity, and the organization will have to develop organizational creative capability, manage the right amount of resources and alternate periods of time constraints with periods of relaxation.

1.2.3. *Factors related to an organization's vision*

The interest of the challenge and the challenge's level of requirement were two of the elements of an organizational climate for creativity. Thus, at the strategic level, a vision and interesting missions, clearly communicated to the members of an organization, act on their motivation to get involved in creative acts. A management style that relies on the vision to define the objectives to be reached seems to be more favorable to the creativity of the employees. Getz and Carney (2013) describe this type of organization as "why" companies, as opposed to "how" companies.

In "why" companies, even if there is an organizational chart, employees are encouraged to be autonomous, to solve everyday problems themselves. In such an organization, managers do not say how to do the work, but rather why it should be done. The whole company then self-organizes into small teams to achieve the objectives of an ambitious vision shared by the majority of the employees. This organizational structure creates individual and organizational flexibility, which is necessary for creativity and innovation (Georgsdottir and Getz 2004). There is a strong relationship between corporate cultures that emphasize creativity and innovation, and an organization's ability to innovate (Alcántara 2010; Jin et al. 2019). An organization that emphasizes innovation goals and values the creativity of collaborators gives the impression that it is important to innovate and that this innovation is part of our mission.

Thus, a culture of creativity and innovation with a focus on goals as a management style is probably a condition that promotes long-term creativity in teams. In video game studios, a culture of creativity characterized by a dominant discourse on the need to be creative, the presence of a creative leader and the possibility of taking risks to develop ideas is strongly present in studios that devote a lot of time and energy to the development of new ideas (Parmentier and Picq 2016).

1.2.4. *Factors related to management methods*

Studies on creative environments have shown the importance of the role of management in creating meaning and translation between different professions (Simon 2006) and in structuring collaboration in creative work (Napier and Nilsson 2006).

Moreover, the organizational climate approach clearly indicates the determining role of managers in the construction of an organizational climate that is conducive to creativity (Amabile et al. 1996; Isaksen and Ekvall 2010), or in the development of creativity-killing practices (Amabile 1998; Amabile et al. 2002). The manager who implements a creativity-friendly management style defines the objectives that take into account both the constraints of the project and the type of work to be done. Based on these objectives, they let the teams decide what work to do and how to do it, as in Getz and Carney's "why" companies. They are instrumental in helping teams solve problems with his considerable expertise (Parmentier and Picq 2016). They foster the development of a climate of confidence and mutual support that facilitates the proposal and discussion of ideas.

In such a climate, employees listen to each other and discuss ideas in a constructive manner. In this case, the manager's role is to frame the debates and avoid any outbursts. This reduces the risk of proposing an idea that could be badly received, because of its embryonic state and how it is badly defined. In order to encourage creativity in teams, the manager takes on the role of facilitator to develop a climate of trust and mutual support and to guide the team towards collective problem solving.

1.3. Organizational routines of creative capabilities

Creative processes unfold at the individual and collective levels according to very similar sequences: preparation, incubation, illumination and verification at the individual level (Poincaré 1908; Wallas 1926; Lubart 2001) and problem identification, preparation, generation, validation and selection of ideas at the group level (Amabile 1988). The phases of these processes do not necessarily follow one another in a linear fashion; for example, there may be a reformulation of the problem during the idea generation phase and numerous back and forth between the phases. Finally, if the ideas generated do not solve the identified problem, the process starts again, in order to obtain more efficient ideas (Amabile 1988). A first organizational approach to these processes would be to deploy these phases in a global process that would involve all collaborators.

Idea management systems (IMS) implement IT processes at the organizational level to collect, improve and evaluate ideas. These systems do not integrate online creativity methods, but allow us to operationalize the online creativity methods as well as the validation and communication of ideas. Being more than just a simple idea box, they enable people to keep track of ideas and sometimes, when these systems are integrated with corporate social networks, to collectively enrich ideas. Good IMSs set up simple and fast processes, involve middle management and measure the performance of the system (Getz and Robinson 2003). At the organizational level, they help develop a culture based on the expression and development of ideas, and they encourage dealing with problems rather than ignoring them. Moreover, when these systems are open, they allow for the implication of customers in the organization's creativity and innovation processes. The processes of organizational creativity extend beyond the boundaries of the company.

This managerial approach to processes, which corresponds to the contributory creativity identified by Unsworth (2001) with closed problems and intrinsic motivation, ignores spontaneous creativity. The members of an organization are constantly confronted with problems to be solved. The solutions to the identified problem exist most often in the work processes, know-how or knowledge carried by the individuals. At all times, in case of a new problem, proactive creativity and the search for a spontaneous solution to an open problem are essential to the search for a solution.

Ford's evolutionary theory, based on creative action, seems to be the most suitable to explain this proactive creativity (Ford 1996). It postulates the existence of processes of variation, selection and retention of ideas at the individual and collective levels. At the individual level, variation consists of the individual choosing the creative act rather than the habit when faced with a given situation, selection consists of retaining the results of the creative act in order to integrate them into modes of action and retention consists of making it a habit. However, Ford does describe the factors influencing the creative action, just not the processes that support it. This approach seems to us, however, less interesting. What would the organizational routines be? What organizational routines would favor the processes of variation, selection and retention of ideas in a sustainable way, thus constituting the foundations of organizational creative capability? Based on the literature on organizational creativity, we propose six types of routines that are deployed at the organizational level: openness, equipment, relaxation, agility, collection, socialization and selection.

Openness routines, found in several of our works (Parmentier and Gandia 2013; Parmentier and Mangematin 2014; Parmentier 2015), open up the boundaries of the internal and external organization and products and services, in order to feed the creativity process into new perspectives on problem identification and to enable mixtures favorable to idea generation. The novelty is defined against the existing ways of thinking and references. It implies the proposal of new frameworks and new points of view that challenge existing reference points. Openness, whether internally or externally, brings the individual into contact with different information and frames of thought, and thus nourishes their ability to detect and reevaluate a problem, to prepare for the generation of ideas and to generate ideas. Openness to a community of users or a community of brands (Jeppesen and Frederiksen 2006; Parmentier 2015), openness to a creative territory (Simon 2009; Grandadam et al. 2013; Deschamps and Szostak 2016), a favorable position in networks for both the individual and the organization (Perry-Smith 2006) are all behaviors and factors favorable to the creative act. Similarly, the openness of the product and service introduces the possibility for users to modify and customize the offering according to their needs and uses, thus offering a new perspective on its nature and functions (Parmentier and

Mangematin 2014). Openness can also be internal when members of an organization performing different activities connect and share their ideas and perspectives. Thus, forms of organizational ambidexterity are likely to feed new ideas to members of an organization (Parmentier and Mangematin 2009). More generally, openness consists of making the organization's boundaries porous, in order to feed the creativity process with new perspectives both in terms of problem identification and new ideas through cross-fertilization.

Equipment routines equip members of the organization and external members linked to the organization with methods, tools and means to carry out creative acts. It is a matter of training employees in creativity methods so that they can appropriate the methods and take the initiative to organize creativity sessions if necessary. Creativity training is part of the organizational context for creativity by encouraging creative behaviors (Woodman et al. 1993), and improves the performance of brainstorming sessions, which thus generate more and better ideas (Baruah et al. 1993). Equipping also involves making available and training in tools that allow for rapid visualization and testing of an idea and gathering feedback on ideas: user toolbox for innovation (Parmentier and Gandia 2013); online focus group (Rolland and Parmentier 2013); simulation tools; and rapid prototyping tools (those found in FabLabs: 3D printers, Arduino controllers, material cutting tools, etc.).

Slack routines leave margins in organizational slack resources to allow creativity to unfold. At the individual level, creativity needs time to incubate so that the problems identified and the information collected can unconsciously lead to ideas. Similarly, an organization that is constantly under stress with a maximum use of resources, and especially of available time, tends to limit the creativity of its members (Amabile et al. 2002). Creativity needs uncertainty and room to maneuver so that combinations of information and ideas can take place. The organizational slack is a stock of resources (Penrose 1959). However, slack is important for maintaining the proper functioning of the organization (Cyert and March 1963); it acts as a shock absorber to absorb internal and external shocks, and allows for the initiation of change (Bourgeois III 1981). It is also an important element for innovation, since it allows for experimentation and creation in contexts where these behaviors would be rejected by the organization (Cyert and March 1963). Thus, the time not dedicated to organizational projects for engineers at 3M and Google allows for the expression of problems and solutions not detected by the organization's classic routines. In the same way that increasing the density of creative forces increases innovation performance, to some extent, when it can make use of the organizational slack (Chen and Huang 2010). Thus, organizational slack seems necessary for creative work, as Woodman et al. (1993, p. 314) hypothesize by linking creative performance with the availability of slack. Cohendet and Simon (2007) have called this slack in creative organizations: the creative slack. They identify access to communities of specialists within a large video game studio as a pool of resources that can be accessed at any time by production teams in order to discuss, evaluate and disseminate the ideas generated in development projects.

Organizational agility routines allow the organization to detect and adapt quickly and efficiently to changes in its internal and external environments (Charbonnier-Voiron 2011; Lee and Lee 2017) and they act on the organizational creativity (Darvishmotevali et al. 2017). They require the development of three abilities: an ability of monitoring the market to detect changes, an ability of exploiting the knowledge and information collected to introduce changes in the organization and an ability of reacting quickly to changes in the environment (Charbonnier-Voiron 2011). Agility involves continuous learning (Dove 1999), including experimentation to learn quickly (Conboy et al. 2009; Hill et al. 2014) and result in innovations (Hill et al. 2014). Agility also manifests itself in project management methods, the agile methods which allow teams to develop autonomy, flexibility, cooperation and trust, thus fostering the creativity of team members (Conboy 2009; Kakar 2017). Thus, agility routines allow the organization to quickly identify problems, threats and opportunities that may impact an organization and provide methods and devices that allow it to respond on the creative potential of the members of an organization.

Idea-gathering routines organize the flow of ideas at the organizational level. Ideas emerge from individuals, in isolation or in groups, and must flow, mix with others or even be stored to be integrated into more mature concepts and, ultimately, into innovations (Hargadon and Sutton 2000). This organization of flows can take simple forms with storage in cardboard boxes, thus constituting the memory of all ideas generated in the company as is the case at Creaholic (Pichault and Picq 2013). By relying on information systems, idea management systems (IMS) implement IT processes at the organizational level to collect, improve and evaluate ideas. These systems do not integrate online creativity methods, but they allow for the validation and communication of ideas. More than a simple idea box, they allow us to keep track of ideas, and even, when these systems are integrated to social networks, to collectively enrich ideas. Adapted IMSs implement simple and fast processes, involve middle management and measure the performance of the system (Getz and Robinson 2003). At the organizational level, they help us to develop a culture based on the expression and development of ideas, and they encourage dealing with problems rather than ignoring them (Getz and Robinson 2003).

Socialization routines provide spaces for discussion of ideas and solutions to problems. The creative individual tests our ideas in order to obtain an evaluation of our relevance and to enrich us with the expertise of colleagues (Zhou and George 2001). Communication about ideas is an integral part of the creativity process (Amabile 1996). It promotes the involvement of participants in the preparation, generation and validation of ideas (Binnewies et al. 2008). It also favors their overall creativity when the organizational support for creativity is high (Zhou and George 2001). Moreover, new ideas inevitably emerge in collaboration during the creative process. For example, in improvisational theater, collective creation is built collaboratively from small individual creation (Sawyer and DeZutter 2009). This situation, where the outcome is not predictable, where each participant contributes one after the other, corresponds well to a process of socialization of ideas in which ideas are shared and enriched in discussion without anticipating the outcome. The space for the socialization of ideas could take the form of time dedicated to the discussion of ideas, or even the provision of time for discussion when management practices leave a lot of room for interaction between the members of a unit. The size of the network, the central position of the idea creator in the organization's internal social networks and the position of intermediary in networks external to the organization favors the socialization of ideas. The virtualization of interactions in spaces dedicated to the discussion of ideas is also a form that favors the socialization of ideas. It takes the form of a corporate social network in the company and a dedicated discussion forum in user and brand communities. In online user communities, virtualization facilitates the contribution of lead users' expertise (Mahr and Lievens 2012; Parmentier and Gandia 2013), and more generally peer feedback on ideas (Franke et al. 2008).

Idea evaluation routines are key to selecting the best ideas for the company. Beyond the evaluation criteria that are commonly based on the novelty, feasibility, relevance and finish of ideas (Dean et al. 2006), the management of this evaluation can have a strong impact on the creativity of groups in organizations. Indeed, the succession of individual and then collective evaluation seems to be the most efficient way to select good ideas (Girotra et al. 2010). Moreover, regular evaluation of ideas during collective creative work supports participants' commitment and guides creative work (Harvey and Kou 2013). Finally, feedback from managers and colleagues plays an active and positive role in prototyping (Harrison and Rouse 2015). The gender composition of the evaluation group can also strongly influence the evaluation of ideas, with women and men having different assessments of the value of ideas (Parmentier and Le Loarne-Lemaire 2018). Evaluation thus occupies a central role in the generation and selection of ideas; clear and fair communication of criteria is likely to stimulate the creativity of individuals and groups; the organization thus displays the importance it places on ideas.

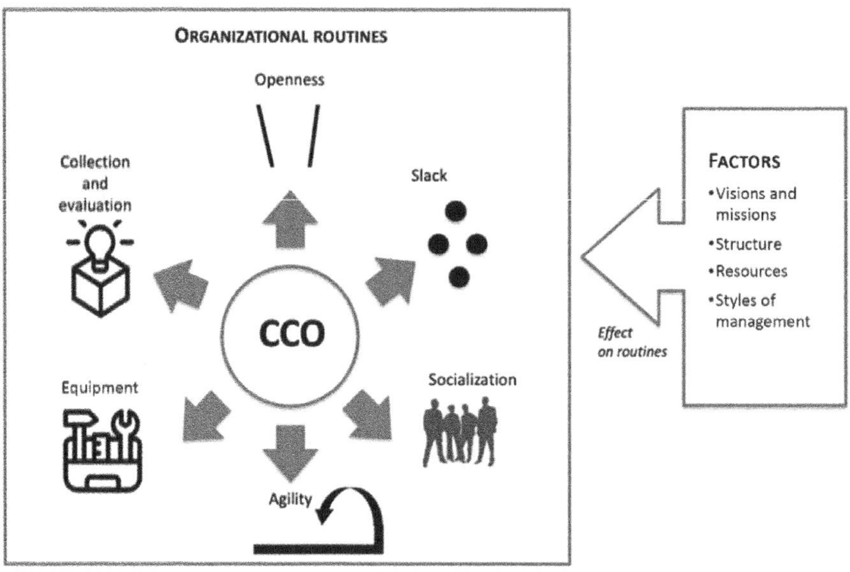

Figure 1.1. *Routines and organizational factors of creative capabilities. For a color version of this figure, see www.iste.co.uk/parmentier/organizational.zip*

At the organizational level, openness, equipment, slack, agility, socialization, collection and evaluation of idea routines will promote the choice of creative action over routine and habit at the individual level, and facilitate the evaluation of its outcome in order to select the most interesting creative actions for the individual and the organization (see Table 1.4). Similarly, the factors contributing to the creative capabilities of organizations, by acting on creativity at all levels of the organization, will facilitate the implementation of these routines. We thus propose a model for the manifestation of organizational creative capability (see Figure 1.1).

Routine	Definition	Authors
Openness	Opening the boundaries of the organization and the products and services, in order to feed the creativity process into new perspectives on problem identification, and promote cross-fertilization.	Jeppesen and Frederiksen (2006), Perry-Smith (2006), Parmentier and Mangematin (2009, 2014), Simon (2009), Grandadam et al. (2013), Parmentier and Gandia (2013), Parmentier (2015) and Dechamp and Szostak (2016).
Equipment	Equipping the organization with methods, tools and means to carry out creative acts.	Woodman et al. (1993), Baruah and Paulus (2008), Parmentier and Gandia (2013) and Rolland and Parmentier (2013).
Slack	Leaving room in the resources, creative slack, to allow creativity to unfold.	Cyert and March (1963), Woodman et al. (1993), Cohendet and Simon (2007) and Chen and Huang (2010).
Agility	Organizing the detection and the quick and efficient adaptation to changes in the internal and external environments.	Conboy et al. (2009), Charbonnier-Voiron (2011), Hill et al. (2014), Darvishmotevali et al. (2020), Kakar, (2017) and Lee and Lee (2017).
Collection	Organizing the flow of ideas at the organizational level.	Hargadon and Sutton (2000) and Getz and Robinson (2003).
Socialization	Creating spaces for discussion of ideas and solutions.	Zhou and George (2001), Binnewies et al. (2008), Franke et al. (2008), Sawyer and DeZutter (2009), Mahr and Lievens (2012) and Parmentier and Gandia (2013).
Evaluation	Organizing the evaluation of ideas at the organizational level.	Dean et al. (2006), Girotra et al. (2010), Harvey and Kou (2013), Harrison and Rouse (2015) and Parmentier and Le Loarne-Lemaire (2018).

Table 1.4. *Organizational routines of creative capabilities*

At the BNP Paribas Group's insurance company, starting in 2008, the insurance branch implemented a real strategy to develop creativity in the organization. BNP Paribas Cardif, with its 10,000 employees, offers savings and protection products in 37 countries to 90 million customers. In the early 2010s, the new head of innovation wanted to develop a culture of innovation and creativity within the company. She set up a progressive approach to innovation based on creativity, which has built up a real creative capability in this company over the long-term. Their approach includes some of the routines and factors described in this chapter. First, they took stock of the existing situation with the help of an annual innovation prize. Using an application, they collected the projects that had led to an innovative solution (collection and evaluation process). A pre-jury then selected a list of nominees who were presented to the grand jury, which was made up of members of the Comex, country directors and functional directors. The winners are rewarded with innovative visit programs or study trips to different European countries. The number of projects submitted for this award has gradually increased from 36 projects at the launch of the award to 283 projects in 2014, of which 42 were nominated for the innovation award. Following the award, the nominated projects are compiled in an innovation book to involve all Cardif employees in the innovation process and to disseminate these innovative solutions to the entire company (socialization process). In a second phase, they set up a process to propose a new way of finding solutions. The idea was to go beyond the classic meeting and problem-solving approaches by developing an in-house creativity session facilitation service with the creation of a place specially equipped for this type of activity ("La Fabrique"). More than 60 workshops per year were organized by the innovation unit made up of three full-time employees. They also decided to train managers in creativity methods and knowledge of their creative profile (FourSight). Thus, they set up a creativity training course for managers with seven to eight sessions per year to spread these methods throughout the organization (equipment process). Creativity was part of the four values of the BNP Paribas group: reactivity, creativity, commitment, ambition (vision and mission factors) and the principle of innovation was integrated as one of the five managerial principles taken into account in the annual evaluation interview (management factors). To consolidate this approach, they have created a club of facilitators that meets once a month to demonstrate new techniques and exchange practices (equipment routines and socialization). In addition, Cardif also opens its ideation and innovation process (opening routine) by organizing 48-hour jam sessions that mix employees with external speakers (sociologists, designers, innovation players in other industries), and "Sharing Days", which are co-creation sessions with partners and prospects to create prototypes for future collaborations.

Box 1.1. *Innovation through the creativity approach at BNP Paribas Cardif*

1.4. References

Adner, R. and Helfat, C.E. (2003). Corporate effects and dynamic managerial capabilities. *Strategic Management Journal*, 24(10), 1011–1025

Alcántara, H.T.R. (2010). Model and culture creators of innovation in organizations. *Revue Sciences de Gestion*, 75, 109–130.

Altintas, G. (2009). Capacités dynamiques : revue de littérature, limites et voies de recherche. *Conférence AIMS*.

Amabile, T.M. (1988). A model of creativity and innovation in organizations. *Research in Organizational Behavior*, 10, 123–167.

Amabile, T.M. (1996). *Creativity in Context: Update to the Social Psychology of Creativity*. Westview Press, Boulder.

Amabile, T.M., Conti, R., Coon, H., Lazenby, J., Herron, M. (1996). Assessing the work environment for creativity. *Academy of Management Journal*, 39(5), 1154–1184.

Amabile, T.M., Hadley, C.N., Kramer, S.J. (2002). Creativity under the gun. *Harvard Business Review*, 80(8), 52.

Amit, R. and Schoemaker, P.J.H. (1993). Strategic assets and organizational rent. *Strategic Management Journal*, 14(1), 33–46.

Andriopoulos, C. (2003). Six paradoxes in managing creativity: An embracing act. *Long Range Planning*, 36(4), 375.

Barney, J. (1991). Firm resources and sustained competitive advantage. *Journal of Management*, 17(1), 99.

Baruah, J. and Paulus, P.B. (2008). Effects of training on idea generation in groups. *Small Group Research*, 39(5), 523–541.

Binnewies, C., Ohly, S., Niessen, C. (2008). Age and creativity at work. *Journal of Managerial Psychology*, 23(4), 438–457.

Bourgeois III, L.J. (1981). On the measurement of organizational slack. *Academy of Management Review*, 6(1), 29–39.

Brion, S., Mothe, C., Sabatier, M. (2008). L'impact-clé des modes de management pour l'innovation. *Revue française de gestion*, 187, 177–194.

Burns, T. and Stalker, G.M. (1961). *The Management of Innovation*. Tavistock Publications, London.

Burt, R.S. (2004). Structural holes and good ideas. *American Journal of Sociology*, 110(2), 349–399.

Charbonnier-Voirin, A. (2011). The development and partial testing of the psychometric properties of a measurement scale of organizational agility. *M@n@gement*, 14(2), 119–156.

Chen, C.J. and Huang, Y.F. (2010). Creative workforce density, organizational slack, and innovation performance. *Journal of Business Research*, 63(4), 411–417.

Cohen, W.M. and Levinthal, D.A. (1990). Absorptive capacity: A new perspective on learning and innovation. *Administrative Science Quarterly*, 35(1), 128–152.

Cohendet, P. and Simon, L. (2007). Playing across the playground: Paradoxes of knowledge creation in the videogame firm. *Journal of Organizational Behavior*, 28(5), 587–605.

Cohendet, P. and Simon, L. (2016). Always playable: Recombining routines for creative efficiency at Ubisoft Montreal's Video Game Studio. *Organization Studies*, 27(3), 614–632.

Collis, D.J. (1994). Research note: How valuable are organizational capabilities? *Strategic Management Journal*, 15, 143–152.

Conboy, K., Wang, X., Fitzgerald, B. (2009). Creativity in agile systems development: A literature review. In *Information Systems – Creativity and Innovation in Small and Medium-Sized Enterprises*, Dhillon, G., Stahl, B.C., Baskerville, R. (eds). Springer, Berlin, 122–134.

Cyert, R.M. and March, J.G. (1963). *A Behavioral Theory of the Firm*. Prentice Hall, Hoboken.

Damanpour, F. (1991). Organizational innovation: A meta-analysis of effects of determinants and moderators. *Academy of Management Journal*, 34(3), 555–590.

Danneels, E. (2008). Organizational antecedents of second-order competences. *Strategic Management Journal*, 29(5), 519–543.

Darvishmotevali, M., Altinay, L., Köseoglu, M.A. (2020). The link between environmental uncertainty, organizational agility, and organizational creativity in the hotel industry. *International Journal of Hospitality Management*, 87, 102–499.

Dean, D.L., Hender, J.M., Rodgers, T.L., Santanen, E.L. (2006). Identifying quality, novel, and creative ideas: Constructs and scales for idea evaluation. *Journal of the Association for Information Systems*, 7(10), 646–698.

Dechamp, G. and Szostak, B. (2016). Organizational creativity and the creative territory: The nature of influence and strategic challenges for organizations. *M@n@gement*, 19(2), 61–88.

Dewett, T. (2007). Linking intrinsic motivation, risk taking, and employee creativity in an R&D environment. *R&D Management*, 37(3), 197–208.

Dove, R. (1999). Knowledge management, response ability, and the agile enterprise. *Journal of Knowledge Management*, 3(1), 18–35.

Eisenhardt, K.M. and Martin, J.A. (2000). Dynamic capabilities: What are they? *Strategic Management Journal*, 21(10/11), 1105.

Ekvall, G. (1991). The organizational culture of idea management: A creative climate for the management of ideas. In *Managing Innovation*, Henri, J. and Walker, D. (eds). Sage Publications, London, 177–190.

Ekvall, G. (1996). Organizational climate for creativity and innovation. *European Journal of Work & Organizational Psychology*, 5(1), 105.

Feldman, M.S. and Pentland, B.T. (2003). Reconceptualizing organizational routines as a source of flexibility and change. *Administrative Science Quarterly*, 48(1), 94–118.

Ford, C.M. (1996). A theory of individual creative action in multiple social domains. *Academy of Management Review*, 21(4), 1112–1142.

Franke, N., Keinz, P., Schreier, M. (2008). Complementing mass customization toolkits with user communities: How peer input improves customer self-design. *Journal of Product Innovation Management*, 25(6), 546–559.

Georgsdottir, A.S. and Getz, I. (2004). How flexibility facilitates innovation and ways to manage it in organizations. *Creativity and Innovation Management*, 13(3), 166–175.

Getz, I. and Carney, B.M. (2013). *Liberté & Cie*. Flammarion, Paris.

Getz, I. and Robinson, A.C. (2003). Innovate or die: Is that a fact? *Creativity & Innovation Management*, 12(3), 130.

Girotra, K., Terwiesch, C., Ulrich, K.T. (2010). Idea generation and the quality of the best idea. *Management Science*, 56(4), 591–605.

Govind Menon, A. (2008). Revisiting dynamic capability. *IIMB Management Review (Indian Institute of Management Bangalore)*, 20(1), 22–33.

Grandadam, D., Cohendet, P., Simon, L. (2013). Places, spaces and the dynamics of creativity: The video game industry in Montreal. *Regional Studies*, 47(10), 1701–1714.

Grant, R.M. (1991). The resource-based theory of competitive advantage: implications for strategy formulation. *California Management Review*, 33(3), 114–135.

Han, J., Han, J., Brass, D.J. (2014). Human capital diversity in the creation of social capital for team creativity. *Journal of Organizational Behavior*, 35(1), 54–71.

Hargadon, A. and Sutton, R.I. (2000). Building an innovation factory. *Harvard Business Review*, 78(3), 157–166.

Harrison, S.H. and Rouse, E.D. (2015). An inductive study of feedback interactions over the course of creative projects. *Academy of Management Journal*, 58(2), 375–404.

Harvey, S. and Kou, C.Y. (2013). Collective engagement in creative tasks: The role of evaluation in the creative process in groups. *Administrative Science Quarterly*, 58(3), 346–386.

Hill, L.A., Brandeau, G., Truelove, E., Lineback, K. (2014). *Collective Genius: The Art and Practice of Leading Innovation.* Harvard Business Review Press, Boston.

Isaksen, S.G. and Ekvall, G. (2010). Managing for innovation: The two faces of tension in creative climates. *Creativity and Innovation Management*, 19(2), 73–88.

Isaksen, S.G. and Lauer, K.J. (2002). The climate for creativity and change in teams. *Creativity & Innovation Management*, 11(1), 74.

Isaksen, S.G., Lauer, K.J., Ekvall, G., Britz, A. (2001). Perceptions of the best and worst climates for creativity: Preliminary validation evidence for the situational outlook questionnaire. *Creativity Research Journal*, 13(2), 171–184.

Jeppesen, L.B. and Frederiksen, L. (2006). Why do users contribute to firm-hosted user communities? The case of computer-controlled music instruments. *Organization Science*, 17(1), 45–63.

Jill, E. and Perry-Smith, J.E. (2006). Social yet creative: The role of social relationships in facilitating individual creativity. *The Academy of Management Journal*, 49(1), 85–101.

Jin, Z., Navare, J., Lynch, R. (2019). The relationship between innovation culture and innovation outcomes: Exploring the effects of sustainability orientation and firm size. *R&D Management*, 49(4), 607–623.

Kakar, A.K. (2017). Assessing self-organization in agile software development teams. *Journal of Computer Information Systems*, 57(3), 208–217.

Lauer, K.J. (1994). The assessment of creative climate: An investigation of the Ekvall Creative Climate Questionnaire. PhD Thesis, University of New York, New York.

Lee, S. and Lee, D. (2017). The role of agility in the relationship between use of management control systems and organizational performance: Evidence from Korea and Japan. *Journal of Applied Business Research*, 33(3), 521–538.

Lubart, T.I. (2001). Models of the creative process: Past, present and future. *Creativity Research Journal*, 13(3/4), 295–308.

Mahr, D. and Lievens, A. (2012). Virtual lead user communities: Drivers of knowledge creation for innovation. *Research Policy*, 41(1), 167–177.

McKelvie, A. and Davidsson, P. (2009). From resource base to dynamic capabilities: An investigation of new firms. *British Journal of Management*, 20, 63–80.

Napier, N.K. and Nilsson, M. (2006). The development of creative capabilities in and out of creative organizations: Three case studies. *Creativity & Innovation Management*, 15(3), 268–278.

Nelson, R. and Winter, S.G. (1982). *An Evolutionary Theory of Economic Change*. Harvard University Press, Cambridge.

Noblet, J.P. and Simon, É. (2010). La capacité d'absorption, un état de l'art. *Management & Avenir*, 35(5), 33–50.

Parmentier, G. (2015). How to innovate with a brand community. *Journal of Engineering & Technology Management*, 37, 78–89.

Parmentier, G. and Gandia, R. (2013). Managing sustainable innovation with a user community toolkit: The case of the video game Trackmania. *Creativity and Innovation Management*, 22(2), 195–208.

Parmentier, G. and Le Loarne-Lemaire, S.L. (2018). La créativité sous influence du genre : comment le genre de l'individu influe sur la créativité de groupe dans les organisations. *Innovations*, 57(3), 39–58.

Parmentier, G. and Mangematin, V. (2009). Innovation et création dans le jeu vidéo. *Revue française de gestion*, 191, 71–87.

Parmentier, G. and Mangematin, V. (2014). Orchestrating innovation with user communities in the creative industries. *Technological Forecasting & Social Change*, 83, 40–53.

Parmentier, G. and Picq, T. (2016). Managing creative teams in small ambidextrous organizations. *International Journal of Arts Management*, 19(1), 15.

Penrose, E. (1959). *The Theory of the Growth of the Firm*. Oxford University Press, Oxford.

Perry-Smith, J.E. (2006). Social yet creative: The role of social relationships in facilitating individual creativity. *Academy of Management Journal*, 49(1), 85–101.

Pichault, F. and Picq, T. (2013). Le rôle des RH dans l'entreprise tendue vers l'innovation. The role of HR in the innovation-oriented company. *Keys and Questions*, 39(233), 161–182.

Poincaré, H. (1908). L'invention mathématique. *Bulletin de l'Institut Général Psychologique*, 8(3), 2–15.

Rolland, S. and Parmentier, G. (2013). Bulletin board focus groups as a tool for co-creation. *International Journal of Market Research*, 55(6), 809–827.

Rosso, B.D. (2014). Creativity and constraints: Exploring the role of constraints in the creative processes of research and development teams. *Organization Studies*, 35(4), 551–585.

Rothaermel, F.T. and Hess, A.M. (2007). Building dynamic capabilities: Innovation driven by individual, firm, and network-level effects. *Organization Science*, 18(6), 898–921.

Sawyer, R.K. and De Zutter, S. (2009). Distributed creativity: How collective creations emerge from collaboration. *Psychology of Aesthetics, Creativity, and the Arts*, 3(2), 81–92.

Shin, S.J., Kim, T.Y., Lee, J.Y., Bian, L.I.N. (2012). Cognitive team diversity and individual team member creativity: A cross-level interaction. *Academy of Management Journal*, 55(1), 197–212.

Simon, L. (2006). Managing creative projects: An empirical synthesis of activities. *International Journal of Project Management*, 24(2), 116.

Simon, L. (2009). Underground, upperground et middle-ground : les collectifs créatifs et la capacité créative de la ville. *Management International*, 13, 37–51.

Somsing, A. and Belbaly, N.A. (2017). Managerial creativity: The roles of dynamic capabilities and risk preferences. *European Management Review*, 14(4), 423–437.

Szostak, B. (2006). La profession de designer. Une source légitime de créativité. *Revue française de gestion*, 161, 125–138.

Teece, D.J. (2007). Explicating dynamic capabilities: the nature and microfoundations of (sustainable) enterprise performance. *Strategic Management Journal*, 28(13), 1319–1350.

Teece, D.J., Pisano, G., Shuen, A. (1997). Dynamic capabilities and strategic management. *Strategic Management Journal*, 18(7), 509–533.

Unsworth, K. (2001). Unpacking creativity. *Academy of Management Review*, 26(2), 289–297.

Wallas, G. (1926). *The Art of Thought*. Harcourt Brace, New York.

Woodman, R.W., Sawyer, J.E., Griffin, R.W. (1993). Toward a theory of organizational creativity. *Academy of Management Review*, 18(2), 293–321.

Zhou, J. and George, J.M. (2001). When job dissatisfaction leads to creativity: Encouraging the expression of voice. *Academy of Management Journal*, 44(4), 682–696.

Zhou, J., Shin, S.J., Brass, D.J., Choi, J., Zhang, Z.X. (2009). Social networks, personal values, and creativity: Evidence for curvilinear and interaction effects. *Journal of Applied Psychology*, 94(6), 1544–1552.

Zollo, M. and Winter, S.G. (2002). Deliberate learning and the evolution of dynamic capabilities. *Organization Science*, 13(3), 339–351.

2

Building Openness to Develop Organizational Creative Capability

The rise of digital and online platforms has fostered the emergence of "open organization" (Meige 2017). In line with the open innovation paradigm (Chesbrough 2003), innovation thrives on opening up the boundaries of the organization to partners, customers and users. Beyond the mere openness of the innovation process, the openness of the organization now includes all the relationships that the organization maintains with external actors to create value. This openness makes it possible to outsource production, support or innovation activities, as well as to acquire new ideas and knowledge. Openness is thus a crucial vector of creativity for organizations.

However, opening up calls for challenges. Organizations must manage their organizational boundaries (Pénin and Burger-Helmchen 2012), the degree of openness and associated governance (Felin and Zenger 2014) or even the absorption of what has been acquired outside the organization (Ruiz et al. 2020). While openness may promote organizational creativity, it is not easy to implement and requires the development of an organizational capability. This is built by adopting routines and management systems that promote external ideas, their evaluation and their integration into the organization's innovation processes.

Further, this chapter aims to bridge the gap between the organization's capability to open up and its creative capabilities. In the first section, we

---

Chapter written by Émilie RUIZ and Guy PARMENTIER.

show the anchoring of organizational openness in the tradition of open innovation. In the second section, we return to the modalities of openness, underlining the difficulties that organizations may encounter in order to understand openness as a capability. Finally, with the help of various examples, we present the main openness mechanisms currently implemented by organizations and illustrate them with concrete examples.

2.1. Open innovation as the beginning of openness

Open organization and the key role of openness in the strategy of any organization have their origins in the concept of open innovation (Meige 2017). Open innovation is "purposeful inflows and outflows of knowledge to accelerate innovation internally while also expanding the markets for the external use of innovation" (Chesbrough 2006, p. 1). Introduced by Chesbrough (2003), the open innovation paradigm claims that firms can no longer exclusively innovate internally, but must also draw on new sources of external knowledge, thus inviting them to open their organizational boundaries (Chesbrough 2003; Laursen and Salter 2006; West and Bogers 2014).

Although formalized in 2003, the open innovation paradigm is based on older observations. Its emergence follows the limitations of the closed innovation model, which consisted of relying on large internal R&D efforts to protect against competition (Jullien and Pénin 2014). Widely adopted by companies from the post-war period up to the 1980s (Vanhaverbeke 2006), closed innovation had begun to open up long before Chesbrough formalized the concept.

Closed innovation implies an internal logic in which the innovating firm trusts internal capabilities in order to innovate successfully (Chesbrough 2006). In this paradigm, the boundaries of the firm are tight and strictly closed, and the entire innovation process, from R&D to market launch, takes place internally. Conversely, in the open innovation model, the company's boundaries are more porous and permeable and allow the company to innovate thanks to both internal and external flows.

In opposition to closed innovation, open innovation underlies two logics. On the one hand, the inbound logic (or outside in) points out the fact that the company opens up to external knowledge. More precisely, it is "the practice of leveraging the discoveries of others: companies need not and indeed should not rely exclusively on their own R&D" (Chesbrough and Crowther 2006, p. 229). In this case, the firm acquires knowledge and ideas from stakeholders in its internal and external environments (Isckia and Lescop 2011) in order to create value. To do this, Dahlander and Gann (2010) indicate that companies must develop mechanisms for sourcing and acquiring external knowledge in order to increase their internal growth. In other words, the company scans its environment with the idea of finding innovation opportunities with others. The main advantage of inbound open innovation lies in the access to a wide variety of sources for the firm (Dahlander and Gann 2010). The literature shows that access to all these resources poses several challenges for the firms, notably related to the maintenance of relationships with external stakeholders (Remneland Wikhamn and Styhre 2019) or the difficulty of integrating external ideas (Salter et al. 2014). To address these challenges, Laursen and Salter (2006) identify two elements that firms need to consider when engaging in inbound open innovation: 1) external search breadth, defined as "the number of external sources or search channels that firms rely upon in their innovative activities" (Laursen and Salter 2006, p. 134); (2) external search depth, which is "the extent to which firms draw deeply from the different external sources or search channels" (Laursen and Salter 2006, p. 134).

On the other hand, the outbound or inside-out logic suggests that the company optimizes its property rights (like licensing). "Open innovations" suggest that "instead of relying entirely on internal commercial channels, companies may seek out external organizations with business models that are better suited to commercializing a given technology" (Chesbrough and Crowther 2006, p. 229). In this logic, the company transfers ideas and technologies that it has created in order to better exploit them, with a view to capturing value. In other words, the firm generates profits by transferring property rights to others. In this case, Dahlander and Gann (2010) identify disclosure and assignment as two mechanisms supporting outbound open innovation. Here again, the authors identify difficulties, notably related to *licensing* management or potential information leaks. However, by making outbound open innovation *inbound*, Dahlander and Gann (2010) show that companies have more control over their openness to their external environment, allowing them to gain legitimacy in relation to this environment.

In these open innovation phenomena, openness, whether inbound or outbound, promotes the circulation of ideas and knowledge that can feed the creativity of individuals and work groups at all levels of organizations. Creativity needs to be fed with knowledge and ideas in order to develop, as the componential model of creativity by Amabile (1996) emphasizes. This model highlights the central role of knowledge in the creative process. Moreover, openness brings different information and frameworks of thought to organizations, which feeds their ability to detect and re-evaluate a problem, prepare for idea generation and generate ideas. Openness thus helps to overcome the fixation effect (Ward 1994), which limits individual creativity. This is because the cognitive mechanisms of ideation often use recurrent categories and ways of thinking to limit the cognitive load and make reasoning more efficient. In the outgoing logic, open innovation encourages the formalization of ideas, which is also favorable to individual creativity, since formalization allows ideas to be shared and enriched during interactions with others, and even allows new ideas to be formed from these ideas, since this formalization constitutes new knowledge in itself.

To turn it into an organizational capability, i.e. to move from individual creativity to a recurrent collective creativity at all levels of the organization, this openness must be organized and established through processes, routines and systems that will bring ideas and knowledge to the members of the organization and develop their creative skills. It is a question of strategically managing the boundaries according to the organization's objectives (search for efficiency, power, knowledge, identity coherence and digital development) and developing devices to capture and absorb ideas in its processes, products and services.

2.2. The modalities of openness

In this section, we highlight three major modalities of openness that can raise difficulties for organizations: managing organizational boundaries, managing the governance of openness and managing the absorption of knowledge gained through openness.

2.2.1. *Boundaries management*

Openness is dependent on the management of the boundaries of an organization. An organizational boundary is a demarcation between the organization and its environment, which can be set according to four organizational objectives: efficiency, power, competence and identity (Santos and Eisenhardt 2005).

The efficiency boundary is used to delimit the transactions carried out by the organization. It is thus set according to the organization's transaction costs. When transaction costs are high and transaction outcomes are uncertain, an organization tends to internalize its activities. Conversely, when transaction costs are low and the outcome of the transaction is controllable, the organization outsources part of its activities. These activities can be related to idea generation and the search for solutions. It may be more efficient and less costly to externalize these types of activities. For example, the video game producer Nadeo only provides about 10 tracks in its car racing game, Trackmania. The remaining tracks are created directly by players using a car racing track creation toolkit. In this way, players have created several hundred thousand tracks over a period of 10 years, which would have required hundreds of additional employees for the producer if the producer had to create these tracks with an internal team (Parmentier and Gandia 2013). Integrating original and playful racing tracks to enrich the Trackmania game has allowed this small company of about 10 people to enter their game into the video game world cup alongside major licenses, such as Counter-Strike (Valve Software), Warcraft (Blizzard), Quake (ID Software) or even Pro Evolution Soccer (Konami).

The power boundary is set according to the competitive intensity. The more active agents there are that limit the organization's performance in its field, the more likely it is that the organization will resort to vertical and horizontal integration to better control the value network. In the creative industries, access to ideas and control is crucial. If the generators of valuable ideas and content are scarce, organizations will tend to attach themselves to the key players who generate them. This is, for example, what is happening in the film and TV industry with the development of large subscription Video-On-Demand (VOD) platforms. Acquiring a catalog of original series and films based on good ideas is crucial. We are thus witnessing fierce battles to buy catalogs of successful films and licenses (e.g. Disney has bought Marvel Studios, Lucasfilm and 20th Century Fox), acquire the rights to great novels (e.g. Netflix has brought the Roald Dahl Story Company) or identify original series that will make the platforms successful, as Netflix is doing by betting on programs sometimes rejected by its rivals. The recent example of Squid Game, the best Netflix start-up in the world since the platform's creation, whose script was rejected for more than 10 years before Netflix saw its potential, shows the importance of mastering key resources in the event of strong competition, either through insourcing or long-term exclusive contracts.

The identity boundary is set according to identity elements (values, culture, brand image, etc.). Openness then depends on the identity of the organization. Firstly, some organizations, because of their sector of activity or their culture, are relatively closed. We often witness phenomena of rejection owing to the fact that an idea is too far from the culture, language and values of the organization. A crowdsourcing platform can be very effective in capturing ideas, but ineffective in disseminating them within the organization when these ideas come from partners, who are culturally very distant (e.g. ideas from users for an engineering company), and the identity front is too strong. Thus, only ideas that are in line with the organization's culture and values can be adopted. In the same way, partnerships or the acquisition of external actors will be guided by the organization's identity.

The knowledge and skills boundary, finally, is set according to the organization's skills portfolio. The internalization of competencies takes place when these competencies allow the organization to guarantee the efficacy of its strategic activities within stable markets or to innovate better within unstable markets. However, some skills are difficult to integrate, because they are intermittent and very rare. To return to the example of Trackmania, beyond the production force, agents brought ideas that the company's employees could not have had. These ideas could only emerge because there was a large mass of ideas generated by the thousands of agents to produce the hundreds of thousands of tracks, and because these players had very diverse experiences and skills. For an organization, it is impossible to fully integrate this great diversity of experience and skills. However, the organization can (and should) integrate a minimum of the skills it is open to in order to identify external ideas and thus create value. In the case of Trackmania, the experienced team of developers and graphic designers, who are also video game players, allowed the studio to identify valuable ideas to make the game evolve towards the players' expectations. However, it should be noted that this boundary is the one that can play out least favorably to the capture of external ideas. Indeed, in order to integrate external ideas, organizations must develop absorptive capacities (see section 2.3). The challenge is then to develop integration mechanisms (internal coordination with the innovation actors, external coordination with the ideators and socialization in the organization of the selected ideas) (Ruiz et al. 2020) in order to benefit from them.

Openness allows the externalization of ideas and the capture of external ideas with different objectives depending on the type of boundary. For the efficiency boundary, the objective is to reduce the costs of idea generation by using external creatives. For the power boundary, the objective is to control or attach creative people in a context where creativity is vital or scarce. For the knowledge boundary, the objective is to capture ideas and concepts that internal teams cannot create because of a lack of knowledge or even a lack of individual creative capability. For the identity boundary, the objective is to capture ideas that are aligned with the strong culture of the organization. The opening of the boundaries to develop creative capabilities is therefore done according to the objectives of openness.

With the development and massive use of digital technologies, it seems important to us to integrate the digital boundary into the typology of Santos and Eisenhardt (2005), particularly when it comes to dealing with openness. This boundary, although it echoes all the organizational boundaries, is set according to the organization's data acquisition and security strategy. At the level of ideation, openness is nowadays most often achieved through digital platforms such as crowdsourcing devices, online community portals, development toolkits offered by organizations and APIs (Application Programming Interfaces). Digital technology enables and facilitates the creation of true innovation ecosystems, which allows an organization to capture valuable external ideas and innovate with and through external partners.

The case of Schneider Electric's Exchange platform is a case emblematic of this digital boundary. It illustrates the value of opening up to capture donations, content, software and services developed by external partners via a digital co-creation platform. The platform brings together multiple players in the energy and automation industry: end-users, system integrators, technology companies, machine manufacturers, entrepreneurs, electrical control panel manufacturers, etc. With the support of Schneider Electric experts, these players co-create solutions together and promote their expertise. The platform also integrates a marketplace to commercialize the software solutions that have been developed.

2.2.2. *Managing the governance of openness*

The openness of these boundaries concerns activities that are delegated to third parties, who provide services, intermediary products, technologies and content. Openness also concerns corporate governance. A major example relates to social and solidarity economy organizations, which are particularly open. By virtue of their activities, they include many stakeholders in their social and environmental action in their board of directors or in open digital platforms when the various stakeholders of the platform are invited to participate in strategic decisions. Governance is sometimes open at the level of exchange regulation when these organizations provide moderation and voting tools to regulate exchanges and negative behaviors (Gandia and Parmentier 2020).

It is rare, however, that openness is total and concerns all boundaries, implying a balance as to the degree to which the organization wishes to open up (Chesbrough 2003; Felin and Zenger 2014; Bogers et al. 2017) and the implementation of simultaneous internal and external mechanisms (Ruiz et al. 2020). Openness thus carries a real balancing challenge for organizations, as too much openness leads to opportunism, inequalities in the distribution of the value created and conflicts of intellectual property, while a lack of openness deprives organizations of opportunities to capture knowledge and ideas that can fuel the creativity of individuals and teams. The literature on open innovation mainly considers technological openness with industrial partners (Chesbrough 2006), but this type of openness forces a distribution of value between partners and does little to prevent the risks associated with openness. Other studies distinguish between openness and closure according to the content of the openness. For example, in multi-space video game platforms, the openness of content (scenarios, graphics and events) promotes idea generation and value creation via network effects, while the openness of the technology used by the game ensures the protection of the company's assets (Parmentier and Gandia 2016).

This can be illustrated by sharing economy platforms, which distribute openness and closure according to the type of boundary mobilized in the type of openness. Thus, within these platforms, the openness of content is associated with the boundary of efficiency and control, the openness of governance to the boundary of power and identity, and the openness of technology to the boundary of skills (Gandia and Parmentier 2020).

Depending on the strategy of the organization, this management of openness results, in the end, in keeping control of key resources without totally holding them internally, while encouraging the creativity of users and/or teams.

2.2.3. *Knowledge absorption management*

As we have seen, being open is not enough. It certainly makes it possible to identify new ideas, but to create value with these ideas, a certain number of organizational modalities linked to openness must be managed. Boundary management, mentioned earlier, has highlighted the need to develop absorptive capacities to benefit from ideas identified outside the organization. Absorptive capacity is defined as "the ability of a firm to recognize the value of new information, to assimilate it, and to apply it for business purposes" (Cohen and Levinthal 1990, p. 128). More specifically, it is a "set of organizational routines and organizational processes by which the firm acquires, assimilates, transmits and exploits knowledge, with the aim of producing a dynamic" (Zahra and George 2002, p. 186). It is important to remember that openness certainly allows organizations to identify new ideas, but without these absorptive capacities, the organization will not be able to benefit from the knowledge carried by the ideas identified externally. Openness therefore implies developing absorptive capacities.

Complementing the seminal work of Cohen and Levinthal (1990), Zahra and George (2002) differentiate between two types of absorptive capacities: potential (PACAP) and realized (RACAP) capacities. These absorptive capacities develop over four distinct phases:

– Acquisition: the ability of a company to identify and acquire critical external knowledge.

– Assimilation: the routines and processes that allow the company to analyze, interpret and understand information from an external source.

– Transformation: the ability of a company to develop and redefine its routines to facilitate the combination of knowledge that the company already possesses with newly acquired and assimilated knowledge.

– Exploitation, which concludes the process of developing absorption capabilities. It involves "applying" the identified knowledge to exploit it.

Potential absorptive capacities develop during the first two stages of acquisition and assimilation, while realized absorptive capacities develop during transformation and exploitation. In terms of openness, this distinction between potential and realized absorptive capacities is important insofar as Ruiz et al. (2020) indicate that open organizations encounter more difficulties in developing realized absorptive capacities.

In other words, openness allows organizations to easily identify and evaluate knowledge from external ideas, but poses challenges when it comes to appropriating, i.e. transforming, integrating and exploiting it. Openness thus requires the implementation of openness and integration mechanisms that must be balanced. These are mechanisms of internal coordination, such as interfaces involving various functions of the organization or internal turnover, mechanisms of internal socialization, such as means and shared experiences, and external integration mechanisms, such as the coordination with the ideators.

2.3. The main openness devices that promote creativity

In parallel with the theoretical enthusiasm for organizational openness over the last 15 years, empirical and managerial practices have also become much more diverse. Without claiming to be exhaustive, we propose here to present the main mechanisms of openness that promote creativity and illustrate them with emblematic examples.

One of the most classic, and probably the oldest, openness devices involve the collaboration of several organizations working on R&D or innovation projects, fostering knowledge creation (Teece 1989). The literature has shown that organizations that develop numerous links with a variety of organizations (small and large companies, suppliers, universities, etc.) are more innovative than those that limit these links (Powell et al. 1999). Studies initially focused on the positive effect of the network on the production of knowledge, especially in high-tech industries that produce and use a large amount of knowledge intensively (Powell et al. 1996). The extension of studies of the effect of collaboration and networking to the service and creative industries has highlighted that collaboration projects in R&D and innovation between organizations also have an effect on the production and circulation of ideas. In creative cities, collaboration between organizations and between creative individuals and organizations is conducive to the creation of new ideas that have an impact on the economy (Cohendet et al. 2010). Collaborative projects, when they are part of a global innovation strategy, generate not only new knowledge, but also new ideas that increase the creativity of teams and fuel the innovation process.

> Creative cities are cities in which the economy is partly based on the activity of a creative class of active individuals with a high level of creative skills. In these cities (Montreal, Barcelona, Lyon, etc.), the circulation of knowledge and ideas between communities of artists, artisans and organizations, is a great source of creativity for businesses. Establishing a presence in a creative city with one or various creative communities is thus likely to reinforce the creative capabilities of a company. For example, in Montreal, the video game studio Ubisoft is developing numerous local links with the design, development and graphics communities in order to feed itself with new ideas and new perspectives to design truly creative games.

Box 2.1. *Creative cities*

In the rationale of the digital boundary that we discussed earlier, another openness device that is often implemented is crowdsourcing. This consists, for an organization, of outsourcing a task to a vast number of individuals, the crowd, through an open call on the Internet (Howe 2006).

Among the typologies of crowdsourcing identified, creative activity crowdsourcing is one that allows companies to identify new ideas (Ruiz 2016). In this framework, it is a matter of an organization identifying a general theme, a tendance or a problem, and opening itself up to the crowd to identify ideas responding to it, thus leading the organization to pull the crowd into its innovation processes (Ruiz et al. 2017). This type of device allows any organization many advantages: accessing many ideas and knowledge (Pénin and Burger-Helmchen 2012), detecting the commercial potential of an idea or project (Schlagwein and Bjørn-Andersen 2014), reducing costs and risks, more so than with a more traditional device (Schenk and Guittard 2012), and doing remote information research (Piezunka and Dahlander 2015). In other words, it is about the organization fetching knowledge and ideas that are distant from its initial knowledge base. Indeed, by approaching individuals with early uses (lead users) or extremely creative individuals, organizations move away from the classic open innovation partners (Lauren and Salter 2006).

In 2001, Procter & Gamble, a leader in the consumer goods market through numerous brands such as Oral B, Mr. Clean, Gilette, etc., launched the Connect + Develop platform. This platform enables any player outside Procter & Gamble, particularly consumers or potential consumers, to participate in the company's innovation activities. The platform, managed by Procter & Gamble, offers an "innovation" portal, which invites the public to share ideas related to the company's activities, but without a guideline. Among the products produced by the crowdsourcing platform, Procter & Gamble's crowdsourcing platform includes the Magic Eraser (Mr. Clean) and the Pulsonic connected toothbrush (Oral B).

Box 2.2. *Connect + Develop (Procter & Gamble)*

In line with the crowdsourcing of creative activities, companies sometimes turn to communities. A community is generally understood as a voluntary and regular gathering of individuals around a common subject or interest (Amin and Cohendet 2005). Among the various existing communities of innovation (Sarazin et al. 2021), there is a category of communities that organizations can call upon to identify new ideas and foster their creativity communities (Franke and Shah 2003). These communities are characterized by an experience when using a product, service or consumer activity and a high level of commitment to it or to the brand that carries it (Dubouloz et al. 2021). The members are indeed heterogeneous, insofar as they have different experiences of use and knowledge of the product (Dubouloz et al. 2021). User communities are open creative devices that allow the organizations that solicit them to improve the user experience, identify problems related to a product or develop skills related to its use (Parmentier and Mangematin 2014; Dubouloz et al. 2021). If this openness device does not directly develop the internal creativity of teams, it is nonetheless a device for organizational creativity by facilitating the emergence of new knowledge, ideas and content internally, based on ideas captured externally, which will lead to the evolution of the organization's products and services, and sometimes the organization itself.

Launched in 2003, Trackmania is a simple and fun car racing game that integrates tools for creating circuits and organizing online car races. Quickly, a community of gamers was created, with sites and forums to exchange tips and tricks, tracks and cars. In 2007, more than three million accounts were opened and 45,000 players registered in the producer's forums. The community has played a major role in the evolution of the game and its success. The first version of Trackmania did not integrate track trading and competitor ranking. Gamers created tools and new game modes. Tom was the creator of the first community website, and he developed a track exchange site, a feature that was not included in the first version of the game. Benz organized the first competitions even though there was no player ranking in the original version. Starbuck created Funclips, a video contest made from video captures of the races. The community brought innovations and ideas for innovations that the producer has incorporated into the various versions of the game: gamer ranking, car customization tools, race video capture tools, track swapping and integration of gamer minisites into the game. All of these innovations have made the game more social, more intense and more interesting.

Box 2.3. *Trackmania*

The multi-sided platform is another openness device that can foster user creativity and enrich product and service offerings. A platform is a socio-technical environment that provides an online market space for users to transact value with applications and software. Airbnb's rental services or Apple's iPhone applications are based on this type of platform. The platform is multi-sided when different user groups create value for each other through their presence and activities. Each user group brings together individuals with common needs, expectations, skills and propensity to pay (Parmentier and Gandia 2016). Users, by contributing to the making of the service, bring many valuable ideas and thus enrich the core service.

For example, on Airbnb, renters offer atypical accommodations (treehouse, bubble house, house on water, etc.) and accommodations with decoration unique to the renters (Parmentier and Gandia 2017). These offerers therefore contribute to the diversity of offers and some of them can be considered creative. The same phenomenon can be found on Apple's app platform, where external developers have come up with services that carry creative ideas concretized in an innovative app, such as apps for tracking sky constellations or measuring heart rate with the camera. Developers are a great external source of creativity that helps create value for the iPhone. While not all multi-sided platforms are creativity and innovation-oriented, the contribution of users to the service nevertheless encourages the emergence of new ideas, content and applications that are not anticipated by the organization that developed the platform. Thus, these are devices of organizational creativity, which act on the originality of the offer and push the organization to adapt to better integrate the novelties proposed by the users on the platform.

Based on a multi-sided platform, Airbnb offers an online service for booking tourism services that is fundamentally open to contributions from external players. The platform has four interdependent sides: travelers, renters, experience providers and service providers. Each side brings value to the users of the other sides and thus contributes to the overall value of the service. Renters provide accommodation for short or long stays. Experience providers offer tourist services such as guided tours, sports activities, private shows, etc. Travelers are potential customers for the accommodation and tourist experience offers. Service providers provide services that make life easier for renters (concierge, housekeeping, photography, etc.). The presence and activity of the four user groups on the platform bring value to the other groups. Some of these users bring their creativity to the platform by proposing atypical accommodations, new tours or new services.

Box 2.4. *Airbnb*

While openness is increasingly linked to the digital boundary, and therefore primarily virtual, physical collaborative spaces still allow for openness to foster creativity. These physical spaces (although sometimes complicated by online spaces) now take many forms and allow us to foster creativity (Dandoy 2021). These include: 1) FabLabs, a contraction of fabrication laboratory, which are small-scale workshops offering open access to (personal) digital fabrication; 2) living labs, bringing together a set of multidisciplinary experts who develop, deploy and test, in a real or realistic environment, new technologies and strategies in response to the transformation of the world; 3) Hacker and Makerspaces, open collaborative spaces where people with common technological interests meet and innovate; and 4) coworking spaces, allowing individuals to work together according to rules, interactions, feelings, individuals and place (Mérindol et al. 2016; Dandoy 2021).

Inspired by FabLabs, several companies have launched their own internal labs. This is what Groupe SEB has done by creating the SEBLab, a true "laboratory dedicated to creativity and materialization". Located at the company's headquarters, the SEBLab is a place for experimentation and has all the tools needed to identify, create, prototype, test and sometimes even validate the potential of new products. The aim of the space is also to bring together teams from different functions and sometimes external players around innovation issues.

Box 2.5. *The SEBLab*

In addition to the identification of ideas and in line with crowdsourcing, crowdfunding is a particular type of platform dedicated to the financing of projects[1]. The primary vocation of these platforms is to collect funds from individuals to finance projects, new products or the creation of companies. They open up the company's financial boundaries by pre-selling the product to be financed or selling shares in the company. However, these platforms can also be an openness device to collect ideas from potential users when they post comments on the project presentation page or when the company creates a community of users following the funding. Compulsion Games, which published the game We Happy Few, used the Kickstarter platform to raise funds and was able to raise $335,000 CAD in its campaign. More than 7,400 contributors paid for access to an alpha version of the game, including 2,000 who paid more than $60 CAD. Following this fundraiser, Compulsion Games created a community of gamers who, for a year, provided information on bugs in the different versions and gave ideas, expectations and difficulties encountered in the game. During this period, the studio has made regular updates, newsletters on the evolution of the game and the life of the development team of Compulsion Games (Parmentier 2019). The platform crowdfunding form was clearly used here as an openness device to create a community of gamers around the game and capture as many ideas and as much information as possible to make a game that pleases most players.

2.4. Conclusion

Studies on open innovation have shown that it is a source of value creation by capturing technologies, knowledge and ideas outside of the organization. This openness also has important consequences on organizational creativity by feeding the organization with new ideas and concepts from external actors. However, they require a careful choice of the type of boundaries to be opened (efficiency, power, knowledge and identity) according to the strategic objectives and the competitive environment. Moreover, the level of openness must be carefully managed to avoid opportunism and intellectual properties. In this respect, digital platforms are interesting tools to manage openness with many partners, while adjusting the level of openness according to the type of boundary and the elements shared. It is also essential to develop absorptive capacities, and thus ensure that the

1 For example, see: www.kickstarter.com or en.ulule.com.

ideas captured are indeed valuable ideas that really feed the organization's innovation and renewal processes.

Nevertheless, to make it a true organizational capability, i.e. a sustainable capability that acts permanently on the creativity of the organizational creativity, openness needs management devices and routines that ensure its concrete realization and effectiveness through, for example, crowdsourcing, collaborative spaces or connections with creative communities in creative cities. These openness systems often allow access to a large quantity and variety of ideas that inspire the teams in place or directly feed the innovation process. They also encourage the formalization of idea management. This means formally organizing processes for capturing, evaluating and transforming ideas.

However, to make it a capability that contributes to the creative capabilities of an organization, openness also poses new challenges. Managing a large quantity of ideas is expensive. This raises the problem of finding new ways to facilitate management and lower costs. Identifying ideas of value for the organization in a large mass of ideas is also a great difficulty, and in this respect, artificial intelligence technologies could be a promising tool to automate the selection (Von Hippel and Kaulartz 2021). Finally, another important challenge lies in the integration of ideas into the processes of innovation and organizational renewal. The absorption of ideas by the organization requires the development of specific mechanisms to identify, transform and exploit them. In a context of openness, with the help of digital platforms, the good coordination of idea senders and the socialization of ideas are particularly important during acquisition, and the establishment of interfaces between the idea capture device and the rest of the organization is fundamental during the assimilation and exploitation of ideas (Ruiz et al. 2018).

Many questions remain to be answered in order to fully understand the role and contribution of the capability for openness to organizational creative capability. Nevertheless, is openness essential to developing creative capabilities? In the video game industry, there are many examples of development studios that are not very open to the outside world, but are still very creative, showing that openness is not a necessary capability. However, it may be that in other industries, and depending on the socio-economic environment, openness is a central component of creative ability. Future research will need to determine which environmental and strategic conditions require the boundaries of the organization to be opened up to develop its creative capabilities. There is also the question of how openness is maintained over time and whether it continues to contribute to creative capabilities. Indeed, it is possible that the external actors mobilized become exhausted or do not renew their ideas. It will therefore be necessary to explore the conditions that allow these actors to remain creative and contribute to organizational creative capability in a sustainable manner. Finally, future research could also look at the effects of openness on other components of creative capabilities, such as the internal collection of ideas, their socialization and their evaluation.

2.5. References

Amabile, T.M. (1996). *Creativity and Innovation in Organizations*, Volume 5. Harvard Business School, Boston.

Amin, A., and Cohendet, P. (2005). Geographies of knowledge formation in firms. *Industry and Innovation*, 12(4), 465–486.

Bogers, M., Zobel, A.K., Afuah, A., Almirall, E., Brunswicker, S., Dahlander, L., Ter Wal, A.L. (2017). The open innovation research landscape: Established perspectives and emerging themes across different levels of analysis. *Industry and Innovation*, 24(1), 8–40.

Chesbrough, H.W. (2003). *Open Innovation: The New Imperative for Creating and Profiting from Technology*. Harvard Business Press, Cambridge.

Chesbrough, H.W. (2006). *Open Business Models: How to Thrive in the New Innovation Landscape*. Harvard Business Press, Cambridge.

Chesbrough, H.W. and Crowther, A.K. (2006). Beyond high tech: Early adopters of open innovation in other industries. *R&D Management*, 36(3), 229–236.

Cohen, W.M. and Levinthal, D.A. (1990). Absorptive capacity: A new perspective on learning and innovation. *Administrative Science Quarterly*, 35(1), 128–152.

Cohendet, P., Grandadam, D., Simon, L. (2010). The anatomy of the creative city. *Industry and Innovation*, 17(1), 91–111.

Dahlander, L. and Gann, D.M. (2010). How open is innovation? *Research Policy*, 39(6), 699–709.

Dandoy, A. (2021). Community management practices in coworking spaces: Being the ‘catalyst’. In *New Ways of Working: Organizations and Organizing in the Digital Age*, Mitev, N., Aroles, J., Stephenson, K.A., Malaurent, J. (eds). Palgrave Macmillan, Cham, 401–427.

Felin, T. and Zenger, T.R. (2014). Closed or open innovation? Problem solving and the governance choice. *Research Policy*, 43(5), 914–925.

Franke, N. and Shah, S. (2003). How communities support innovative activities: An exploration of assistance and sharing among end-users. *Research Policy*, 32(1), 157–178.

Gandia, R. and Parmentier, G. (2020). Managing open innovation through digital boundary control: The case of multi-sided platforms in the collaborative economy. *Journal of Innovation Economics & Management*, 159–180.

Howe, J. (2006). The rise of crowdsourcing. *Wired Magazine*, 14(6), 176–183.

Isckia, T. and Lescop, D. (2011). Une analyse critique des fondements de l'innovation ouverte. *Revue française de gestion*, 1(210), 87–98.

Jullien, N., and Pénin, J. (2014). Innovation ouverte : vers la génération 2.0 (Open innovation: Toward the 2.0 generation). *Encyclopédie de la Stratégie*, Vuibert.

Laursen, K. and Salter, A. (2006). Open for innovation: The role of openness in explaining innovation performance among UK manufacturing firms. *Strategic Management Journal*, 27(2), 131–150.

Meige, A. (2017). L'innovation ouverte est morte, vive l'organisation ouverte ! [Online]. Available at: https://www.hbrfrance.fr/chroniques-experts/2017/01/14257-linnovation-ouverte-est-morte-vive-lorganisation-ouverte/.

Mérindol, V., Bouquin, N., Versailles, D. W., Capdevila, I., Aubouin, N., Le Chaffotec, A., Chiovetta, A., Voisin, T. (2016). Le Livre blanc des Open Labs. Quelles pratiques ? Quel changements en France ? PBS Paris Business School, Paris.

Parmentier, G. (2019). Compulsion Games. In *Business models et trajectoires stratégiques à l'ère digitale. 12 cas de studios de développement de jeu vidéo*, Demil, B. (ed.). PLS Presses de Mines, Paris

Parmentier, G. and Gandia, R. (2013). Managing sustainable innovation with a user community toolkit: The case of the video game Trackmania. *Creativity and Innovation Management*, 22(2), 195–208.

Parmentier, G. and Gandia, R. (2016). Gérer l'ouverture dans un business model multiface : le cas du jeu vidéo en ligne. *Revue française de gestion*, 42(254), 107–128.

Parmentier, G., and Gandia, R. (2017). Redesigning the business model: From one-sided to multi-sided. *Journal of Business Strategy*, 38(2), 52–61.

Parmentier, G. and Mangematin, V. (2014). Orchestrating innovation with user communities in the creative industries. *Technological Forecasting & Social Change*, 83, 40–53.

Pénin, J. and Burger-Helmchen, T. (2012). *Crowdsourcing* d'activités inventives et frontières des organisations. *Management International*, 16, 101–112.

Piezunka, H., and Dahlander, L. (2015). Distant search, narrow attention: How crowding alters organizations' filtering of suggestions in crowdsourcing. *Academy of Management Journal,* 58(3), 856–880.

Powell, W.W. (1996). Inter-organizational collaboration in the biotechnology industry. *Journal of Institutional and Theoretical Economics (JITE)/Zeitschrift für die gesamte Staatswissenschaft*, 197–215.

Powell, W.W., Koput, K.W., Smith-Doerr, L., Owen-Smith, J. (1999). Network position and firm performance: Organizational returns to collaboration in the biotechnology industry. *Research in the Sociology of Organizations*, 16(1), 129–159.

Remneland Wikhamn, B. and Styhre, A. (2019). Managerial challenges of outbound open innovation: A study of a spinout initiative in AstraZeneca. *R&D Management*, 49(4), 652–667.

Ruiz, E. (2016). Crowdsourcing pour innover : proposition d'un modèle d'adoption, le cas de Raidlight. *Gestion 2000*, 33(4), 31–57.

Ruiz, É., Brion, S., Parmentier, G. (2017). Les barrières à la mise en œuvre du crowdsourcing pour innover. *Revue française de gestion*, 43(263), 121–140.

Ruiz, É., Brion, S., Parmentier, G. (2020). Absorbing knowledge in the digital age: The key role of integration mechanisms in the context of crowdsourcing for innovation. *R&D Management*, 50(1), 63–74.

Salter, A., Criscuolo, P., Ter Wal, A.L.J. (2014). Coping with open innovation: Responding to the challenges of external engagement in R&D. *California Management Review*, 56(2), 77–94.

Santos, F.M. and Eisenhardt, K.M. (2009). Constructing markets and shaping boundaries: Entrepreneurial power in nascent fields. *Academy of Management Journal*, 52(4), 643–671.

Sarazin, B., Cohendet, P., Simon, L. (2021). Communities of innovation: A synthesis. In *Communities of Innovation: How Organizations Harness Collective Creativity and Build Resilience*, Cohendet, P., Rao, M., Ruiz, É., Sarazin, B., Simon, L. (eds). World Scientific, Singapore, 3–26.

Schenk, E. and Guittard, C. (2012). Une typologie des pratiques de Crowdsourcing : l'externalisation vers la foule, au-delà du processus d'innovation. *Management International*, 16, 89–100.

Schlagwein, D. and Bjorn-Andersen, N. (2014). Organizational learning with crowdsourcing: The revelatory case of LEGO. *Journal of the Association for Information Systems*, 15(11), 3.

Teece, D.J. (1989). Inter-organizational requirements of the innovation process. *Managerial and Decision Economics*, 35–42.

Vanhaverbeke, W. (2006). The interorganizational context of open innovation. In *Open Innovation: Researching a New Paradigm*, Chesbrough, H., Vanhaverberke, W., West, J. (eds). Oxford University Press, Oxford, 205–219.

Von Hippel, E. and Kaulartz, S. (2021). Next-generation consumer innovation search: Identifying early-stage need-solution pairs on the web. *Research Policy*, 50(8), 1–14.

Ward, T.R. (1994). Structured imagination: The role of category structure in exemplar generation. *Cognitive Psychology*, 27(1), 1–10.

West, J. and Bogers, M. (2014). Leveraging external sources of innovation: A review of research on open innovation. *Journal of Product Innovation Management*, 31(4), 814–831.

Zahra, S.A. and George, G. (2002). The net-enabled business innovation cycle and the evolution of dynamic capabilities. *Information Systems Research*, 13(2), 147–150.

3

Methods, Tools and Spaces for Revealing Employee Creativity

Materiality holds a central place in creativity management. One only needs to observe the number of differently colored Post-it notes exchanged during brainstorming sessions or the multiple templates used by managers and consultants to reevaluate the organization's strategy, develop new products, or innovate business models to realize this. The management of creative processes increasingly involves the use of various artifacts and methods, each with its preferred tools, to stimulate, structure, and unveil the creativity of the organization's collaborators. Furthermore, we are witnessing a growing trend of spaces dedicated to creativity in organizations, such as rooms equipped with whiteboards for ideation. These spaces are designed to encourage internal collaboration, collaboration with external stakeholders, or to immerse employees in a more playful or unconventional environment to boost their creativity. This materiality enables managers to "*equip*" individuals and teams to foster creative behavior in the workplace. In this context, "*equipping*" refers to providing methods, tools, artifacts, and other organizational techniques for facilitating creative activities. It also implies training staff in creativity methods, so that they can take ownership of the creative techniques and take the initiative to organize creativity sessions when necessary. While numerous articles and examples showcase various methods, tools, and spaces, there is limited integrative work that discusses

---

Chapter written by Romain RAMPA and Guy PARMENTIER.

For a color version of all the figures in this chapter, see www.iste.co.uk/parmentier/organizational.zip.

the advantages and challenges of equipping individuals and collectives in organizations.

This chapter aims to identify the effects and limitations of equipment on the organizational creative capabilities, as well as what is still to be learned from these materials and cognitive equipment for creativity. We will document the methods, present examples of innovative spaces and tools that have been implemented by companies, and we will also discuss recent work that is beginning to address this materiality of creativity. In the first section, our work will focus on cognitive equipment by looking at the benefits that organizations can get from training their employees in different theories and methods of creation. The second section will address the question of the improvement of spaces, and physical and even virtual places, which can help to stimulate creativity. The third section will question in a more general way the different functions that artifacts and tools can have in the service of creativity. We will conclude with a discussion on the interest of the notion of equipping and the management of materiality to address the issue of organizational creative capabilities.

3.1. Cognitively equipping for creativity: training and methods

One of the primary levers frequently employed by organizations to stimulate and structure the creativity of individuals and teams is the use of design and creativity methods and training employees to use these methods to develop their creative skills. Indeed, training is considered one of the most vital processes in the strategic management of human resources (Delaney and Huselid, 1996; Gómez et al. 2004). It plays a pivotal role in maintaining and enhancing individual, group, and organizational capabilities and can significantly contribute to the organizational change process (Valle et al. 2000). Hence, it is not surprising that training in creative methods and tools can be an effective means of developing employees' design skills. Research in this area explores how training in innovative design (Hatchuel et al. 2011) or design thinking (Glen et al. 2014) can enhance employees' ability to work on ill-defined problems or situations with a high degree of uncertainty and exhibit creativity.

The literature documents numerous benefits and advantages of training individuals in creativity theories and methods. As Valgeirsdottir and Onarheim (2017) highlight in their review of creativity training programs, creativity training is increasingly gaining traction in organizations to nurture their creative capabilities. Numerous studies have been conducted to illustrate the impact of such programs on enhancing individual creative abilities by demonstrating tangible benefits in divergent thinking (Karwowski and Soszynski, 2008), self-efficacy (Mathisen and Bronnick, 2009), and creative problem-solving skills (Im et al. 2015). Generally, these studies indicate that this form of training enables people to overcome fixation effects (Hatchuel et al. 2011) and become more comfortable experimenting in unfamiliar territory. It equips individuals with new cognitive skills, as well as new heuristics and strategies for demonstrating creative behaviors.

By providing employees with new tools, methodologies, and theories, innovation and creativity training can have a ripple effect across groups. For instance, Gillier et al. (2010) demonstrate that the use of design methods enables different teams to be better equipped to identify knowledge gaps, synergies between their projects, and new stakeholders for creating value in exploration projects. Kurtmollaiev et al. (2018) showed that training in design thinking methods and tools generally increases teams' ability to make sense of and seize new opportunities, strengthening their willingness to explore unknown territories. Baruah and Paulus (2008) have demonstrated that brainstorming training significantly enhances teams' capacity to generate original and varied ideas in terms of both quantity and quality. Therefore, innovation and creativity training tend to help groups overcome collective fixation effects and think outside the box.

Moreover, Rampa and Agogué's (2021) article argues that by training employees in creative and design methodologies, they can familiarize themselves by working together on common methodologies and adopt an exploratory approach. Leifer et al. (2001) also point out that innovation methodologies emphasizing "trial and error" approaches allow teams to discover unexpected and new values along the way.

Finally, Gillier et al. (2015) mention that recent design theories, such as C-K theory, can help individuals appreciate their new ideas in terms of goals to be achieved, potential spin-offs, new knowledge, and expertise for the organization, thereby strengthening their ability to generate ideas that encompass new forms of value.

Of course, these effects are nuanced based on the methodologies deployed and taught to employees. Without delving into the details of the different methods, we can briefly examine the significance of three major creation methodologies that managers often use to equip individuals and teams in their organizations: C-K theory, CPS, and design thinking.

3.1.1. *The C-K theory and the DKCP method*

The starting point of the C-K theory is that when creating new objects, such as products, services, or business models, we must begin with what the theory refers to as "concepts." These concepts can take various forms, whether it's a designer's brief, an architect's vision, or an ambitious technological objective. Essentially, we need to start with propositions that do not have logical statuses initially, meaning we cannot determine if these statements are true or false at the outset. The form of these propositions may evolve as designers explore different possibilities.

On the other hand, being creative and designing new objects also requires us to engage, integrate, and explore existing "knowledge," which does have a logical status, meaning we can determine the truth or falsity of these propositions.

The C-K theory integrates these two realms – the known (comprising existing knowledge and the individuals who possess it) and the unknown (consisting of the concepts) – to create a formal theory of exploration into the unknown with the goal of designing new objects (Le Masson et al. 2014). The key idea is that these two spaces, despite their distinct structures, interact through consistent and expansive mechanisms. They simultaneously generate both new objects and new knowledge.

To illustrate, consider the frequently cited example of designing a boat that can fly (the unknown). In this case, designers can explore different approaches, such as a boat that flies like a helicopter (knowledge base 1), like an airplane (knowledge base 2), or like a flying fish (knowledge base 3). They can delve deeper into each of these options, gaining more knowledge about the underlying concepts to discover an innovation that is both feasible and valuable.

This process involves transitioning from the unknown to the known. It is the ongoing interchange between the realm of the unknown and the realm of the known that leads to the simultaneous expansion of concepts (desirable unknowns to work on) and knowledge to be explored, resulting in the creation of new objects that challenge prevailing design norms and open up new paths for design.

For a more in-depth understanding of the theory's scientific foundation, please refer to Hatchuel et al. (2013). Figures 3.1 and 3.2 provide a simplified representation of the general mechanics of innovative design work using C-K theory.

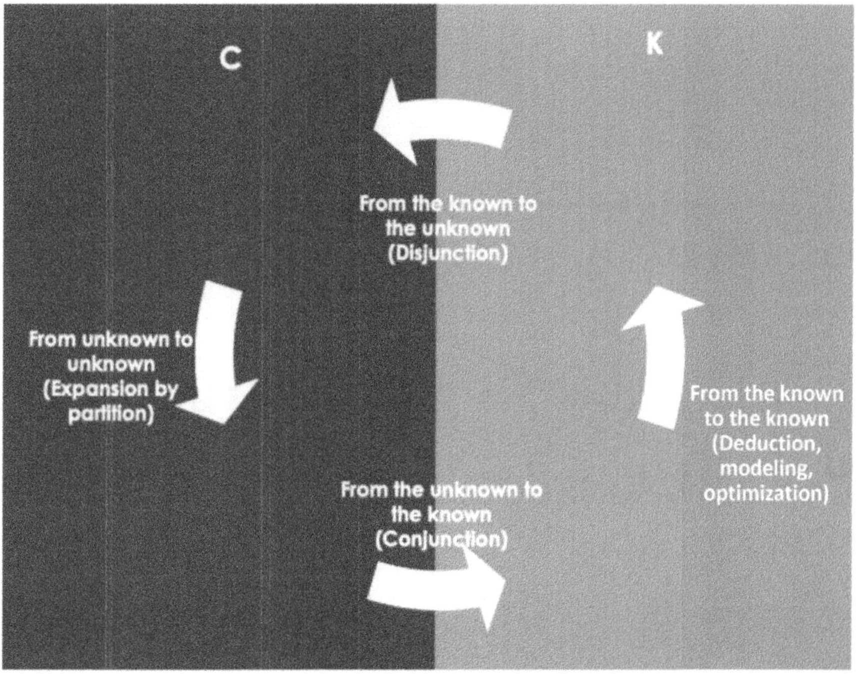

Figure 3.1. *Logics mobilized by C-K theory to address the types of expansion possible in any design work*

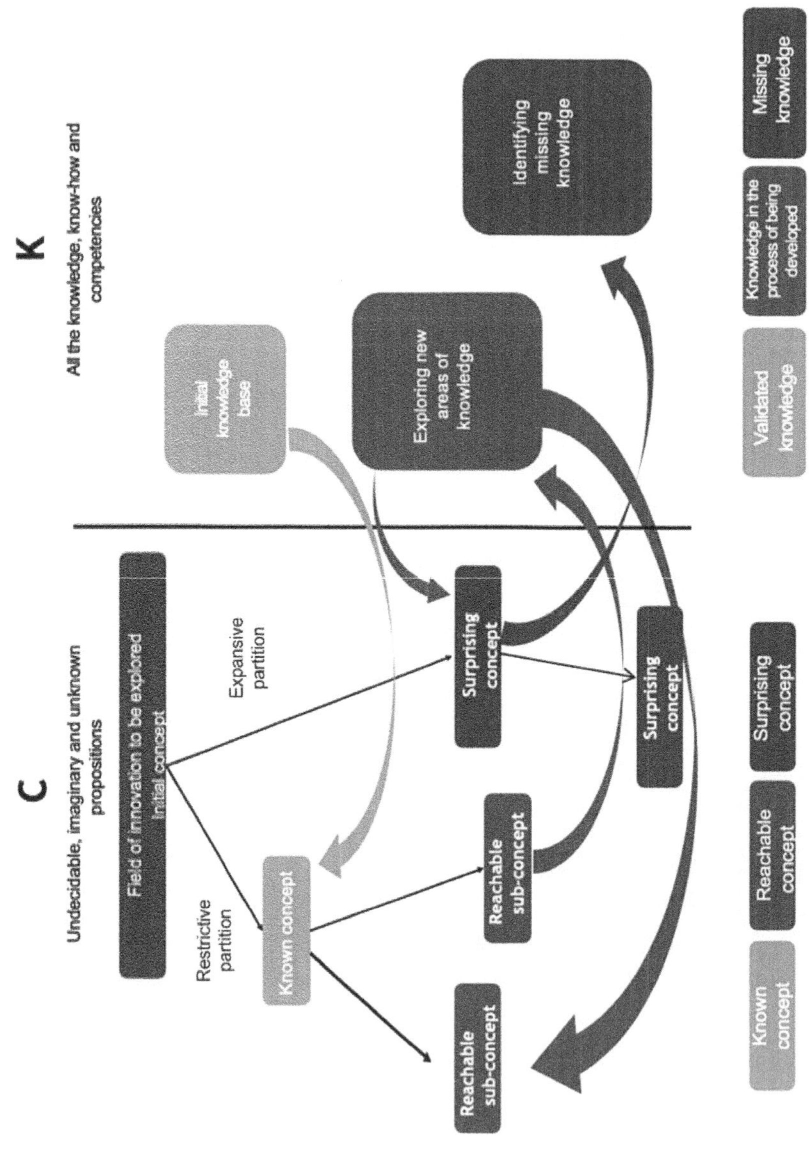

Figure 3.2. *General mechanics of innovative design work with C-K theory*

The C-K theory is used to identify avenues of innovation to explore, as well as to decide on priority avenues to pursue and to use the new insights learned during the explorations to deepen ideas and explore new avenues. There are many variations of the theory in methods.

The best-known and most widespread method in organizations is the DKCP method, inspired by the C-K theory, which promotes collaborative co-design moments that allow leaving behind the dominant designs in large groups. This method is broken down into four phases:

1) An initial diagnostic phase to pose the problem, formulate one or more briefs, and begin to identify some relevant actors for the process.

2) The "K" phase, which aims to extend the initial common knowledge on a given topic.

3) The "C" phase, which aims to provide a large number of ideas and creative alternatives within the defined scope of innovation.

4) The "P" phase, which aims to build a design strategy based on the results of the first two phases (see more details in Elmquist and Segrestin 2009; Le Masson et al. 2009; Laousse and Hooge 2018).

The benefits for organizations of equipping individuals and teams with training in C-K theory and methods are numerous. In particular, individuals can develop new heuristics that lead them not to think in terms of ideas and instead design solution spaces that allow them to more quickly identify the different alternatives that can be considered to respond to a problem, a need, or an original concept.

Moreover, after having explored different alternatives, the visual tree structure of C-K allows groups to keep track of the design reasoning that led them to choose one solution over another, and to more easily justify the value of their ideas. Furthermore, the strength of C-K methods is that they force groups to explore new knowledge and even to develop new knowledge after having identified pockets of missing knowledge.

At Safran, the C-K theory was used to redesign helicopter engines to achieve very high fuel consumption gains, far superior to any innovation developed up to that point.

At SNCF, the use of the DKCP method, applying the principles of C-K theory to large groups, is widespread. They have held more than 100 workshops involving dozens, even hundreds of people, to rethink train maintenance, the use of drones and exoskeletons, and mobility.

At Thales, the use of C-K led to a European innovation award for cockpit demonstrators. Since then, several teams have used this method to think outside the box and develop new products.

At Hydro-Québec's research institute, the use of C-K has made it possible to map out numerous breakthrough paths and to develop an ambitious technological roadmap in the energy field.

Box 3.1. *Examples of companies that use C-K methods*

3.1.2. *Creative problem solving (CPS)*

CPS (Creative Problem Solving) was originally conceived by Alex Osborn and Sid Parnes. Alex Osborn, the founder of the advertising agency BBDO, aimed to stimulate the ideation of his employees and enable them to better communicate their ideas in response to the financial crisis and the declining creative climate that his agency faced in 1939. He is most renowned for inventing the brainstorming method, which is actually just a small component of the broader creativity method detailed in the book "Applied Imagination" (Osborn 1953). This method was later adopted by Treffinger et al. (2006) and is now utilized by numerous consultants and facilitators of creative sessions in organizations.

CPS is a method for discovering original solutions to specific problems. The method clearly identifies and defines the difficulties to stimulate the generation of creative ideas and transform them into actionable solutions, while fostering a creative environment conducive to crafting an original solution suited to the situation.

It comprises three phases and seven steps (see Figure 3.3). The process commences with a situation analysis, involving the identification of existing needs, clarification of the problem's nature, and the decision on the approach to solve the problem. This step is central and can be revisited throughout the problem-solving process. The process proceeds to a problem clarification phase, which includes vision exploration and challenge formulation activities. It then advances to creative transformation, involving idea generation and solution formulation activities, and concludes with implementation, encompassing exploration of acceptance and action plan formulation activities (as per the 2018 version of CPS promoted by the European CREA association). At each stage, participants can reevaluate the situation, backtrack, and recommence the process.

For instance, if it becomes evident that the chosen solution might not be well-received by potential users, participants can return to the creative transformation stage. Similarly, if the challenges are clearly defined from the outset, the process can directly commence with the creative transformation phase.

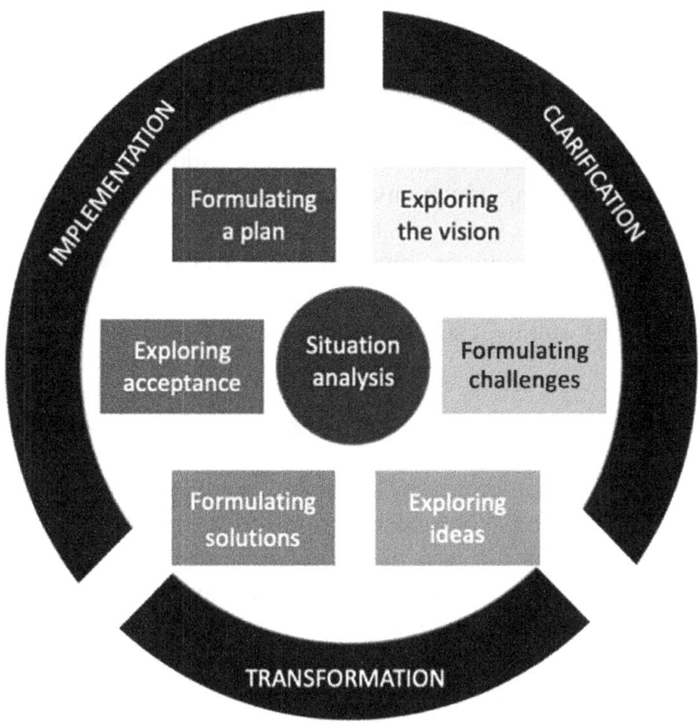

Figure 3.3. *CPS processes and activities*

Each activity in CPS is marked by a divergent thinking phase, aimed at generating as many options as possible, and a convergent thinking phase to select the most relevant ones (Guilford 1967). For instance, the process of formulating challenges involves identifying the gaps that must be filled (the challenges) to achieve the envisioned future. Through divergent thinking, this activity can yield numerous challenge formulations, which are then analyzed in detail using convergent thinking to select the challenge(s) that correspond to the most critical problems.

CPS also underscores the distinct roles of the client (the problem owner), the resource group (responsible for problem-solving), and the facilitator (managing the process and tool selection). It emphasizes the importance of fostering conditions that encourage openness to novelty in a secure climate, along with a willingness to take risks, i.e. recognizing the existence of the problem and the required changes.

The comprehensive method stresses the importance of clarifying the problem before generating solutions. These stages of problem exploration and identification have been recognized as pivotal steps in the creative process (Mumford et al. 1991; Lubart 2001). Additionally, the method promotes metacognition, which involves observing thought processes by clearly identifying the types of thoughts used. Finally, it encourages collective problem solving by enabling the group to create a creative environment that nurtures imagination and the expression of ideas, all with a clear objective of fostering a shared identity for all.

3.1.3. *Design thinking or empathy at the service of creation*

Design thinking, championed by engineer David Kelley and designer Tim Brown, is a methodology that gained prominence in Silicon Valley in the late 1990s. It positions the user as the focal point of the design process, aiming to craft innovative solutions through a comprehensive understanding and definition of user needs and problems.

The core goal of design thinking is to mitigate ambiguity and risk in creative solutions by directly or indirectly engaging customers or stakeholders in the design process. Employing this approach enables decisions to be rooted in what future customers genuinely desire, rather than solely relying on historical data or making uncertain gambles based on intuition.

As Beverland and colleagues expressed:

> Design thinking is characterized by trial-and-error learning through iterative forms, prototyping, and trials that test a range of possible solutions with end-users and other project stakeholders (Beverland et al. 2015, p. 593).

Design thinking is inherently user-centric, yet it doesn't confine itself to a narrow perspective. Many companies employ design thinking to deliver enriching and tailored experiences for their customers.

Depending on the version, design thinking can be segmented into three, four, or five stages (refer to Table 3.1). Fundamentally, it commences with a discovery phase, aiming to generate a set of key observations that enhance the understanding of the context, usage, needs, and challenges of users and stakeholders regarding a problem or initial desire to address. Following the identification of the challenges faced by users, an ideation phase ensues, exploring diverse solutions and alternatives to effectively address the identified problems or needs.

Typically, one or more prototypes are developed to amalgamate and refine ideas, facilitating internal and external discussions with users to enhance the end product or potentially go back to the drawing board. The learning phase, grounded in feedback, is pivotal and at the core of this approach, which should be viewed as iterative and non-linear.

Actors	Key steps
IDEO	Inspiration, ideation, implementation
IBM	Understanding, exploring, prototyping, evaluating
Stanford Design School	Empathy, definition, ideation, prototyping and testing

Table 3.1. *The different models of the design thinking stages*

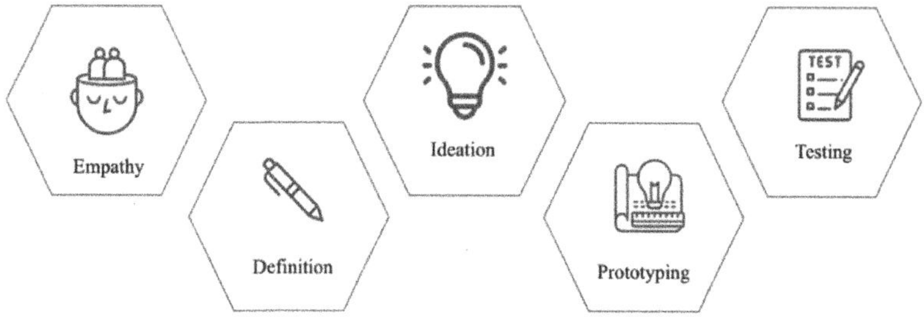

Figure 3.4. *A visual summary of the design thinking steps*

One fascinating aspect of this method is the significance it places on visualizing and materializing ideas. This enables tinkering, refinement, and collaborativc cxploration around tangible objects, fostering greater creativity. As Boni et al. (2009, p. 409) aptly describe, "shifting from abstract thinking to visualizing ideas and then building upon those visualizations is at the core of design for innovation. "

Another key feature is that, much like approaches associated with the C-K theory, this method tends to encourage multidisciplinary collaboration, cultivating creativity and knowledge expansion among individuals who transform into designers.

A third central point is that design thinking prioritizes prototyping and testing phases, facilitating rapid learning. This methodology is widely acknowledged for its ability to make teams highly agile in the design and implementation of new products and services.

Ultimately, the reason design thinking has gained such recognition is because it brings companies closer to the needs, expectations, and frustrations of users. This alignment increases the likelihood of generating original and genuinely valuable solutions.

3.1.4. *Cognitively equipping: issues and limits to be taken into account*

In our discussion, we've highlighted the value of training an organization's employees in various methods and theories related to creativity and innovation, along with introducing three of the main methods that organizations can leverage to equip their staff. However, it's essential to acknowledge that methods and training, while crucial, are not the only elements at play. Several boundary conditions frame their effectiveness.

First and foremost, while the methods themselves are intriguing, the individuals who employ them are equally vital. Special attention should be given to the selection of individuals who will undergo training (as not all may need it) and those who will participate in initiatives guided by these methods. Frequently, it becomes necessary to involve external actors in these explorations. Here, the organization's capability to open up and integrate ideas from external sources comes into focus. Moreover, specific actors, such as facilitators or boundary spanners, can play pivotal roles in these processes.

Secondly, the benefits of these methods and training depend on the actual competence that individuals develop. Training alone is insufficient; it is essential to practice using new methods and tools in low-pressure settings. This allows individuals and groups to enhance their competence independently and foster a sense of self-efficacy in their creative abilities.

Thirdly, knowing when to employ specific methods and tools for different problems or needs is crucial. The choice of method depends on the nature of the task. For example, the C-K method is suitable for seeking disruptive innovation or mapping new fields for the organization, while design thinking is better suited for identifying and exploring well-defined needs or client segments. Additionally, the CPS method can be valuable for clarifying problems. It's not just about the method itself; what matters is the range of approaches that individuals and teams can mobilize in diverse situations.

Fourth, proactive training initiatives signal to teams and individuals that the organization values and gathers original and useful ideas. Such strategies lay the foundation for nurturing the organization's creative capabilities by providing individuals and groups with the cognitive resources to collaboratively foster creativity. These trainings also signify that creativity is a core competency that the organization aims to develop.

Finally, beyond methods and training, the intriguing aspect of this intangible form of equipping an organization's creative capabilities is how it fosters a common language for discussing exploration and creation. This shared language aids in breaking down silos between different business units and disciplines within the organization, making the creative process more efficient by quickly identifying challenges and the tools to address them. However, to establish this common language, there is a certain threshold in terms of trained individuals for it to truly permeate the organization. Therefore, the organization should carefully select the right people and include individuals from different teams and divisions to facilitate this dissemination.

3.2. Establishing and developing fertile spaces for creativity

The role of physical spaces in stimulating, preparing, and influencing creative behaviors is of significant importance. Recent literature has placed a particular focus on both the internal and external spaces within organizations that foster a fertile ground for innovation. The layout of spaces, the arrangement of places, and the functions attributed to different areas possess the power to shape interactions and behaviors among individuals and colleagues within them. As far back as 1996, Amabile et al. emphasized that "physical environments designed to be cognitively and perceptually stimulating can enhance creativity."

However, there is still a lack of comprehensive research on this topic, as acknowledged by some authors working in this field (De Paoli et al. 2019). Some studies on designing spaces for creativity have yielded intriguing findings. For example, research has shown that the color blue in spaces can promote creativity (Mehta and Zhu 2009; Kombeiz and Steidle 2018) by creating a vibrant and stimulating ambiance. Similarly, validating an implicit intuition, other researchers have recently found that a well-lit working environment positively affects the work atmosphere and indirectly stimulates the creativity of individuals working there (Lan et al. 2021). Furthermore, studies, such as those by Plambech and Konijnendijk (2015), demonstrate that the presence of plants and natural elements in offices tends to foster greater curiosity and a more flexible thinking pattern.

Mellard and Parmentier (2020), in their study of a coworking space with a strong emphasis on creativity, identified space design as a critical factor for workers. They found that a warm, well-lit, and relaxing space layout encouraged exchanges, conviviality, and the interaction of people with diverse backgrounds, irrespective of hierarchical connections. This encouraged the sharing of experiences and ideas, promoting a relaxed work atmosphere conducive to knowledge exchange and the spontaneous emergence of ideas. However, individuals also require enclosed spaces to work without visual and auditory distractions when focused attention is needed. As Capdevila (2015) articulates, "the combination of open spaces with spaces that provide privacy is an element that supports collective innovation."

The social facilitator and meeting aspects of spaces have been a focal point of study in the literature, examining how they impact employee creativity. This has led to the significant growth of coworking spaces, alternative environments to traditional office spaces, as well as FabLabs, Living Labs, and other Makerspaces. Notably, spaces like "La Ruche," a collective workspace designed to support and nurture social entrepreneurs in an open and collaborative setting (Fabbri and Charue-Duboc 2013), have emerged. Such spaces promote the pooling of ideas and collective efforts to address individual challenges. In a broader sense, coworking spaces, similar to communal and open spaces within companies, facilitate interdisciplinary collaboration by bringing together people with diverse knowledge bases and ideas (Fabbri and Charue-Duboc 2016; Samani and Alavi 2020). This phenomenon gives rise to serendipitous encounters and fosters creativity within work environments.

The I-Lab at Air Liquide

In 2013, following a trip to California by its CEO and VP of Innovation, Air Liquide decided to create an internal FabLab, the I-Lab (Ruiz 2021). The goal was to be able to support employees with new tools and methodologies and to allow those in the organization to have a more agile and flexible space. The place has a videoconference room, a creativity room with whiteboards and equipment at disposal, as well as a place for prototyping with a 3D printer, a laser cutter and other equipment facilitating experimentation and innovation (including a 3D screen). It is an experimentation laboratory that aims to test the feasibility of ideas more quickly, in addition to providing a framework for the development of new ideas.

The ProtoSpace network at Airbus

Inaugurated in 2014, Airbus' first ProtoSpace has seen the price of its success, and there are now several networks of ProtoSpace spaces that have sprung up across the company's various sites. The advantage of these spaces is that they provide real design spaces, where employees can think about and develop future concepts. These spaces are designed to encourage creativity and cooperation. But they also to have a prototyping lab, where employees can bring their concepts to life with access to a wide range of materials and resources, as well as a wide range of tools and technologies (3D scanners, virtual reality headsets, 3D impression, and more conventional tools, etc.). In addition, since a virtual network between the locations has been set up with a common sharing platform, designers can easily share their models, digital files of their projects for 3D printing, as well as various solutions they have developed on the company's digital platform.

Box 3.2. *Two examples of corporate OpenLabs*

Companies are increasingly establishing open spaces dedicated to collaboration with users and external actors, as well as rapid prototyping laboratories equipped with various tools for quick experimentation and testing of new ideas. Mérindol et al. (2016) refer to these spaces as corporate OpenLabs, designed to foster individual and collective initiatives driven by employees within a creative framework (see Box 3.2). The creation of these spaces aims to provide employees with diverse environments for activities that extend beyond their usual routines. They offer dedicated spaces for collaboration with both internal and external partners and areas for the design and experimentation of new solutions (Lô 2017).

Through the implementation of these open and shared spaces or by relocating employees to external coworking spaces, companies aim to promote collaboration and offer their employees the opportunity to work in aesthetically pleasing and enjoyable offices. These spaces often feature amenities that encourage relaxation and informal discussions, as well as dedicated rooms for specific activities such as creativity, games, meetings, concentration, and even relaxation (Bouncken et al. 2021).

Although workplace design and spatial layout significantly influence the creativity of individuals and groups, there is still a shortage of research in this area, primarily due to methodological challenges. Distinguishing the relationship between material and social contexts can be complex. Additionally, empirically testing the impact of relocating to a new workspace on creativity can be challenging due to potential measurement biases linked to other organizational factors or the disruptive nature of changing work locations (Maheshwari and Werd 2019).

Nevertheless, certain factors related to workspace design have been shown to have a profound impact on employee well-being and motivation, consequently influencing creativity. These include the size of the space, access to natural light, and the arrangement of locations (Dul et al. 2011; Hoff and Öberg 2015). Spaces that reduce distractions and ambient noise tend to be more conducive to sustaining employee creativity, as creativity often demands increased attention and focus (Stokols et al. 2002). Lastly, flexibility and modularity of spaces, along with the ability to strike a balance between private and collaborative areas, have a positive impact on creativity (Martens 2011; Hoff and Öberg 2015).

3.2.1. *The advent of virtual spaces?*

The rapid shift to telecommuting for many employees in 2020 has brought virtual spaces and platforms into the spotlight, prompting a surge of interest in their potential to foster collective ideation activities and either enhance or diminish organizational creativity. Several studies, mostly conducted from 2010 onwards, had already explored this question, often through laboratory experiments or by examining multinational organizations with geographically dispersed teams. The collective body of work suggests that creativity in virtual spaces can be hampered by coordination and communication challenges, which can have a negative impact on both individual and team creativity (Painter et al. 2016). However, it has been observed that establishing a climate of trust among participants and defining norms for communication within virtual spaces, such as rules for speaking time and respectful interactions, can serve as effective strategies to mitigate this negative relationship (Han et al. 2017).

An interesting aspect of virtual spaces is their potential to provide anonymity under certain conditions. However, research on this subject has yielded mixed results. For instance, one study suggests that utilizing platforms that allow anonymity can enhance individual contributions and the originality of ideas by reducing status and power biases in the organization (Chang 2011). Conversely, another study indicates that anonymity can reduce individuals' motivation to contribute ideas when contributions can be identified and acknowledged (Chen et al. 2014).

To address this ambivalence, recent research highlights that the relationship between virtual spaces and creativity may vary at the individual level depending on the personality and traits of the employees (Bourgeois-Bougrine et al. 2020). This research suggests that individuals with a higher risk tolerance may find it easier to express uninhibited creativity in virtual environments, displaying greater divergent thinking and idea expression. In contrast, those with lower risk tolerance may feel more at ease expressing their ideas in physical environments.

Although studies conducted during the pandemic are expected to shed further light on the factors that influence creativity in virtual contexts, some early lessons have emerged in this crisis context. Firstly, individuals need to feel comfortable with the functionality of virtual platforms. The stress and ambiguity often associated with these platforms stem from individuals' abilities to confidently navigate the various options and interfaces available to generate ideas, such as Teams, Zoom, Miro, Klaxoon, and others.

Secondly, it is increasingly important to employ written forms of communication in virtual spaces to express, critique, and improve ideas. Virtual spaces can introduce communication barriers, such as difficulty conducting simultaneous conversations, limited nonverbal communication, and increased background noise. The written word becomes particularly crucial when dealing with medium and large groups.

Thirdly, given the challenges of fostering informal communication in virtual settings, building a climate of trust within workgroups and facilitating discussions is paramount. This includes regulating speaking time, reinitiating discussions, and reducing authority bias, among other measures.

Lastly, virtual spaces offer opportunities to implement interaction modalities and playful elements that are often harder to incorporate in physical spaces, such as the creation of avatars, virtual worlds, or immersion in virtual reality. Early research in this area shows a promising and positive impact on the originality of ideas generated within these virtual worlds (Bonnardel et al. 2016; Guegan et al. 2016; Gong et al. 2021).

3.3. The role of physical tools and equipment

Objects play various roles in the creative processes of organizations, supporting, framing, and stimulating the creative behavior of individuals and teams.

Firstly, artifacts and tools serve to stimulate and frame the emergence of new ideas. The creative spark, the moment when an idea is born, is often facilitated by multisensory stimuli conveyed by physical artifacts in individuals' immediate surroundings (van Iterson et al. 2017; Parmentier et al. 2017). Some organizations provide their employees with various types of artifacts to catalyze and frame these moments and facilitate conversational practices. For instance, at Salomon's shoe department, rooms are filled with a variety of objects, materials, shoes, past prototypes, and more. These artifacts are not merely decorative but are actively used to fuel discussions among employees. In this setting, no creative process occurs without objects systematically placed at the center of discussions. Similarly, in the game Trackmania, user toolkits have been employed to collect, share, and rapidly visualize user ideas (Parmentier and Gandia 2013).

Secondly, artifacts can function as organizational memory, helping to strengthen and preserve the knowledge pool of individuals and teams. For instance, at Créaolica, a company specializing in designing new objects, employees randomly access shoeboxes filled with tools and remnants from past projects to stimulate memories and experiences, thus facilitating the search for new ideas (Garel 2019). This concept extends to a wide range of creativity tools such as personae, mindmaps, and canvases, which serve as both reservoirs of organizational memory, tools for reflection, and spaces for discussion. This aspect is closely related to the concept of the creative pool, which is explored in another chapter of this book.

Finally, the equipment and tools at hand are instrumental in visualizing ideas quickly, learning, discussing, iterating on concepts, and testing them. To facilitate this, simulation and rapid prototyping tools have become increasingly available for the swift implementation and testing of ideas. These tools encompass 3D printing, Arduino controllers, material cutting tools, and more (Georgiev et al. 2017; Garnier 2020). With these resources, ideas transition from being purely conceptual to partially material, enabling individual designers to initially evaluate and refine concepts more effectively. Tangible manifestations of ideas move them from the confines of designers' minds to a physical medium, allowing them to validate the forms of value they incorporate and assess their reception among various stakeholders (Stigliani and Ravasi 2012).

3.4. Discussion and conclusion

In the realm of organizational creative capabilities, equipment holds a distinctive and pivotal role, offering managers the most direct means to impact their collectives and groups. Equipment for creativity supplies the frameworks and cognitive resources necessary for individuals and teams within an organization to manifest creative behaviors.

Our chapter delves into a deeper understanding of how managers can equip their organizations, training them in creativity methods, crafting or providing access to spaces (both physical and virtual) conducive to creativity, and leveraging material tools and artifacts. This chapter also delves into the effects and boundary conditions that frame these diverse approaches to equipping. We categorize these effects into direct and indirect consequences of equipping within an organization, situating the concept within the broader context of other creative capabilities.

Our chapter demonstrates that equipment plays a profoundly instrumental role in organizations, directly affecting individuals, teams, and the community within the organization. Cognitive equipment serves as a vital tool in developing creative skills for both individuals and organizational collectives.

Training and the implementation of new creative and design methods foster divergent thinking and new heuristics in individuals while bolstering their sense of creative self-efficacy, two attributes central to Amabile's model (2011). Cognitive equipment also directly enables collectives to more effectively select and evaluate creative ideas.

Physical equipment also plays a prominent direct role by providing support for visualizing, discussing, and selecting ideas. This support is central to organizational memory, aiding in the easy retrieval of knowledge and ideas to stimulate the creativity of collaborators. In addition, organizational spaces play a key role in materializing ideas, providing areas for experimentation and rapid prototyping.

Beyond the numerous direct effects of equipment, it is the indirect effects that hold particular interest. Cognitive equipment, if training and methods become widespread, can facilitate the development of a common language within the organization for discussing creation and exploration (Rampa and Agogué 2021).

Physical equipment can stimulate both internal and external collaboration, providing dedicated spaces that promote interdisciplinarity and thus stimulate the exchange of knowledge and information. These spaces also have the power to influence the organization's atmosphere, which significantly affects the well-being and motivation of individuals, creating a playful, warm, and stimulating environment conducive to the emergence of creative behavior (Dobson and McKendrick 2018).

Moreover, both physical and cognitive equipment can send a powerful signal if the organization employs proactive strategies to develop them and values, welcomes, and promotes creativity. This signal can have a profound impact on the organization's culture and the actual utilization of these creative spaces. It's worth noting that the extent of this impact depends on how the organization perceives and integrates creativity into its core functions and identity. Figure 3.5 summarizes these various direct and indirect effects, illustrating how equipment influences the creative capabilities of organizations.

However, equipment occupies a unique position among the dimensions that constitute organizational creative capability. Much of the value of equipment is intertwined with other dimensions of the model. Factors such as the organization's level of socialization and openness play a crucial role in determining the effective use of physical creativity spaces, fostering collaboration and interdisciplinarity.

Organizational agility is vital in understanding the frequency and importance of experimentation and rapid prototyping within these spaces. Cognitive equipment and employee training can only fully enable value creation if the organization establishes formal or informal idea management mechanisms and provides room to maneuver in terms of time and resources.

Creative slack also influences how the material artifacts of the organization support its organizational memory, making it easier to reactivate prior knowledge and ideas in the service of the organization's creativity.

We can draw a parallel between equipment and Amartya Sen's concept of "capabilities". Equipment represents the foundational aspects of creative capabilities, offering the potential for organizational actors to exhibit creative behaviors. However, it does not function in isolation; it acts as the bedrock that enables other dimensions to be more generative and robust, granting greater or lesser possibilities for action within the organization. Like any foundation, it may be prudent for the organization to start with equipment to initiate and cultivate creative capabilities.

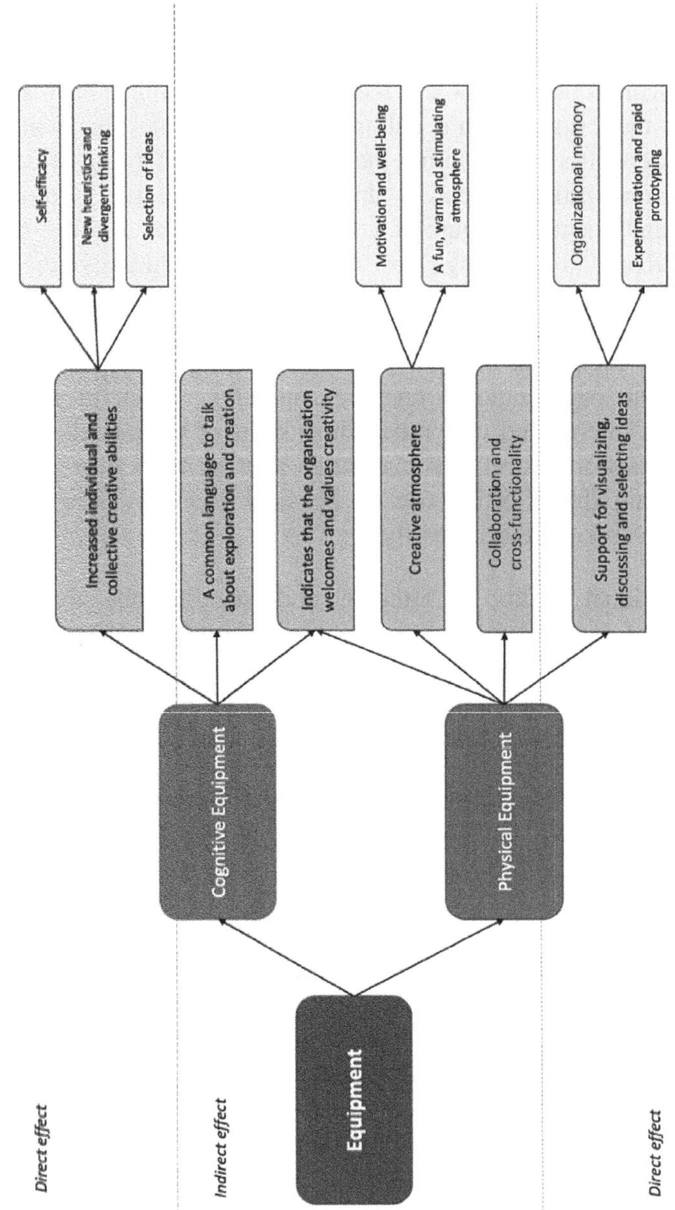

Figure 3.5. *A synthesis of the direct and indirect effects of equipment on organizational creativity*

3.5. References

Amabile, T.M. (2011). *Componential Theory of Creativity.* Harvard Business School, Boston.

Amabile, T.M., Conti, R., Coon, H., Lazenby, J., Herron, M. (1996). Assessing the work environment for creativity. *Academy of Management Journal*, 39(5), 1154–1184.

Baruah, J. and Paulus, P.B. (2008). Effects of training on idea generation in groups. *Small Group Research*, 39(5), 523–541.

Beverland, M.B., Wilner, S.J.S., Micheli, P. (2015). Reconciling the tension between consistency and relevance: Design thinking as a mechanism for brand ambidexterity. *Journal of the Academy of Marketing Science*, 43(5), 589–609.

Boni, A.A., Weingart, L.R., Evenson, S. (2009). Innovation in an academic setting: Designing and leading a business through market-focused, interdisciplinary teams. *Academy of Management Learning & Education*, 8(3), 407–417.

Bonnardel, N., Forens, M., Lefevre, M. (2016). Enhancing collective creative design: An exploratory study on the influence of static and dynamic personas in a virtual environment. *The Design Journal*, 19(2), 221–235.

Bouncken, R.B., Aslam, M.M., Qiu, Y. (2021). Coworking spaces: Understanding, using, and managing sociomateriality. *Business Horizons*, 64(1), 119–130.

Bourgeois-Bougrine S., Richard P., Burkhardt J.-M., Frantz B., Lubart T. (2020). The expression of users' creative potential in virtual and real environments: An exploratory study. *Creativity Research Journal*, 32(1), 55–65.

Capdevila, I. (2015). Les différentes approches entrepreneuriales dans les espaces ouverts d'innovation. *Innovations*, 3, 87–105.

Carrier, C., Cadieux, L., Tremblay, M. (2010). Créativité et génération collective d'opportunités. *Revue française de gestion*, 7, 113–127.

Chang, C.M. (2011). New organizational designs for promoting creativity: A case study of virtual teams with anonymity and structured interactions. *Journal of Engineering and Technology Management*, 28(4), 268–282.

Chen, F., Zhang, L., Latimer, J. (2014). How much has my co-worker contributed? The impact of anonymity and feedback on social loafing in asynchronous virtual collaboration. *International Journal of Information Management*, 34(5), 652–659.

Delaney, J.T. and Huselid, M.A. (1996). The impact of human resource management practices on perceptions of organizational performance. *Academy of Management Journal*, 39(4), 949–969.

De Paoli, D., Sauer, E., Ropo, A. (2019). The spatial context of organizations: A critique of creative workspaces. *Journal of Management & Organization*, 25(2), 331–352.

Dobson, S. and McKendrick, J. (2018). Intrapreneurial spaces to entrepreneurial cities: Making sense of play and playfulness. *The International Journal of Entrepreneurship and Innovation*, 19(2), 75–80.

Dul, J., Ceylan, C., Jaspers, F. (2011). Knowledge workers' creativity and the role of the physical work environment. *Human Resource Management*, 50(6), 715–734.

Elmquist, M. and Segrestin, B. (2009). Sustainable development through innovative design: Lessons from the KCP method experimented with an automotive firm. *International Journal of Automotive Technology and Management*, 9(2), 229–244.

Fabbri, J. and Charue-Duboc, F. (2013). Un modèle d'accompagnement entrepreneurial fondé sur des apprentissages au sein d'un collectif d'entrepreneurs : le cas de La Ruche. *Management International*, 17(3), 86–99.

Fabbri, J. and Charue-Duboc, F. (2016). Les espaces de coworking-Nouveaux intermédiaires d'innovation ouverte ? *Revue française de gestion*, 42(254), 163–180.

Garel, G. (2019). Organizing innovative design or how to remain an explorer: The case of Creaholic. In *Management of Extreme Situations: From Polar Expeditions to Exploration-oriented Organizations*, Lièvre, P., Aubry, M., Garal, G. (eds). ISTE Ltd, London, and John Wiley & Sons, New York, 105–120.

Garnier, C. (2020). Les FabLabs, un réseau mondial et en croissance d'organisations collaboratives : une analyse des modes de coordination intra et inter-organisationnels. PhD Thesis, Institut Polytechnique de Paris, Paris.

Georgiev, G.V., Sánchez Milara, I., Ferreira, D. (2017). A framework for capturing creativity in digital fabrication. *The Design Journal*, 20(1), S3659–S3668.

Gillier, T., Piat, G., Roussel, B., Truchot, P. (2010). Managing innovation fields in a cross-industry exploratory partnership with C–K design theory. *Journal of Product Innovation Management*, 27(6), 883–896.

Gillier T., Hooge S., Piat G. (2015). Framing value management for creative projects: An expansive perspective. *International Journal of Project Management*, 33(4), 947–960.

Glen, R., Suciu, C., Baughn, C. (2014). The need for design thinking in business schools. *Academy of Management Learning & Education*, 13(4), 653–667.

Gómez, P.J., Lorente, J.J.C., Cabrera, R.V. (2004). Training practices and organisational learning capability: Relationship and implications. *Journal of European Industrial Training*, 28(2/3/4), 234-256.

Gong, Z., Nanjappan, V., Soomro, S. A., Georgiev, G.V. (2021). Virtual brainstorming and creativity: An analysis of measures, avatars, environments, interfaces, and applications. *Proceedings of the Design Society*, 1, 3399–3408.

Guegan, J., Buisine, S., Mantelet, F. et al. (2016). Avatar-mediated creativity: When embodying inventors makes engineers more creative. *Computers in Human Behavior*, 61, 165–175.

Guilford, J.P. (1967). *The Nature of Human Intelligence*. McGraw-Hill, New York.

Han, S.J., Chae, C., Macko, P., Park, W., Beyerlein, M. (2017). How virtual team leaders cope with creativity challenges. *European Journal of Training and Development*, 41(3), 261-276.

Hatchuel, A., Le Masson, P., Weil, B. (2011). Teaching innovative design reasoning: How concept–knowledge theory can help overcome fixation effects. *Artificial Intelligence for Engineering Design, Analysis and Manufacturing*, 25(1), 77–92.

Hatchuel, A., Weil, B., Le Masson, P. (2013). Towards an ontology of design: Lessons from C–K design theory and Forcing. *Research in Engineering Design*, 24(2), 147–163.

Hoff, E.V. and Öberg, N.K. (2015). The role of the physical work environment for creative employees – a case study of digital artists. *The International Journal of Human Resource Management*, 26(14), 1889–1906.

Im, H., Hokanson, B., Johnson, K.K.P. (2015). Teaching creative thinking skills: A longitudinal study. *Clothing and Textiles Research Journal*, 33(2), 129–142.

van Iterson, A., Clegg, S., Carlsen, A. (2017). Ideas are feelings first: Epiphanies in everyday workplace creativity. *M@n@gement*, 20(3), 221–238.

Karwowski, M. and Soszynski, M. (2008). How to develop creative imagination? Assumptions, aims and effectiveness of role play training in creativity (RPTC). *Thinking Skills and Creativity*, 3(2), 163–171.

Kombeiz, O. and Steidle, A. (2018). Facilitation of creative performance by using blue and red accent lighting in work and learning areas. *Ergonomics*, 61(3), 456–463.

Kurtmollaiev, S., Pedersen, P.E., Fjuk, A., Kvale, K. (2018). Developing managerial dynamic capabilities: A quasi-experimental field study of the effects of design thinking training. *Academy of Management Learning & Education*, 17(2), 184–202.

Lan, L., Hadji, S., Xia, L., Lian, Z. (2021). The effects of light illuminance and correlated color temperature on mood and creativity. *Building Simulation*, 463–475.

Laousse, D. and Hooge, S. (2018). Refaire société par la création de communautés d'innovation. Le cas des ateliers SpotLAB sur les nouvelles mobilités en régions. *Revue française de gestion*, 44(272), 85–102.

Le Masson, P., Hatchuel, A., Weil, B. (2009). Design theory and collective creativity: A theoretical framework to evaluate KCP process. *DS 58-6: Proceedings of ICED 09, the 17th International Conference on Engineering Design, Vol. 6, Design Methods and Tools (pt. 2)*, Palo Alto.

Le Masson, P., Weil, B., Hatchuel, A. (2014). *Théorie, méthodes et organisations de la conception*. Transvalor-Presses des Mines, Paris.

Leifer, R., O'Connor, G.C., Rice, M. (2001). Implementing radical innovation in mature firms: The role of hubs. *Academy of Management Executive*, 15(3), 102–113.

Lô, A. (2017). Un FabLab d'entreprise pour favoriser l'ambidextrie des salariés. Étude de cas chez Renault. *Revue française de gestion*, 43(264), 81–99.

Lubart, T.I. (2001). Models of the creative process: Past, present and future. *Creativity Research Journal*, 13(3/4), 295–308.

Maheshwari, A.K. and Werd, M.R.P. (2019). Architecture and creativity: Examining the impact of Maharishi Vastu on workplace creativity. *Creativity Research Journal*, 31(4), 371–376.

Martens, Y. (2011). Creative workplace: Instrumental and symbolic support for creativity. *Facilities*, *29*(1/2), 63-79.

Mathisen, G.E. and Bronnick, K.S. (2009). Creative self-efficacy: An intervention study. *International Journal of Educational Research*, 48(1), 21–29.

Mehta, R. and Zhu, R.J. (2009). Blue or red? Exploring the effect of color on cognitive task performances. *Science*, 323(5918), 1226–1229.

Mellard, M. and Parmentier, G. (2020). La créativité dans les espaces de coworking : le cas de "La Cordée". *Innovations*, 61(1), 67–88.

Mérindol, V., Bouquin, N., Versailles, D., Capdevila, I., Aubouin, N., Le Chaffotec, A., Chiovetta, A., Voisin, T. (2016). Le Livre blanc des Open Labs. Quelles pratiques ? Quel changements en France ? PBS Paris Business School, Paris.

Mumford, M.D., Mobley, M.I., Uhlman, C.E., Reiter-Palmon, R., Doares, L.M. (1991). Process analytic models of creative capacities. *Creativity Research Journal*, 4(2), 91–122.

Osborn, A.F. (1953). *Applied Imagination: Principles and Procedures of Creative Problem Solving*. Charles Scribner's Sons, New York.

Painter, G., Posey, P., Austrom, D., Tenkasi, R., Barrett, B., Merck, B. (2016). Sociotechnical systems design: Coordination of virtual teamwork in innovation. *Team Performance Management*, *22*(7/8), 354-369.

Parmentier, G. and Gandia, R. (2013). Managing sustainable innovation with a user community toolkit: The case of the video game Trackmania. *Creativity and Innovation Management*, 22(2), 195–208.

Parmentier, G., Szostak, B., Rüling, C.C. (2017). Introduction au dossier thématique : créativité organisationnelle : quels enjeux en management stratégique dans un contexte mondialisé ? *Management International*, 22(1), 12–18.

Plambech, T. and van den Bosch, C.C.K. (2015). The impact of nature on creativity. A study among Danish creative professionals. *Urban Forestry & Urban Greening*, 14(2), 255–263.

Rampa, R. (2020). Émergence et organisation d'une fonction d'innovation disséminée : ethnographie d'un institut de recherche en mutation. PhD Thesis, HEC Montréal.

Rampa, R. and Agogué, M. (2021). Developing radical innovation capabilities: Exploring the effects of training employees for creativity and innovation. *Creativity and Innovation Management*, 30(1), 211–227.

Ruiz, E. (2021). Entre différenciation et intégration : favoriser l'innovation d'exploration grâce au Fab Lab interne, le cas de l'i-Lab (Air Liquide). *Innovations*, 65(2), 219–245.

Samani, S.A. and Alavi, S.M.S.Z. (2020). Does the design of the workplace affect individual creativity. *Performance Improvement*, 59(5), 6–16.

Sen, A. (2003). Development as capability expansion. In *Readings in Human Development : Concepts, Measures and Policies for a Development Paradigm,* Fukuda-Parr, S., Shiva Kumar, A.K. (eds). Oxford University Press, New Delhi, New York, 3–16.

Stigliani, I. and Ravasi, D. (2012). Organizing thoughts and connecting brains: Material practices and the transition from individual to group-level prospective sensemaking. *Academy of Management Journal*, 55(5), 1232–1259.

Stokols, D., Clitheroe, C., Zmuidzinas, M. (2002). Qualities of work environments that promote perceived support for creativity. *Creativity Research Journal*, 14(2), 137–147.

Tierney, P. and Farmer, S.M. (2002). Creative self-efficacy: Its potential antecedents and relationship to creative performance. *Academy of Management Journal*, 45(6), 1137–1148.

Treffinger, D.J., Isaksen, S.G., Stead-Dorval, K.B. (2006). *Creative Problem Solving: An Introduction*. Prufrock Press Inc., Wako, TX.

Valgeirsdottir, D. and Onarheim, B. (2017). Studying creativity training programs: A methodological analysis. *Creativity and Innovation Management*, 26(4), 430–439.

Valle, R., Martin, F., Romero, P.M., Dolan, S.L. (2000). Business strategy, work processes and human resource training: Are they congruent? *Journal of Organizational Behavior*, *21*(3), 283-297.

Williams, P. (2002). The competent boundary spanner. *Public Administration*, 80(1), 103–124.

Yström, A., Agogué, M., Rampa, R. (2021). Preparing an organization for sustainability transitions. The making of boundary spanners through design training. *Sustainability*, 13(14), 8073.

4

Creative Slack Enabling Ideas to Emerge, to be Stored and Transform

In recent years, the notion of creative slack has emerged in innovation management literature to describe the stock of material and immaterial resources that can be mobilized for organizational creative capabilities (Cohendet and Simon 2007, 2016; Harvey et al. 2013; Parmentier et al. 2017). According to these authors, the formation of creative slack is one of the central components explaining organizational creative capabilities, as it enables individuals, teams, and communities within the organization to tap into previously untapped or underutilized resources in order to guide or redirect the company's projects with creative ideas.

Cohendet and Simon (2007) illustrate, for example, how in the field of video games, Ubisoft consistently excels in innovation by incorporating unused or underused creative ideas developed by different teams and communities within the organization as part of their daily work. Others, like 3M, have a policy that encourages employees to explore new ideas, as exemplified by this quote from one of the company's employees (Garud et al. 2011):

> I'll now make a confession: the 15% parts of the 15% rule is essentially meaningless. Some of our technical people use much more than 15% of their time on projects of their own choosing. Some use less than that; some use none at all… The number is not so important as the message, which is this: the system has

Chapter written by Romain RAMPA and Guy PARMENTIER.

> some slack in it. If you have a good idea, and the commitment to squirrel away time to work on it, and the raw nerve to skirt your lab manager's expressed desires, then go for it.

However, like many new concepts, the definition of *creative slack* is not widely agreed upon today. To the extent that two main visions of what creative slack is in practice have emerged. Some, like Ubisoft, view it as a reservoir of creative micro-ideas that accumulate and come to life thanks to the individuals and communities of the company. In this conception, ideas can be stored in formal idea management systems or remain in the collective memory, thanks, for example, to the war stories that innovation communities share. On the other hand, others, more akin to 3M, consider creative slack primarily as the flexibility that individuals and teams have to generate, develop, and experiment with new and creative ideas. They utilize time and resources that are unused or underused by the organization or, in some cases, divert these resources, almost like pirates (Augsdorfer 2008; Criscuolo et al. 2014; Globocnik and Salomo 2015).

These two major perspectives, each with its own appeal, have rarely been questioned and challenged. This chapter aims to fill this gap. It will enable us to demystify and deconstruct the concept of creative slack by first tracing its historical origins. Then, it will explore the implications and attractiveness of these two primary visions of the concept. This will allow us to delve into the ramifications of these two perspectives and illustrate them with concrete cases before attempting to conclude and draw more general implications for enhancing organizational creative capability through creative slack.

4.1. The origins of the slack concept

The concept of creative slack has its origins in the notion of organizational slack, which was introduced by Penrose (1959). Penrose argued that a company gradually accumulates a stock of resources (financial, material, knowledge, relationships, etc.) that exceeds what it can currently mobilize in its ongoing activities. This surplus of resources can be redirected and combined to support the company's growth or respond to new market opportunities. According to Penrose, these surplus resources that constitute organizational slack "are, for the enterprising firm, at the same time a challenge to innovate, an incentive to expand, and a source of competitive advantage" (Penrose 1959, p. 76).

For Penrose, organizational slack is a driving force for a company's growth, enabling it to expand, reconfigure its existing capabilities, and enhance its knowledge base. This is why Penrose is often regarded as a precursor to the concept of dynamic capabilities (Teece and Pisano 1994; Kor and Mahoney 2004).

Following Penrose's pioneering work, other researchers in economics and management have explored the concept of organizational slack and its connections to firm performance and adaptability. Bourgeois and Singh (1983) introduced the idea of breaking down slack into three main categories: available slack, recoverable slack, and potential slack. Available slack pertains to resources that remain untapped in the organization's daily operations. Recoverable slack includes resources that have been utilized in the organization's activities but can be easily redeployed or haven't been fully exploited. Potential slack encompasses resources that the organization can potentially access through its environment. This categorization helps differentiate the various ways in which companies can leverage slack.

Regarding creative and innovative capabilities, researchers have demonstrated that organizational slack has a favorable relationship with innovation up to a certain point, beyond which it becomes unfavorable (resembling a U-shaped relationship) (Nohria and Gulati 1996). A certain degree of slack can facilitate the exploration and experimentation of ideas, but excessive slack can harm the company's performance by leading to inefficient resource allocation and risk-averse behavior.

It is only more recently that the concept of creative slack has emerged to describe the role of these surplus resources in relation to organizational creative capabilities more precisely (Cohendet and Simon 2016; Parmentier et al. 2017). This notion has been broken down into two main concepts, which we will explore in the following sections: creative slack as a reservoir of ideas and creative slack as a space for creative maneuvering.

4.2. Creative slack as a pool of ideas

In looking at creative industries that have the property of having to constantly manage new projects with creative content, Cohendet and Simon (2007) found that firms in the field were accustomed to drawing on a myriad of innovative ideas and proposals that had been developed by individuals and teams during the organization's past activities. Elaborating on Penrose's concept, they argue that one of the drivers of firms' creative capabilities is precisely the creative slack that they manage to develop, nurture and maintain (Cohendet and Simon 2007, 2016; Harvey et al. 2013). As a source of growth and renewal, they define this *slack* as a pool of unused or underused micro-creative ideas that have been developed by the different teams and individuals of the organization in the course of their daily activities.

Figure 4.1. *The different possible components of the creative pool according to the degree of advancement of the ideas. For a color version of this figure, see www.iste.co.uk/parmentier/organizational.zip*

This notion astutely acknowledges the collection of proposals, ideas, and new insights (refer to Figure 4.1 for a breakdown of the potential components of this reservoir) that are conceived and developed by individuals and teams both within and outside the organization's projects. Only some of these ideas will be directly appreciated by the organization. This array of creative opportunities can then be harnessed by individuals and teams within the organization to make more informed decisions, select new projects, or inject innovation into ongoing projects. This concept of slack underscores the importance of supporting its cultivation and maintenance to facilitate the generation, evaluation, and refinement of fresh ideas.

Furthermore, Hargadon and Sutton (1998), in their pioneering article on the mechanisms behind IDEO's excellence in new product development, already highlighted this concept without explicitly labeling it as "creative slack." They point out that a central element of IDEO's creative capabilities is its constant acquisition and storage of new ideas and insights that designers can subsequently utilize in new projects (for more details, see Box 4.1).

AT IDEO, engineers and designers are strongly encouraged to go to trade shows, events and networks to seek out new knowledge and ideas. The goal is to accumulate knowledge and be inspired by technological solutions and models that are constantly being proposed by other organizations and bring them back in-house. Within the organization, employees then share their stories and learnings in the manner of communities, often even bringing back technical objects to present them, introduce them into the company and bring their stories to life.

Thanks to this progressive accumulation, enriched by the discoveries, ideas and learnings from past projects, IDEO has been able to build up a large creative slack over time. The firm manages to keep it alive thanks to its culture of sharing, a very low team turnover and a propensity to constantly mobilize various technical objects. Indeed, IDEO's engineers often bring back many objects from outside the company that serve to remind them of past stories and ideas. IDEO's designers are largely able to be creative because of this accumulation of objects that they constantly mobilize to initiate new projects or find inspiration in ongoing projects.

Hargadon and Sutton (2000) refer to this as knowledge and idea brokering to explicate this phenomenon to IDEO by mentioning that designers systematically use old ideas as raw material for new ideas. In addition, IDEO employees have a natural facility for finding old ideas that can be used in new places, new ways and new combinations. The researchers illustrate this aspect with a quote from Edison: "To invent, you need a good imagination and a pile of junk."

Box 4.1. *Absorbing and storing new knowledge and ideas at IDEO*

There is an interesting parallel between this reservoir of creative ideas and accumulated insights and the literature on improvisation, particularly in jazz (Barrett 1998; Moorman and Miner 1998). In jazz, musicians draw from their repertoire to craft new music. As Vera and Crossan (2005) express, this repertoire provides access to musical resources that facilitate adaptation and recontextualization for the purpose of improvisation. In music, as well as in other domains like cooking, individuals tap into this pool of past knowledge and ideas to adapt, innovate, and make more informed decisions based on the immediate requirements of their context.

Creative slack is not exclusive to companies in the creative industries; all organizations develop it as part of their daily operations. The larger an organization's creative slack, the more it can harness this reservoir of creative potential to fuel projects that contribute to its growth and renewal. However, as Cohendet and Simon point out, "the creative slack is shaped by the culture of the firm and is primarily understood through the organization's internal language" (Cohendet and Simon 2007, p. 600). While there are methods to foster it, such as by facilitating the emergence of internal communities (Cohendet et al. 2008), working on socialization mechanisms (Hargadon and Bechky 2006), or promoting external openness, the organization's culture can also impede or inhibit creative slack or its utilization to some extent. Manifestations like "*not invented here*" syndrome (Antons and Piller 2015), the existence of silos, or frequent turnover can indeed have a negative impact on the creative slack that an organization can develop.

In fact, as we will explore in the subsequent sections, there are several ways to manage and nurture this creative slack by leveraging formal mechanisms and structures. Through a formal approach, the organization can utilize tools, techniques, and processes to accumulate the ideas and discoveries of individuals and teams in systems, allowing for storage and measurement. In the informal domain, the responsibility for this reservoir is often delegated to communities within the organization. These communities ensure that creative slack thrives and expands, particularly by promoting a significant redundancy of past ideas within the stories shared among these specialist groups.

4.2.1. *The creative slack as a formal idea pool*

The formal idea pool represents the initial approach for managing, preserving, and accessing creative slack. It has become the focal point for a growing number of organizations seeking efficient means to store and access ideas. In fact, what company wouldn't aspire to have the capability to locate within an idea management system, often facilitated by software or a reference document, all the ideas generated by the individuals and teams within the organization during their activities? With such a platform in place, the company could harness it to make more informed decisions, initiate new projects, or guide teams toward unexplored paths based on past ideas. Several platforms, including Brightidea, are readily available today to streamline communication, capture, and manage this reservoir of opportunities and ideas to which people can contribute virtually.

Within Hydro-Québec's research institute, more commonly known as IREQ, a platform to capture, develop and formally manage the ideas of the research center's researchers and engineers is currently being developed. Dubbed "the garden of ideas", or "the idea pool", this platform was designed to collect ideas from all employees, launch challenges, advance emerging ideas, and map and analyze the existing pool of ideas.

The formal tool thus meets the needs and expectations of several stakeholders: the ideators in search of validation, feedback and recognition.

Managers, in order to analyze existing idea portfolios, select new existing idea portfolios, new projects and identify talent among the platform's contributors.

Researchers and engineers looking for ideas to start new projects get inspired or ask for help on the platform.

The tool is associated with an idea management process that gives ideators the opportunity to meet with a select committee to discuss their ideas, get feedback and advice, and potentially be matched with a sponsor to help sell the idea to corporate selection platforms.

Box 4.2. *The garden of ideas at IREQ*

These formal idea systems are often complemented by processes for effectively capturing, translating, and selecting the ideas that are entered into the platform. They offer the advantage of granting access to valuable data that can be used for various analyses, research, talent identification, or even to initiate new ideation processes by mapping domains that are seldom explored by the organization's ideators.

While the establishment of such an idea pool may appear ideal, this approach is not without its limitations. Firstly, the creation and maintenance of such a formal platform come with costs. Beyond the expenses associated with the platform itself, it's primarily the investment of time and effort from individuals required to articulate, clarify, and formalize their ideas within the platform that proves to be significant (Beretta 2019). The risk here is either an influx of "Post-it" ideas that are poorly defined and understood or, conversely, highly developed ideas with abundant information that demanded a substantial amount of time from the idea creators for formalization, discouraging many from contributing their ideas to the pool (Naggar 2015).

Secondly, for the idea creators, the motivation to share their ideas lies in the hope that their ideas will be recognized and selected by the organization. However, the idea selection process is also costly, especially when managers have to evaluate numerous ideas with varying degrees of definition. Crowdsourcing provides an example in this regard. For instance, Cisco spent several months evaluating the thousands of ideas submitted during its 2008 call for proposals, even though the company could already rely on user votes and comments to aid in idea selection (Jouret 2009). This selection process is critical because, much like traditional idea suggestion boxes, formal idea management systems create expectations and excitement. If people's efforts are not at least partially acknowledged and rewarded, it can lead to disengagement.

Lastly, the quantity and quality of the ideas that the formal pool can accommodate also hinge on the organization's climate. To make this system effective, the initial reluctance of employees to share their ideas with others, especially their boldest ones, needs to be overcome. Anonymity may encourage such sharing (Connolly et al. 1990), but it can complicate the process of recognizing and rewarding the idea creators. On the other hand, the quality of ideas and engagement on the platform is also influenced by the level of participation from contributors–individuals who are not the original idea creators but actively contribute to enhancing, recognizing, and improving the ideas of others through their comments and interactions on the platform (Phang et al. 2015). Yet, once again, this necessitates a culture of sharing and incentives to ensure that this active involvement and effort are also duly acknowledged.

4.2.2. *Creative slack as the informal idea pool*

While the formal idea pool relies on systems and processes, the informal creative pool is built upon communities, individuals, and socialization mechanisms to operate. Cohendet and Simon (2007) argue that, following the Ubisoft model, there's no need for expensive platforms and systems to formalize ideas when communities of specialists consistently exchange creative micro-ideas that individuals and teams generate during their projects. These ideas are absorbed and stored in the collective memory of these communities, which share both successful and unsuccessful strategies, attempts, and unconventional ideas that emerge. By fostering interdisciplinarity within the organization, these communities rely on their shared history and moments of socialization to create redundancy and keep this reservoir of ideas constantly replenished and enriched through the company's activities (Brown and Duguid 1991; Cohendet and Llerena 2003).

The value of this informal exchange of real-life experiences, learning while in action, new routines, and ideas lies in the fact that individuals can appropriate and reinterpret these stories, drawing upon their personal experiences to recombine and reutilize these ideas, routines, and lessons to meet their current needs. Informal slack is particularly advantageous during times of crisis, as demonstrated by Cohendet and Simon (2016), because it can offer the raw material for devising and implementing appropriate and innovative responses.

These socialization processes help preserve ideas and knowledge within the organization at a lower cost (Harvey et al. 2013). In contrast, as expressed by Mérindol and Versailles (2007, p. 61):

> In essence, the form and content of what is conveyed by these spaces of exchange escape management and rely on the communicational and relational qualities of the individuals who participate in these exchanges.

In the case of informal creative slack, managers relinquish some control and analytical tools for overseeing these exchanges. They must ensure that individuals are afforded time and privileged opportunities to participate in these social activities. Values such as benevolence, sharing, and collaboration must be fostered so that the pool can thrive and continue to evolve with the contributions of different communities and teams within the organization.

While the strength of informal creative slack lies in the quality of the connections and interactions that individuals, teams, and communities develop both internally and externally, this model is not either without limitations. Because knowledge and ideas remain largely implicit, they are heavily reliant on individuals and the collective memory cultivated by communities. There are two primary risks associated with maintaining and accessing this pool of knowledge and ideas.

The first risk pertains to the departure of individuals. Without formalization, a portion of the slack inevitably departs with employees who leave the organization. Additionally, even if individuals can sustain the slack, there is a need to generate enough redundancy by promoting a rich culture of informality to avoid losing a portion of this diverse collection of creative ideas, some of which are bound to be lost over time.

The second challenge is the management of interactions, which is inherently complex. Once again, it is crucial to rely on a culture of sharing and trust to keep this informal slack dynamic. This dynamic nature makes it difficult to control through formal means.

Ubisoft has decided to create business communities within its organization to build bridges between project teams and help the different areas of the company grow in parallel (developers, game designers, artists, etc.). These communities of specialists are encouraged to network and share with each other, especially during events like Cool Tuesday, where individuals can share their experiences, war stories, projects and ideas.

A community manager appointed by his peers to represent the community is responsible for bringing ideas and knowledge that are of interest to the organization, and acts as a bridge to obtain resources, time or support for their community.

The advantage of this model, according to Cohendet and Simon (2007, 2008, 2016), is that it allows for the feeding and maintenance of a creative slack at a lower cost, which is, moreover, enriched by the relays that the community is encouraged to develop outside through networks and events to capture new ideas that emerge in the active local environment in which the firm is immersed.

Box 4.3. *Specialist communities at Ubisoft*

4.3. Creative slack as room to maneuver

Following this initial exploration of creative slack, other researchers have reinterpreted the concept. Instead of framing slack as a reservoir of creative resources, they now emphasize the value of resource slack intentionally left by organizations to foster creativity (Parmentier et al. 2017; Parmentier 2019).

Drawing upon a wealth of studies in innovation management, it has become clear that encouraging some resource flexibility is beneficial for creating space for autonomy (Gambardella et al. 2020), bricolage (Baker et al. 2003; Baker and Nelson 2005), or agility in a company's processes and routines (Eisenhardt and Martin 2000; Pirola-Merlo 2010). These researchers leverage the second interpretation of Penrose's concept, viewing slack as a space for creativity.

The value of approaching creative slack as a room to maneuver is manifold. Firstly, this space is pivotal to organizational creative capability, allowing room for experimentation (Bourgeon and Demil 1999). It's also essential for individuals and teams within the organization to exhibit flexibility and adaptability (Troilo et al. 2014), as having room for resources enables exploration of different avenues, additional time for solving complex problems, or combining excess resources to generate new solutions. Additionally, this organizational flexibility enables individuals to work with constraints and be more agile when dealing with challenging or unexpected situations.

In reality, the appeal of resource slack for creativity and its implications vary based on the type of space left within the organization. This space can be dedicated or redirected time for creativity. It can also manifest as material or financial resources that individuals and teams can leverage in their projects. Finally, it can be regarded as a room for interpretation and maneuvering within the organization's processes and routines, left for individuals and teams. These different facets will be discussed in the following sections.

4.3.1. *The room for time for creativity*

The concept of allowing dedicated time for employees and teams to nurture and refine their creative ideas is not a new one and has been extensively discussed in the literature (von Hippel et al. 1999; Garud et al. 2011; Agrawal et al. 2018). This allocation of time for creativity is often exemplified by well-known companies like Google and 3M, which have historically permitted their employees to spend 15-20% of their total work hours exploring new ideas, avenues, and solutions (refer to Box 4.4). However, it also extends to the flexibility for employees to occasionally devote time to developing new ideas that don't align with the organization's established roadmap or routines (Augsdorfer 2005; Criscuolo et al. 2014).

Time is a scarce and precious resource within organizations, particularly in environments where managers tend to enforce tight deadlines for the sake of efficiency and performance. However, studies conducted by Amabile et al. (2002a, 2002b) as early as the 2000s demonstrated that significant time pressure had a detrimental effect on individual creativity. Individuals not only require an incubation period to nurture new ideas (Wallas 1926), but ideators also often need time to mature and develop their creative concepts.

This is why organizations that manage to carve out time or preserve room for creativity are better positioned to identify and cultivate more innovative ideas. When we speak of the time margin set aside by the organization, we are essentially referring to the freedom and autonomy granted to employees to explore new ideas and paths.

3M is known for being one of the first companies to voluntarily give employees time to come up with new ideas and develop inventions for the company. It was the first company to declare the famous 15% rule, granting an employee permission to independently exercise some of their time working on a new idea. For a long time, 3M has been one of the most innovative companies in the world, having been consistently ranked in the top three by the Boston Consulting Group. What is less well known, however, is how cutting into the time frame has been damaging to 3M.

In the early 2000s, shareholders appointed James McNerney, a General Electric veteran known for his ability to streamline companies, to lead 3M to improve the performance and efficiency of the group, which was losing momentum from a financial point of view. He introduced Six Sigma as soon as he took the helm of the company and won praise from Wall Street initially by streamlining work processes, eliminating 10% of the workforce and increasing operating margins from 17% in 2001 to 23% in 2005 (Hindo 2007).

But when McNerney tried to apply Six Sigma to 3Ms research and development processes, the result was a dramatic drop in the number of innovative products the company developed over the years. By taking away the time margin and forcing researchers and engineers in the research center to reduce time and variability in the processes as much as possible, the R&D center gradually lost a large part of its creative capability.

As a result, between 2003 and 2007, the company fell in the innovation rankings every year, and while short-term performance was good due to better cost and time control, the long-term prospects for the company were not good. As one employee put it[1], "we all came to the conclusion that there was no chance that something like a Post-it note would ever emerge in this system again."

A new leader, George Buckley, was hired in 2005 to turn things around. Recognizing the value of streamlining methods, he reiterated the need for time and space in the

1 See: https://www.inc.com/linkedin/don-peppers/downside-six-sigma-don-peppers.html.

company's research and development center (ibid.): "Invention is by its very nature a disorderly process.... You can't put a Six Sigma process into that area and say, well, I'm getting behind on invention, so I'm going to schedule myself for three good ideas on Wednesday and two on Friday. That's not how creativity works."

Box 4.4. *3M and time for creativity*

For organizations that intend to purposefully allocate time for employee creativity, a question arises: should they consistently designate a small fraction of time (e.g. 15% weekly) for employees, or allow them more flexible, ad hoc periods to engage in exploratory activities (for several continuous days or weeks)? This is a matter that remains unresolved in the literature. However, Agrawal et al. (2018) advocate for the latter approach, citing the example of Google, which transitioned from a continuous 20% time allocation to establishing an incubation platform, Area 120, enabling idea creators to develop and nurture their concepts over extended periods. Nevertheless, some may argue that during the early stages of an idea, a continuous time period is more conducive to allow the idea creator to incubate their concept, seek knowledge, and engage in other activities that can spark inspiration.

While a time margin appears to be an essential component of organizational creative capability, it can also introduce tensions within the organization. Firstly, companies implementing it must have mechanisms to filter out lower-quality contributions and ideas that will inevitably surface (Agrawal et al. 2018). Therefore, there is merit in utilizing progressive filters to prevent idea creators from dedicating excessive time to ideas of lesser significance. Moreover, beyond time, individuals need to possess creative skills to genuinely leverage the time granted for exploring new ideas (Rampa 2020). Lastly, having a time margin doesn't imply complete freedom from constraints. As shown by Parmentier (2019), constraints can actually be fertile ground for creativity, especially when they are perceived as meaningful. Therefore, it is beneficial to alternate between periods of high-pressure and less intense phases in creative projects that have clear objectives.

4.3.2. *The room for material and financial resources for creativity*

In contrast to the discussion around time allocated for creativity, the relationship between the availability of material and financial resources and the creative performance of individuals and teams is a more debated topic (Suzuki 2018). This type of slack falls under the resource dimension of the conducive creative climate (Amabile et al. 1996), with the notion that easy access to adequate information, material, and budgetary resources is beneficial for individuals and working groups. However, aligning with the early research on organizational slack, which pertains to the excess capacity in terms of machinery, personnel, resource stocks, or cash that a firm can generate (Bourgeois and Singh 1983), some argue for a negative relationship (Latham and Braun 2009), while others suggest a U-shaped relationship (Nohria and Gulati 1996).

Indeed, having surplus resources for exploring and experimenting with new ideas can be highly advantageous, as it reduces constraints and facilitates creativity among teams and individuals. However, counterintuitively, having too few constraints and too many resources can also hinder creativity. Nevertheless, akin to the work on do-it-yourself (DIY) (Baker et al. 2003; Baker and Nelson 2005; Wu et al. 2017), individuals and teams can tap into unused or underused resources available in their environment to creatively recombine or mobilize them. Hence, there’s a need to strike a balance between having a too meager or excessively abundant pool of material and financial resources for creativity.

The article by Dolmans et al. (2014) contributes to refining this debate by suggesting that constraints and resources are not mutually exclusive when it comes to organizational creativity. In reality, the ingenuity that individuals and teams can develop depends more on their perceptions of the perceived levels of resources and constraints at different times. Therefore, it is the perception that individuals hold regarding the balance between slack and constraints that is pivotal, and managers can work to promote a favorable balance conducive to creativity.

4.3.3. *The room for interpretation in processes and routines*

As organizations grow, they often establish formalized processes to facilitate coordination and enhance efficiency in performing their basic functions. These processes may evolve into routines that govern the organization's operations. Even creative activities occasionally benefit from routines to guide actions, particularly in the creative industries where design methods and processes are used to support and frame creative work. These routines allow organizations to conserve cognitive resources and direct them toward the act of creation itself.

Routines have two dimensions: an ostensive dimension that provides a conceptual framework to guide and justify actions, and a performative dimension that involves "specific actions, by specific people, in specific places and times" (Feldman and Pentland 2003, p. 101). The very act of executing a routine can become a creative process that modifies, adapts, and refines the initial routine. Moreover, as articulated by Cohendet and Simon (2016), individuals combine and transform routines to allow for adaptation to unanticipated situations.

In this context, creative slack can manifest at two levels. Firstly, in the formalization of routines, organizations can intentionally leave areas of ambiguity or refrain from formalizing every detail. This grants actors the freedom to interpret routines based on their context and the evolving situations they encounter. This room for interpretation is likely to foster creativity among actors as they have the flexibility to tailor routines to the current situation and, in doing so, invent new approaches. On the other hand, slack can also be expressed through lenient managerial control. In this scenario, the routine is fully formalized, but there is no strict requirement to adhere to it verbatim, allowing room for a degree of variation and innovation.

A case study involving a chain of clothing, jewelry, and accessory stores, as described in research by Sonenshein (2016), vividly illustrates the impact of slack in routines on creativity. This chain aims to create a sense of familiarity in merchandising that is consistent across all stores while allowing room for adaptation to the unique local conditions of each store. The flexibility in interpreting merchandising routines thus permits the creation of distinct atmospheres while preserving a shared identity for all the stores.

The freedom to interpret routines and processes empowers individuals and teams within the organization to not only be more adaptable in their daily activities but also more creative in their approach, thereby influencing the future routines of the organization through their performance. However, similar to the balance sought in resource allocation, there is a need to find equilibrium between a level of control that is overly lax, risking efficiency and collective coordination, and a level of control that is excessively rigid, leaving no room for adaptation.

4.4. The different components of creative slack: implications and limitations

By contrasting the two main perspectives that have emerged regarding the notion of creative slack, our chapter provides an overview of the different components of this concept, which is still very recent in the literature (see Figure 4.2). Far from favoring one or the other of these perspectives, our study shows that both are, in fact, central to the creative capabilities of an organization. The creative resource pool provides access to a myriad of ideas and knowledge that can be used as a starting point to generate, improve, renew, and even select new ideas and solutions. In this sense, it is one of the main organizational levers that the company can rely on to introduce novelty through recombination and make better and faster decisions thanks to a pool of easily accessible creative resources. The room to maneuver for creativity is necessary to give sufficient freedom and resources to individuals and teams to be creative and to mature their ideas. A necessary but insufficient condition, this slack space allows creativity to unfold.

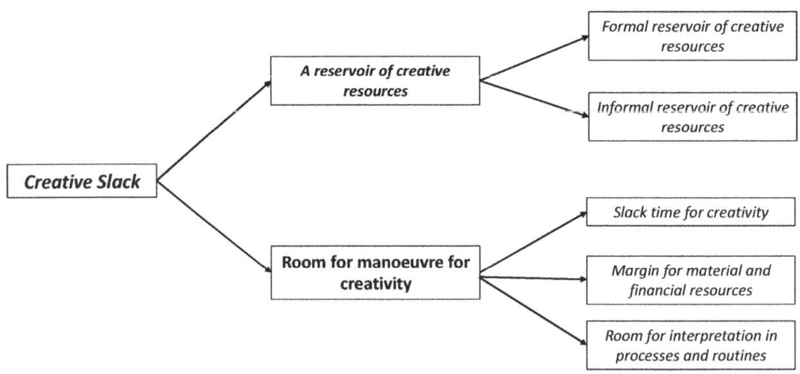

Figure 4.2. *The different components of creative slack*

It is interesting to consider that these two perspectives can, in many ways, complement each other. Indeed, leaving room to maneuver in terms of time and resources for individuals within the company will enable them to generate and develop more ideas that can be added to the organization's formal or informal pool of knowledge and ideas. Similarly, the pool, in turn, will equip individuals and teams to be more effective in their projects, fostering creativity and taking advantage of the latitude and interpretation provided to them.

As we have seen, however, there are limitations that frame the proper functioning of slack, but they also open up great prospects for future research. Firstly, it is challenging, a priori, to determine the optimal amount of slack that optimizes organizational creative capabilities. This notion of balance, which has already been extensively discussed based on Penrose's work, is crucial. It's not easy to establish, for a given organization, how much time should be dedicated to slack for individuals and teams, or how much time the organization can allocate for social interactions to nurture the pool of ideas maintained by communities. As organizations consistently grapple with finding the right equilibrium between creativity and efficiency (Andriopoulos and Lewis 2009), it is imperative for managers to gauge this margin. This can be achieved by alternating, for example, periods of high pressure and relaxation, by earmarking specific exploration periods, or by balancing the autonomy granted to employees with coordination mechanisms in an effort to align everyone's creative endeavors.

Some organizations, like CAE, a leading company in digital simulation for aviation, are already combining these two approaches in innovative ways. At CAE, all individuals have a small budget and dedicated time to explore new ideas. Once that time and budget are exceeded, they must present their idea in a formal way to a manager to get more time and budget to mature their idea, which allows the ideas to be documented in a formal repository. There is then a progressive time margin coupled with a process to formalize an idea pool. The motivation for the ideators to reveal and formalize their ideas comes from obtaining resources and additional time at each step of the process up until the idea transitions into project mode.

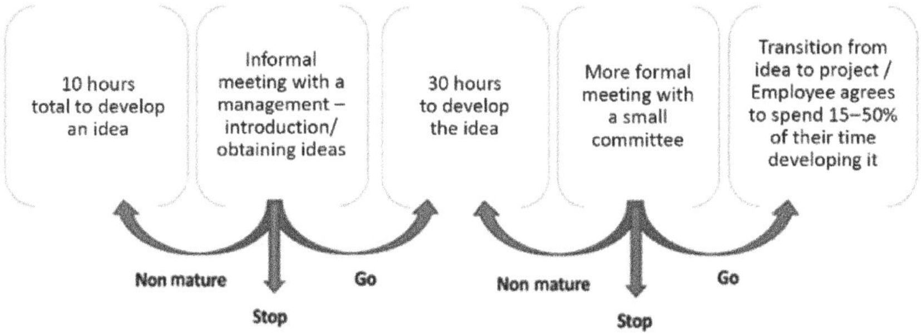

Figure 4.3. *The combination of the room to maneuver and the formal pool at CAE. For a color version of this figure, see www.iste.co.uk/parmentier/organizational.zip*

Box 4.5. *The combination of approaches at CAE*

Secondly, creative slack alone is insufficient. Amassing a stock of creative ideas and knowledge amounts to nothing if individuals and teams lack opportunities to participate in the decision-making process or implement these ideas. The same applies to the leeway within the organization. The freedom and autonomy granted to individuals and teams must translate into tangible action. Furthermore, in his thesis, Rampa (2020) demonstrates that providing time and resources alone is inadequate for developing genuine creative skills. Often, it's necessary to equip organizational actors with new methods of creativity and design. In other words, creative slack offers a range of potentialities, but actors must still have the freedom to exercise them in practice to genuinely cultivate creative capability.

Lastly, it may be useful to consider the conditions conducive to effectively mobilizing creative slack. The creative climate within the organization can play a role by fostering psychological security within teams and promoting a culture that encourages risk-taking and the acceptance of failure. This enables individuals and teams to utilize the room to maneuver, recombine old ideas, explore, and exhibit flexibility. However, these enabling conditions also depend on how creative slack intersects with other attributes that constitute creative capabilities. These attributes encompass systems and processes for managing ideas, the level of openness and internal transparency (employee involvement in decision-making), as well as the social interactions that occur within the organization.

4.5. References

Agrawal, A., Catalini, C., Goldfarb, A., Luo, H. (2018). Slack time and innovation. *Organization Science*, 29(6), 1056–1073.

Amabile, T.M., Conti, R., Coon, H., Lazenby, J., Herron, M. (1996). Assessing the work environment for creativity. *Academy of Management Journal,* 39(5), 1154–1184.

Amabile, T.M., Hadley, C.N., Kramer, S.J. (2002a). Creativity under the gun. *Harvard Business Review*, 80(8), 52.

Amabile, T.M., Mueller, J.S., Simpson, W.B., Hadley, C.N., Kramer, S.J., Fleming, L. (2002b). Time pressure and creativity in organizations: A longitudinal field study. *Working paper.*

Andriopoulos, C. and Lewis, M.W. (2009). Exploitation-exploration tensions and organizational ambidexterity: Managing paradoxes of innovation. *Organization Science*, 20(4), 696–717.

Antons, D. and Piller, F.T. (2015). Opening the black box of "not invented here": Attitudes, decision biases, and behavioral consequences. *Academy of Management Perspectives*, 29(2), 193–217.

Augsdorfer, P. (2005). Bootlegging and path dependency. *Research Policy*, 34(1), 1–11.

Augsdorfer, P. (2008). Managing the unmanageable. *Research-Technology Management*, 51(4), 41–47.

Baker, T. and Nelson, R.E. (2005). Creating something from nothing: Resource construction through entrepreneurial bricolage. *Administrative Science Quarterly*, 50(3), 329–366.

Baker, T., Miner, A.S., Eesley, D.T. (2003). Improvising firms: Bricolage, account giving and improvisational competencies in the founding process. *Research Policy*, 32(2), 255–276.

Barrett, F.J. (1998). Creativity and improvisation in jazz and organizations: Implications for organizational learning. *Organization Science*, 9(5), 605–622.

Beretta, M. (2019). Idea selection in web-enabled ideation systems. *Journal of Product Innovation Management*, 36(1), 5–23.

Bourgeois, L.J. III and Singh, J.V. (1983). Organizational slack and political behavior among top management teams. *Academy of Management Proceedings*, 44–47.

Bourgeon, L. and Demil, B. (1999). Slack organisationnel et innovation : application au secteur hospitalier public. *Conférence de l'AIMS.*

Brown, J.S. and Duguid, P. (1991). Organizational learning and communities-of-practice: Toward a unified view of working, learning, and innovation. *Organization Science*, 2(1), 40–57.

Cohendet, P. and Llerena, P. (2003). Routines and incentives: The role of communities in the firm. *Industrial and Corporate Change*, 12(2), 271–297.

Cohendet, P. and Simon, L. (2007). Playing across the playground: Paradoxes of knowledge creation in the videogame firm. *Journal of Organizational Behavior*, 28(5), 587–605.

Cohendet, P. and Simon, L. (2008). Knowledge-intensive firms, communities, and creative cities. In *Community, Economic Creativity, and Organization*, Amin, A. and Roberts, J. (eds). Oxford University Press, Oxford.

Cohendet, P. and Simon, L. (2016). Always playable: Recombining routines for creative efficiency at Ubisoft Montreal's Video Game Studio. *Organization Studies,* 27(3), 614–632.

Cohendet, P., Grandadam, D., Simon, L. (2008). Réseaux, communautés et projets dans les processus créatifs. *Management International*, 13(1), 29.

Connolly, T., Jessup, L.M., Valacich, J.S. (1990). Effects of anonymity and evaluative tone on idea generation in computer-mediated groups. *Management Science*, 36(6), 689–703.

Criscuolo, P., Salter, A., Ter Wal, A.L.J. (2014). Going underground: Bootlegging and individual innovative performance. *Organization Science*, 25(5), 1287–1305.

Dolmans, S.A., van Burg, E., Reymen, I.M., & Romme, A.G.L. (2014). Dynamics of resource slack and constraints: Resource positions in action. *Organization Studies*, 35(4), 511–549.

Eisenhardt, K.M. and Martin, J.A. (2000). Dynamic capabilities: What are they? *Strategic Management Journal*, 21(10/11), 1105–1121.

Feldman, M.S. and Pentland, B.T. (2003). Reconceptualizing organizational routines as a source of flexibility and change. *Administrative Science Quarterly*, 48(1), 94–118.

Gambardella, A., Khashabi, P., Panico, C. (2020). Managing autonomy in industrial research and development: A project-level investigation. *Organization Science*, 31(1), 165–181.

Garud, R., Gehman, J., Kumaraswamy, A. (2011). Complexity arrangements for sustained innovation: Lessons from 3M Corporation. *Organization Studies*, 32(6), 737–767.

Globocnik, D. and Salomo, S. (2015). Do formal management practices impact the emergence of bootlegging behavior? *Journal of Product Innovation Management*, 32(4), 505–521.

Hargadon, A.B. and Bechky, B.A. (2006). When collections of creatives become creative collectives: A field study of problem solving at work. *Organization Science*, 17(4), 484–500.

Hargadon, A. and Sutton, R.I. (2000). Building an innovation factory. *Harvard Business Review,* 78(3), 157–166.

Harvey, J.-F., Naggar, R., Cohendet, P., Simon, L. (2013). Gérer les idées pour mieux innover. *Gestion,* 38(3), 25–34.

Hindo, B. (2007). At 3M, a struggle between efficiency and creativity. *Business Week*, 11(11), 8–14.

von Hippel, E., Thomke, S., Sonnack, M. (1999). Creating breakthroughs at 3M. *Harvard Business Review Working Paper*, 77(5), 47.

Jouret, G. (2009). Inside Cisco's search for the next big idea. *Harvard Business Review*, 87(9), 43–45.

Kor, Y.Y. and Mahoney, J.T. (2004). Edith Penrose's (1959) contributions to the resource-based view of strategic management. *Journal of Management Studies*, 41(1), 183–191.

Latham, S.F. and Braun, M. (2009). Managerial risk, innovation, and organizational decline. *Journal of Management*, 35(2), 258–281.

Mérindol, V. and Versailles, D. (2017). Développer des capacités hautement créatives dans les entreprises : le cas des laboratoires d'innovation ouverte. *Management International,* 22(1), 58–72.

Moorman, C. and Miner, A.S. (1998). Organizational improvisation and organizational memory. *Academy of Management Review*, 23(4), 698–723.

Naggar, R. (2015). The creativity canvas: A business model for knowledge and idea management. *Technology Innovation Management Review*, 5(7), 50–58.

Nohria, N. and Gulati, R. (1996). Is slack good or bad for innovation? *Academy of Management Journal*, 39(5), 1245–1264.

Parmentier, G. (2019). Creativity under constraint: A management sciences perspective. In *Management of Extreme Situations: From Polar Expeditions to Exploration-oriented Organizations*, Lièvre, P., Aubry, M., Garal, G. (eds). ISTE Ltd, London, and John Wiley & Sons, New York, 121–137.

Parmentier, G., Szostak, B., Rüling, C.C. (2017). Introduction au dossier thématique : créativité organisationnelle : quels enjeux en management stratégique dans un contexte mondialisé ? *Management International*, 22(1), 12–18.

Penrose, E. (1959). *The Theory of the Growth of the Firm*. Revised edition published in 2009. Oxford University Press, Oxford.

Phang, C.W., Kankanhalli, A., Tan, B.C. (2015). What motivates contributors vs. lurkers? An investigation of online feedback forums. *Information Systems Research*, 26(4), 773–792.

Pirola-Merlo, A. (2010). Agile innovation: The role of team climate in rapid research and development. *Journal of Occupational and Organizational Psychology*, 83(4), 1075–1084.

Rampa, R. (2020). Émergence et organisation d'une fonction d'innovation disséminée : ethnographie d'un institut de recherche en mutation. PhD Thesis, Institut Polytechnique de Paris, Paris.

Sonenshein, S. (2016). Routines and creativity: From dualism to duality. *Organization Science,* 27(3), 739–758.

Suzuki, O. (2018). Enabling or constraining? Unraveling the influence of organizational slack on innovation. *Industrial and Corporate Change*, 27(3), 555–575.

Teece, D. and Pisano, G. (1994). The dynamic capabilities of firms: An introduction. *Industrial and Corporate Change*, 3(3), 537–556.

Troilo, G., De Luca, L.M., Atuahene-Gima, K. (2014). More innovation with less? A strategic contingency view of slack resources, information search, and radical innovation. *Journal of Product Innovation Management*, 31(2), 259–277.

Vera, D. and Crossan, M. (2005). Improvisation and innovative performance in teams. *Organization Science,* 16(3), 203–224.

Wallas, G. (1926). *The Art of Thought.* Solis Press, Poole.

Wu, L., Liu, H., Zhang, J.Q. (2017). Bricolage effects on new-product development speed and creativity: The moderating role of technological turbulence. *Journal of Business Research*, 70, 127–135.

5

Agile Methods and Organizational Creativity

One of the priorities expressed for more than 20 years by proponents of so-called "agile" project management methods is to support the creativity of the internal teams that deploy them (Glass 2006; Conboy et al. 2009; Highsmith 2009; Morris et al. 2014). These methods differ from traditional project management and execution models, in particular the waterfall model, in that they have short, iterative and adaptive development cycles lasting only a few weeks and the centrality of the customer within the projects (Lee and Xia 2010). They encompass a set of more than 20 different project management practices and techniques (Rasnacis and Berzisa 2016) – the most widespread being ScrumKanban, or extreme programming (Aldave et al. 2019) – sharing the same core values and principles gathered in the 2001 *Manifesto for Agile Software Development*[1]. According to Highsmith (2009, p. 67), one of the 17 experts who signed this manifesto, "creativity and innovation are the emergent results of well-functioning agile teams".

In a book for practitioners published a few years after the manifesto, the American engineer Glass (2006) argues for a possible compatibility between the notions of agility[2] and creativity:

Chapter written by Florence JEANNOT, Maxime MELLARD and Guy PARMENTIER.

1 Available at: https://agilemanifesto.org/iso/en/manifesto.html.

2 Following Glass (2006), we consider agility as an "umbrella" concept that includes the principles and practices of agile methods. As Cooper and Sommer (2016) point out, adaptation and response to change are common denominators in the various definitions and descriptions of this concept.

> And given that Agile's flexibility allows much more creative freedom than discipline's "dregs of structure", I for one see Agile as much more compatible with creativity than its traditional alternatives (Glass 2006, p. 42).

Furthermore, in reference to Cockburn and Highsmith (2001), both signatories of the agile manifesto, Conboy et al. (2009, p. 123) specify that "agile methodologies deal with unpredictability by relying on people and their creativity rather than on processes". More recently, in a book with the evocative title, *Agile Innovation: The Revolutionary Approach to Accelerate Success, Inspire Engagement, and Ignite Creativity*, Morris et al. (2014) make a direct connection between agile practices and creativity.

However, while the influence of agile methods on creativity is widely discussed in the press and in management literature, as illustrated by the few examples above, only a few research studies have provided proof of its existence. Conboy et al. (2009) were clear on this subject:

> Proponents of agile methods claim that enabling, fostering and driving creativity is the key motivation that differentiates agile methods from their more traditional, bureaucratic counterparts. However, there is very little rigorous research to support this claim (Conboy et al. 2009, p. 122).

Ten years later, Annosi et al. (2020, p. 562) make a similar point, noting that previous work has not empirically examined the "key concepts and underlying relationships" through which agile methods create an environment that fosters innovation and creativity.

Two studies with different methodologies have nevertheless attracted our attention. Petrillo and Pimenta (2010) find that, in the majority of the video game projects they analyzed via a retrospective (or post-mortem) analysis, the use of agile practices is dictated by the organizations' desire to achieve a more creative outcome. However, Petrillo and Pimenta do not shed light on how the agile practices used can improve the creativity of the games produced. More recently, Kakar (2017) showed that the use of agile methods increases the innovation capability of project teams, questioned via a survey, more than traditional management methods. Nevertheless, in this study, the capability for innovation was measured by means of eight questions, only two of which dealt with the creativity of the teams.

In line with this research, this chapter aims to take a closer look at an explanatory (or mediating) process through which agile methods strengthen organizational creativity. More specifically, we propose and test a causal chain linking the implementation of agile methods, organizational creative capability, as defined in the first chapter of this book and the company's creative output. We base our reflection on a review of the relevant literature in organizational management, information systems and social psychology, and on a quantitative study conducted with 70 executives operating in the video game industry. In a few years, this industry has positioned itself at the heart of the entertainment industry by generating growing global revenues[3] (Higuchi and Nakano 2017).

The video game industry, like many of its creative industry cousins[4], is characterized by tensions between the need to rationalize its production processes to the maturity of the sector (Tschang 2007) and the need to be creative to meet the needs and expectations of consumers, who are looking for more and more out-of-the-box experiences (Koutonen and Leppänen 2015). In response to these tensions, some publishers and independent studios[5] have resorted to agile methodologies or practices (Stacey and Nandhakumar 2008; Musil et al. 2010a, 2010b; Koutonen and Leppänen 2013; Higuchi and Nakano 2017). The question of the effect of these methods and practices on the creativity of companies emerging from the video game industry is all the more important because enterprises in this sector need to be creative more than ever to remain competitive (Darchen and Tremblay 2015). This exploratory work also has an interest in focusing on organizational creativity, which is less studied than individual creativity (Blomberg et al. 2017) and empirically testing the effect of agile methods in an industry where they are far less studied than in the computing sector, from which they originated (Musil et al. 2010b).

3 The global video game revenue was estimated at $152.1 billion in 2019 (see: https://newzoo.com). In France, the video game industry generated 4.81 billion euros in revenue in 2018 (see: https://www.sell.fr).

4 With the introduction of multimedia technologies, technology-intensive industries, such as the video game industry, have become an integral part of the creative industries (Aoyama and Izushi 2003).

5 Video game publishers publish and distribute video games. Most game publishers have in-house development teams. Indie studios, often consisting of small teams, develop their own games.

We will start by presenting how agile methods are used in the video game industry. We will continue by discussing the influence of agile methods on the creativity of the video games produced. Then, we will analyze the central role played by organizational creative capability in the explanation of the above-mentioned link between the use of agile methods and the creative production (in this case, of video games). This section will lead us to look at the different components of agile methods that can positively influence the creativity of companies operating in the video game sector. Then, we will present the tests we have carried out on the basis of the data collected. Finally, the discussion of our results will allow us to evoke the theoretical and managerial contributions of this research work and also the limits associated with it.

5.1. The use of agile methods in the video game industry

One of the most dynamic and creative industries today is the video game industry. In recent years, however, it has been facing many challenges. Gamers' expectations for visual appearance, scripting, sound quality and technological novelty, in particular virtual and augmented realities, are continuously growing (Koutonen and Leppänen 2013). Video games must now offer players ever more immersive experiences (Tschang 2007).

Moreover, their increasing complexity involves the use of diverse competitive technical and artistic skills, for example, game design, script writing and computer graphics and large budgets (Musil et al. 2010b). The video game industry has also become a highly competitive and risky sector (Koutonen and Leppänen 2013). Indeed, publishers take a great risk by investing tens of millions of euros in a development project without knowing whether the game will be a success or not. The video game industry also faces extreme market volatility (Rydzewski 2019).

In response to these challenges, video game publishers and independent studios have had to rethink their working methods. To this end, some of them have turned to agile methods (Stacey and Nandhakumar 2008; Musil et al. 2010a, 2010b; Koutonen and Leppänen 2013; Higuchi and Nakano 2017). Originally used in the IT industry, agile methods are characterized by a pragmatic and iterative approach to project management, encouraging self-organization and adapting to change (Rasnacis and Berzisa 2016). They allow companies to operate more smoothly and reduce cycle times, which is particularly important in the video game industry, which is characterized by the need to adapt to the constant evolution of the demands of users. More specifically, the signatories of the agile manifesto have decided to change the way they look at project management by giving more importance to people and their interactions (rather than processes and tools), to the functional character of a software (rather than exhaustive documentation), to collaboration with the customer (rather than contractual negotiation) and, finally, to adaptation to change (rather than plan monitoring).

In the spirit of transparency and cooperation, agile project teams work directly with customers to better understand their expectations and deliver solutions in a fast and incremental way. Communication between multidisciplinary project teams and the client is essential in the agile approach. The initial expectations of customers in terms of functionalities (which are translated in the form of "requirements") are certainly recognized as useful for development, but they are not an end in themselves. In the agile approach, the products or services developed must be able to integrate, throughout the project, the rapid evolution of users' needs and expectations.

In a book for practitioners, Keith (2010) argues that the principles of agile methods are applicable, with minor changes, to the video game industry. The video game industry has similarities with the IT industry because of the similarity of the output produced – which is also a set of programs and procedures – and the development phases.

Drawing on the practices of the Scrum method, Keith presents a four-stage development process, including the design, pre-production, production and post-production of a game. In the design stage, ideas are generated and eventually prototyped within a predefined time frame, and a game concept is selected. During pre-production, the project teams build upon the entertainment components of the concept envisioned in the definition phase and determine the computer resources or assets (sound, image, text and video files) needed to implement them in the game. It is also during this phase that the search for funding takes place. In the production stage, project teams focus on creating an 8- to 12-hour game experience based on the components described in the pre-production phase. A schedule and tasks are established with regular meetings to validate progress and adjust the game production along the way according to the issues identified. Finally, in the post-production phase, the teams finalize the game experience, making incremental improvements to it. According to Darchen and Tremblay (2015), the most creative aspect of video game production appears mainly during the design and pre-production phases.

The use of agile methods in the video game industry is mentioned in different empirical research conducted around the world. For example, more than half of the 20 Finnish independent studios surveyed by Koutonen and Leppänen (2013) use the Scrum in pre-production, production and post-production, and one-third use it in the concept definition phase. Kanban, on the contrary, is used by only one of these studios during concept definition, and extreme programming is not used by any of the studios.

These results corroborate those of Musil et al. (2010b): 77% of the 20 Austrian studios surveyed use an agile method and 61.5% use the Scrum method. They are also consistent with a qualitative study conducted with five Brazilian studios, according to which, agile methods, particularly the Scrum method, are used in the production phase of a video game (Higuchi and Nakano 2017). Stacey and Nandhakumar's (2008) findings are more nuanced, in that these researchers found that the three studios they interviewed in Singapore and London were not deploying agile methods per se, but rather some agile practices.

5.2. The influence of agile methods on the creativity of the video games produced

Numerous studies, mostly conducted in the IT industry, have highlighted the beneficial effects of agile methods on the performance of companies taken (e.g. (Cegarra-Navarro et al. 2016; Lee et al. 2017)), on customer and employee satisfaction (Lee et al. 2017) and also on the quality of the final products (Dybå and Dingsøyr 2008). Closer to our study topic, Koutonen and Leppänen (2013) showed that agile methods and practices, in particular the Scrum method, assured the quality of the games produced, by allowing for faster identification of features that are both entertaining and implementable.

But a quality game is not necessarily a creative product. As we have seen previously, creative game design is a key factor in the video game industry. To our knowledge, no study has, to date, tested the influence of the use of agile methods on the level of creativity of video games.

5.3. The central role of organizational creative capability

Organizational creative capability was defined in the opening chapter of this book as "the ability, using processes and routines, to generate, select and integrate new, appropriate, useful and feasible ideas and solutions to improve, change and renew the organization's processes and products, as well as the organization itself". This definition approaches creativity from the point of view, not of a result, but of an ability. In this sense, it is in line with the pioneering work on creativity, which focused on the creative potential of an individual, in particular that of Guilford (1950), taken up by Torrance (1974). However, as the terminology indicates, organizational creative capability considers creativity in terms of an organization, not in terms of an individual. As such, it also refers to the work on organizational creativity. In particular, Woodman et al. (1993, p. 293) define it as "the creation of a useful and new product, service, idea, procedure or process by individuals working together in a complex social system".

However, while Woodman et al.'s definition of organizational creativity views organizational creativity as an outcome, organizational creative capability focuses on the creative potential that an organization has. This potential is based both on the creative abilities of employees and on the organization's ability to create a climate that is conducive to the generation and expression of ideas. Creative capability can be attributed to the organization as a whole when it specifically implements processes and routines to foster the creativity of its employees.

However, as previously mentioned, agile methods place people, rather than processes, at the heart of projects. Moreover, as Hanssen and Fægri (2008, p. 53) point out, "Agile software development (ASD) can exploit the creative potential of the developers". As a result, studying the organizational creative capability that uses these methods intrinsically leads to an interest in the creative skills of the teams that comprise it. This focus is all the more relevant since, in the video game industry, the development teams are a key resource for companies (Musil 2010a). Moreover, consider that the central role of organizational creative capability requires the analysis of a double relationship. On the one hand, it will be a matter of better understanding the way in which agile methods affect the creative capability of development teams, and therefore the organizational creative capability, and, on the other hand, of analyzing the impact of the latter on the level of creativity, measured in terms of the perceived originality of the games produced.

5.3.1. *The influence of agile methods on organizational creative capability*

With the exception of Kakar (2017), whose results were discussed in the introduction of this chapter, to our knowledge there is no empirical study that has tested the link between agile project management methods and creativity or co-creativity (Dampérat et al. 2019). We will therefore return here to different characteristics of agile methodologies likely to reinforce the creative capabilities of development teams. We group these characteristics around three themes (iterative and incremental development, collaborative devices and tools and management mode) represented in Figure 5.1.

5.3.1.1. *The iterative and incremental approach*

In agile methods, development phases are iterative and short in duration, typically two to four weeks (Cooper and Sommer 2016). A development perimeter including a list of features and fixes to existing code is defined at the beginning of each cycle (or sprint in the Scrum method) and must be fully completed when it ends. Thus, when the project team reaches the end of one cycle, another begins and so on until the finished product that perfectly meets the customer's needs can be delivered. As Cooper and Sommer (2016, p. 519) state, these sprints thus generate a "project heartbeat" for working productively and creatively. There are several reasons why an iterative and incremental approach, as described in agile methods, has a positive effect on the creative abilities of teams.

First, the agile approach encourages development teams to identify the best possible solutions to problems specific to a given cycle (Beecham et al. 2008). As Higuchi and Nakano (2017, p. 117) state, these problems are, in fact, "unstructured", in that most of the time, customers only really become aware of their needs after seeing the version of the software (or video game) delivered at the end of an iteration. The clarification of "requirements", i.e. in the engineering domain, the expectations, as formulated by the customer in terms of functionalities or scenarios that a product or service must meet, which takes place at the beginning of each iteration (Highsmith 2009), places the development teams in a position where they must "clarify the problem", as in the method of creative problem solving (CPS) (Osborn 1953), or "define the needs", as in design thinking (Brown 2009). This is a phase that particularly calls on the creativity of teams (Aldave et al. 2019) and needs to be approached with an attitude worthy of "the greatest explorers, such as Cook, Magellan, Shackleton and Columbus" (Highsmith 2009, p. 68).

Yet, the literature shows that such an exploratory approach, to use the terminology used in extreme programming (Vidgen and Wang 2009), fosters team creativity in later phases of the creative process (Amabile 1988; Lubart 2001; Treffinger and Isaksen 2005).

At each stage, development teams must deliver an intermediate version of the game to the client, including the solutions found to the expectations formulated at the beginning of the cycle (Higuchi and Nakano 2017). In addition, the materialization (or prototyping) of solutions, which brings ideas to be tested and refined to life, is conducive to the creativity of teams (Dampérat et al. 2019).

Moreover, an iterative development process provides regular feedback from the client on the developed versions (Tschang 2007; Dybå and Dingsøyr 2008; Kakar 2017). Now, whether positive or negative, feedback delivered to a team in relation to a task at hand is likely to increase its creativity (Hoever et al. 2018).

Finally, the use of incremental design reduces the number of decisions made upstream of development (Highsmith 2009), and subsequently, the amount of functionalities to be implemented (Hoda et al. 2013). Continuously adjusting the features to be developed, according to the evolving demands of the client, thus avoids workload pressure that can be counterproductive in terms of creativity (Amabile et al. 1996). This adjustment is particularly useful in the video game industry, where crunch time (a term specific to this industry referring to short- and medium-term periods when there is a significant increase in overtime) is frequent (Musil et al. 2010b), notably due to the seasonality of demand.

5.3.1.2. *Collaborative devices and tools*

Agile methods include various devices or artifacts (Cooper and Sommer 2016) that facilitate interactions within an organization. The regular meetings recommended by these methods (Tessem 2014), for example, in the Scrum method, time-box sprints, daily scrums, retrospective meetings and reviews (Cooper and Sommer 2016), strengthen communication and collaborative work (Vidgen and Wang 2009). These meetings facilitate the transfer of information (Stacey and Nandhakumar 2008) and the confrontation of ideas (Tessem 2014), both of which are conducive to the creativity of a team (Ekvall 1996; Isaksen et al. 2001). The differences in perspectives are even more important because agile methods favor multidisciplinary teams (Cockburn and Highsmith 2001; Highsmith 2009; Higuchi and Nakano 2017). Research conducted, in the video game industry in particular (Parmentier and Picq 2016), shows that diversity within a team (e.g. in terms of gender, age, culture, education or technical skills) enhances its creativity (Sethi et al. 2001; Perry-Smith and Shalley 2003; Choi 2007; Shin et al. 2012). In particular, Conboy et al. (2009) identify diversity in agile teams as a source of "creative abrasion," terminology borrowed from Jerry Hirshberg, founder of Nissan's international design office.

Peer programming improves the sharing of tacit knowledge (Melnik and Maurer 2002) and facilitates individual learning (Tessem 2003), both of which have been identified as facilitators of team creativity (Amabile 1988). In addition, this practice builds trust among team members (Melnik and Maurer 2002), which is also conducive to their creativity (Ekvall 1996; Isaksen et al. 2001).

Finally, agile methods mobilize numerous visual tools, such as storyboards, story-cards or product-backlogs, intended to promote communication and coordination of team work (Nerur et al. 2005). These tools enable the prioritization of actions and a better understanding of the customer's expectations at each development cycle (Cooper and Sommer 2016). The latter strengthens the creative capability of a team. In general, visual tools, such as Post-it notes or mind maps, are recognized as facilitating creativity (Brown 2009).

5.3.1.3. *The management method*

In the agile philosophy, in relation to development teams, "in a self-organized team, individuals take accountability for managing their own workload, shift work among themselves based on need and best fit, and take responsibility for team effectiveness" (Highsmith 2009, p. 51). Indeed, the 11th principle of the agile manifesto argues that "the best architectures, specifications, and designs come from self-organizing teams" (Agile 2001).

Different variables related to the self-organization of a team are likely to influence its creative capabilities, starting with autonomy (Dyba and Dingsoyr 2008; Vidgen and Wang 2009; Hoda et al. 2013; Kakar 2017). Numerous research studies, conducted in different organizational contexts, for example, Paolillo and Brown (1978), Bailyn (1985) or, more recently, Joo et al. (2014), indicate that the creativity of a team is greater when it has a "relatively high level of autonomy" (Amabile et al. 1996, p. 1161). Defined as the ability to decide what tasks the team should perform and how they should perform them (Amabile 1988), autonomy in work contributes to increasing the intrinsic motivation of individuals working together (Joo et al. 2010). In this regard, self-determination theory (Ryan and Deci 2000) predicts that an individual's (or group of individuals') perception of autonomy is antecedent to their motivation to perform specific tasks. Intrinsic motivation is a widely recognized factor in stimulating organizational creativity (see, for example, the widely recognized componential model by Amabile (1988)). It is at the heart of the fifth principle of the manifesto signed by the initiators of the agile movement, which recommends "building a project around motivated people" (Agile 2001).

The self-organization advocated by agile methods also refers to the notion of freedom to act (Vidgen and Wang 2009; Hoda et al. 2013; Kakar 2017). The latter is a dimension of organizational climates conducive to creativity (Amabile 1988; Amabile et al. 1996; Ekvall 1996). The results of the study conducted by Isaksen et al. (2001) indicate that the teams perceived as being the most creative, among those made up of students and managers questioned, have developed working methods based on self-organization and freedom of action.

If, adopting an agile approach, development teams freely decide on the actions they need to take to achieve set objectives, they also take responsibility for the results of these same actions. Empowerment of teams is a well-referenced practice in agile methods (Tessem 2003; McAvoy and Butler 2009; Hoda et al. 2013). In particular, McAvoy and Butler (2009) emphasize that, in agile project management, development teams must feel accountable for the value they will need to deliver quickly to the customer.

Research, such as that of Sun et al. (2012), has shown the positive effects of *empowerment* practices on the individual creativity of employees. On the contrary, at the collective level, the relationship between empowerment and creativity has, to date, been the subject of very little research, and the results seem more nuanced (Zhan and Bartol 2015). For example, Maruping and Magni (2012) show that empowerment practices for internal teams only increase the intention to explore new ideas when the learning climate is favorable.

Finally, the principle of self-organization relies on trusting relationships between team members (Dyba and Dingsoyr 2008), which, as we have seen above, are conducive to creativity (Ekvall 1996; Isaksen et al. 2001).

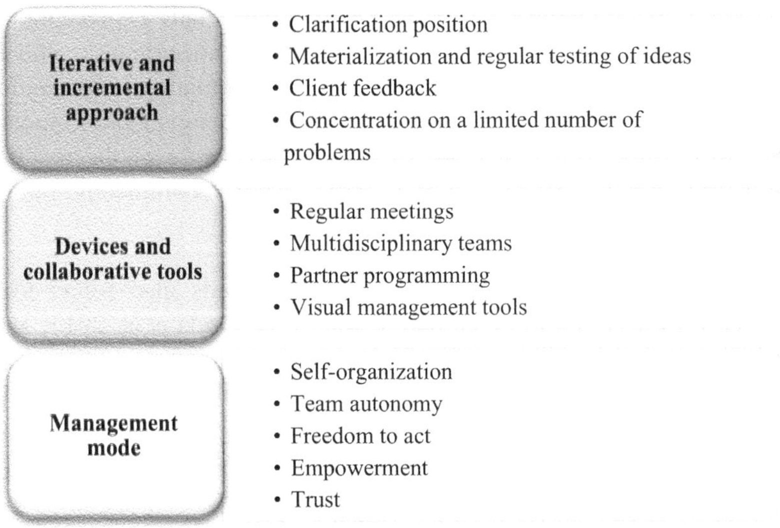

Figure 5.1. *Sources of team creativity within agile methods*

5.3.2. *The influence of organizational creative capability on the creativity of the video games produced*

The presence of a creative capability can be measured by the generation of a large number of ideas and solutions at all levels of the organization and also by the perception that individuals, employees and/or leaders, have of the creativity of the organization in which they work. At the individual level, this perception refers to the concept of creative self-efficacy, defined as "the belief one has the ability to produce creative outcomes" (Tierney and Farmer 2002, p. 1138). Ford (1996) was the first to lay the groundwork for this concept in a model identifying the factors that lead an individual to undertake creative action. The production of new ideas is, in fact, a complex task born of an internal force that encourages individuals to persevere in the face of the challenges specific to creative work (Amabile 1983; Wood and Bandura 1989). Creative self-efficacy beliefs appear to provide such an impetus in the sense that strong beliefs improve the level of persistence and coping that individuals need to demonstrate when faced with difficult situations (Bandura 1977, 1989). Research conducted in organizational settings shows that beliefs of personal creative efficacy increase employees' creative performance (Tierney and Farmer 2002). Such beliefs also exist at the level of a group of individuals through the concept of collective creative efficacy, i.e. "an individual's belief in a team's ability to produce creative results" (Dampérat et al. 2016). Collective creative efficacy beliefs influence the generation and implementation of new ideas (Liu et al. 2015) and increase the creative performance of a team (Salanova et al. 2014; Ali et al. 2019). Following a similar logic, we propose that, at the organizational level, an individual's belief in an organization's ability to produce creative outcomes can be a measure of said organization's creative capability. Given that the perception of creative efficiency is a good predictor of perceived originality of creative production (Dampérat et al. 2016), it is likely that the perception of creative capability is also a good predictor of the perceived originality of the creative output. Consequently, we propose that an organization with high creative capability produces more creative output.

The relationships discussed above based on existing work are grouped into a causal chain shown in Figure 5.2. The latter includes (1) the influence of agile methods (considered as a whole) on the creativity of the games produced, (2) the influence of agile methods on the organizational creative capability and (3) the influence of organizational creative capability on the creativity of produced games.

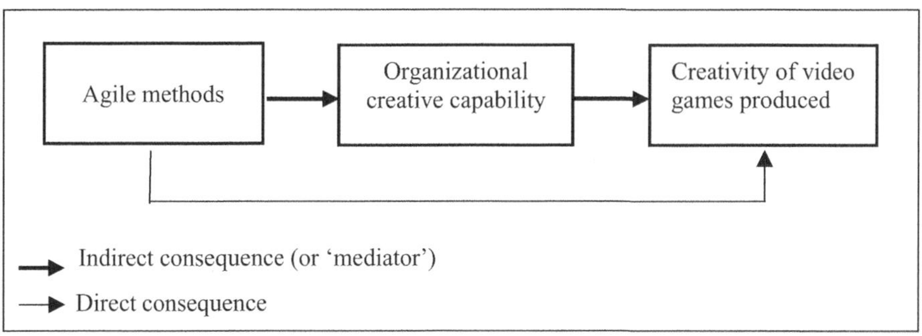

Figure 5.2. *The proposed causal chain*

5.4. An empirical study

A quantitative study was conducted to test the relationships included in Figure 5.2. The process of this study is presented in Box 5.1.

The data was collected at three international events that brought together key players in the video game industry: Game Connection Europe in Paris (October 24–26, 2018), Montreal International Game Summit (November 12–13, 2018) and Game Connection America in San Francisco (March 18–22, 2019). Prior to the events, we scheduled meetings with potential respondents using event platforms. Our final sample consisted of 70 executives, who agreed to answer closed-ended questions measuring the variables included in the proposed model (use of agile methods, creative abilities, organizational skills and perceived originality of the video games produced).

All these executives worked in companies operating in the video game industry. We conducted the questionnaires face-to-face, using a tablet. In order to reduce the social desirability and response bias that may be present in the survey, we, on the one hand, assured the respondents that their answers would remain anonymous and, on the other hand, asked our questions in different orders.

Box 5.1. *Study process*

5.4.1. *Test of the influence of agile methods on the creativity of the video games produced*

We use perceived originality as an indicator of creativity of video games. Dahl et al. (1999) emphasize the importance of originality in measuring a creative production. In Hart and Jacoby's approach, this indicator refers to the innovation dimension of the concept of novelty of a product or service, i.e. "novelty refers to the quality and extent of differences between a product alternative and all other alternatives in that product category" (Hart and Jacoby 1973, p. 839).

Originality was assessed via a mono-item scale adapted from Dampérat et al. (2016): "How would you rate the games produced by your company?", with responses ranging from 1 for "not at all original", to 5 for "very original". The agility of the project management methods used by the surveyed studios was measured via a bimodal qualitative variable: "Does your company use one (or several) agile method(s)?", with response coding of 0 for "no" and 1 for "yes". A Levene (1960) test validated the homogeneity of variances between the two groups. As shown in Table 5.1, the p-value of Levene's test is greater than the 5% significance level, leading to the acceptance of the null hypothesis.

		Workforce	Average	Standard deviation	Levene's statistics	Sig.
Agile methods ***Does your company use one (or more) agile method(s)? (yes/no)***	No	17	3.15	0.70	0.339	0.563
	Yes	53	3.82	0.81		

Table 5.1. *Test of homogeneity of variances*

A *t*-test could thus be performed on the perceived originality variable. As shown in Table 5.2, the results reveal a significant difference in the means between the two answer modalities of the question on the use of agile methods: the mean of perceived originality is statistically different ($t(68) = 3.060$; $p < 0.01$) and higher when agile methods are used ($_{MUuse} = 3.82$) than when they are not ($_{MNon\text{-}Use} = 3.15$).

	Δ averages	ddl	*t-test*	Sig.
Perceived originality ***How do you rate the games produced by your company? (from 1: not at all original, to 5: very original)***	– 0.674	68	3.060	0.003

Table 5.2. *Independent samples test*

This analysis provides empirical evidence that the use of agile methods enhances the creativity of games produced by independent studios. This result is interesting in itself, given the significance for a studio to be creative. But it invites us to look at the mechanisms underlying the relationship that has been uncovered. We will therefore test the causal chain proposed above.

5.4.2. *Empirical test of the proposed causal chain*

The causal chain "organizational creative capability – perceived originality" was tested using mediation analysis. Creative capability was measured holistically through two five-step items adapted from Salanova et al. (2003): "To what extent do you think your company has the capabilities to solve problems creatively?" and "To what extent do you think your company has the capabilities to generate new ideas?" ranging from 1 for "not at all" to 5 for "totally". We created an index of organizational creative capability by averaging the two items. The creation of this index was possible because of the statistically significant correlation between the two items (Pearson's correlation coefficient is 0.277 and the p-value is below the 5% significance level). To test the so-called indirect effect, i.e. the path through organizational creative capability that corresponds to a x b in Table 5.3, we used the re-sampling (bootstrapping) technique included in Hayes' (2013) PROCESS macro.

		Organizational creative capability skills				**Perceived originality**		
		Coefficient	**SE**	**Significance**		**Coefficient**	**SE**	**Significance**
Agile methods	*a*	0.342	0.161	0.038	*c'*	0.465	0.204	0.026
Organizational creative capability	–	–	–	–	*b*	0.609	0.148	0.000
		$R^2 = 0.062$				$R^2 = 0.297$		
		$F(1.68) = 4.470$; $p = 0.038$				$F(1.67) = 14.195$; $p = 0.000$		
		Significance test for indirect effect: a x b = 0.208; 95% CI [LL = 0.050; UL = 0.443]						

Table 5.3. *Results of the mediation analysis*

The results of this analysis revealed that the use of agile methods has a positive and statistically significant effect on organizational creative capability (see Table 5.3: a = 0.342; $t(68) = 2.114$; $p < 0.05$). Controlling for the effect of agile methods, organizational creative capability also has a positive and statistically significant effect on perceived originality of video games (b = 0.609; $t(67) = 4.104$; $p < 0.001$). Controlling for the effect of organizational creative capability, the use of agile methods has a direct effect that remains positive and statistically significant on the perceived originality of video games (c' = 0.465; $t(67) = 2.271$; $p < 0.05$). Even more important, the use of agile methods has a positive and statistically significant indirect effect on the perceived originality of video games through its effect on organizational creative capability (a x b = 0.208), with a 95% confidence interval (CI) excluding zero (95% CI: [LL = 0.050; UL = 0.443]). Thus, we have a mediation in which the effects of agile methods and organizational creative capability explain, in a "complementary" manner, in the sense of Zhao et al. (2010), the perceived originality of video games. The mediating effect of organizational creative capability is thus validated, but it is not total. Therefore, the possibility of one or more mediating variables remains to be considered.

5.5. Discussion

This chapter aimed to better understand the mechanism by which the use of agile methods influences the creative output of companies operating in the video game industry. The results indicate that the use of these methods has a direct and positive effect on the creativity of the games produced. This result is consistent with the several studies that have highlighted the benefits of agile methods in the video game industry, especially on the quality of the games (Koutonen and Leppänen 2013), without having specifically analyzed the effect of these methods on creativity. Above all, our results show that the creative capability of a company is an important construct, as it underlies the influence of agile methods on creative output.

To the best of our knowledge, this research is the first to provide empiric evidence of the mediating effect of organizational creative capability. Note that the proposed model explains nearly 30% of the variance in perceived game originality, which is an encouraging result for an exploratory study[6] for which our only industry reference is a 9.4% explanation of innovative capability by one of the components of agile methods, namely self-organization (Kakar 2017). This percentage counters recent statements by Aldave et al. (2019, p. 1) that agile methods induce little or no creativity: "Agile approaches tend to focus solely on scoping and simplicity rather than on problem solving and discovery". Consistent with the claims made by the pioneers of the agile movement, our results lead to an initial quantification of the impact of agile project management methods on organizational creativity. We believe that the lack of interest in empirical research related to this impact is due to the fact that the IT industry, in which agile methods were initially deployed, has less need for creativity than the video game industry. As Musil et al. (2010) state:

6 As Frost (2019) points out in his statistics book, the percentage of variance explained can only be interpreted with reference to existing work in the field of study.

> Video games as interactive entertainment software can also be regarded as non-utilitarian software products that have affective, experiential qualities which are neither captured by current non-functional requirements nor by any other means.

However, identifying a new antecedent to organizational creativity, as opposed to traditional models, requires robust measures of constructs. This is a current limitation of our work. A qualitative dichotomic variable was used to measure the agility of project management methods implemented in the surveyed companies. Taking a holistic approach, in a future research work, we could adapt an existing method agility scale, including the 10-item scale by Lee et al. (2017) or the 15-item scale by Darvishmotevali et al. (2020), to our study context. A multidimensional approach could also be considered, for example, by considering the frequency of use of agile practices, as well as their scope of application, or by including the different components of agile methods that are likely to increase the creativity of teams, as identified in this chapter, in a more global model that could be tested *via* structural equation modeling.

The measurement of the final dependent variable in our model could also be improved. In social and organizational psychology, there are three main measures of creativity: fluency, flexibility and originality (De Dreu et al. 2008). Fluidity refers to the number of (non-redundant) product or solution ideas generated during the creative process. Flexibility is a measure of an individual's capacity to move beyond traditional product categories and incorporate divergent perspectives into their thinking. Finally, (perceived) originality is a measure of how unusual and differentiating an idea or solution is. This last indicator of creativity is used in various creativity research articles, including Dahl et al. (1999) and Dampérat et al. (2016). Perceived originality is also used in the literature to distinguish between incremental and radical or completely new innovations (Zhao et al. 2012). It is therefore interesting in the video game industry, which is characterized by the need for continuous innovation, either incremental, such as when the game concept is pre-existing (Parmentier and Mangematin 2009), or radical, as in the case of creating a new genre[7] (Tschang 2007). Regarding the choice of evaluation of creative production, several topics of debate exist in the creativity research literature, particularly the number of evaluators to consider. Some researchers have mobilized multiple raters to judge creative outcomes.

7. It refers to a set of games characterized by similar rules (or gameplay).

Others, however, have focused on the evaluation of a team's creative performance by a single individual. This type of evaluation is widely used and accepted in the innovation literature. In our study, we interviewed the company's top managers. Other methods of measuring creative outcomes could be considered in future research. For example, multilevel analyses (Tu 2009; Wang et al. 2016) would allow for the combination of team perspectives and managerial perspectives. The use of test markets could also be a relevant way to test the creativity of ideas or solutions (Soukhoroukova et al. 2012). Finally, as recommended by Tschang (2007), we could use a measure of creativity specifically adapted to video games, as these products are so atypical.

5.6. References

Agile (2001). Manifeste pour le développement de logiciels agiles [Online]. Available at: https://agilemanifesto.org/iso/fr/manifesto.htm.

Aldave, A., Vara, J.M., Granada, D., Marcos, E. (2019). Leveraging creativity in requirements elicitation within agile software development: A systematic literature review. *Journal of Systems and Software*, 157, 1–18.

Ali, A., Wang, H., Khan, A.N. (2019). Mechanism to enhance team creative performance through social media: A transactive memory system approach. *Computers in Human Behavior*, 91, 115–126.

Amabile, T.M. (1983). The social-psychology of creativity: A componential conceptualization. *Journal of Personality and Social Psychology*, 45(2), 357–376.

Amabile, T.M. (1988). A model of creativity and innovation in organizations. *Research in Organizational Behavior*, 10(1), 123–167.

Amabile, T.M., Conti, R., Coon, H., Lazenby, J., Herron, M. (1996). Assessing the work environment for creativity. *Academy of Management Journal*, 39(5), 1154–1184.

Annosi, M.C., Martini, A., Brunetta, F., Marchegiani, L. (2020). Learning in an agile setting: A multilevel research study on the evolution of organizational routines. *Journal of Business Research*, 110(87), 554–566.

Aoyama, Y. and Izushi, H. (2003). Hardware gimmick or cultural innovation? Technological, cultural, and social foundations of the Japanese video game industry. *Research Policy*, 32(3), 423–444.

Bailyn, L. (1985). Autonomy in the industrial R&D laboratory. *Human Resource Management*, 24(2), 129–146.

Bandura, A. (1977). Self-efficacy: Toward a unifying theory of behavioral change. *Psychology Review*, 84(2), 191–215.

Bandura, A. (1989). Regulation of cognitive processes through perceived self-efficacy. *Developmental Psychology*, 25(5), 729–735.

Beecham, S., Baddoo, N., Hall, T., Robinson, H., Sharp, H. (2008). Motivation in software engineering: A systematic literature review. *Information and Software Technology*, 50(9/10), 860–878.

Blomberg, A., Kallio, T., Pohjanpää, H. (2017). Antecedents of organizational creativity: Drivers, barriers or both? *Journal of Innovation Management*, 5(1), 78–104.

Brown, T. (2009). *Change by Design: How Design Thinking Transforms Organizations and Inspires Innovation*. Harper-Collins, New York.

Cameron, M., Ford, M., Jackson, S. (1996). A Theory of creative action individual of individual creative theory action in multiple social domains multiple social domains. *The Academy of Management Review*, 21(4), 1112–1142.

Cegarra-Navarro, J.G., Soto-Acosta, P., Wensley, A.K.P. (2016). Structured knowledge processes and firm performance: The role of organizational agility. *Journal of Business Research*, 69(5), 1544–1549.

Choi, J.N. (2007). Group composition and employee creative behaviour in a Korean electronics company: Distinct effects of relational demography and group diversity. *Journal of Occupational and Organizational Psychology*, 80(2), 213–234.

Cockburn, A. and Highsmith, J. (2001). Agile software development: The people factor. *Software Management*, 34(11), 131–133.

Conboy, K., Wang, X., Fitzgerald, B. (2009). Creativity in agile systems development: A literature review. *Advances in Information and Communication Technology*, 301(1), 122–134.

Cooper, R.G. and Sommer, A.F. (2016). The agile–stage-gate hybrid model: A promising new approach and a new research opportunity. *Journal of Product Innovation Management*, 33(5), 513–526.

Dahl, D.W., Chattopadhyay, A., Gorn, G.J. (1999). The use of visual mental imagery in new product design. *Journal of Marketing Research*, 36(1), 18–28.

Dampérat, M., Jeannot, F., Jongmans, E., Jolibert, A. (2016). La créativite des équipes : l'efficacité créative personnelle et collective et leurs déterminants. *Recherche et Applications en Marketing*, 31(3), 7–28.

Dampérat, M., Jeannot, F., Jongmans, E., Jolibert, A. (2019). Modeling a cocreative process: The contributions of design and management. *Recherche et Applications en Marketing*, 34(3), 111–137.

Darchen, S. and Tremblay, D.G. (2015). Policies for creative clusters: A comparison between the video game industries in Melbourne and Montreal. *European Planning Studies*, 23(2), 311–331.

Darvishmotevali, M., Altinay, L., Köseoglu, M.A. (2020). The link between environmental uncertainty, organizational agility, and organizational creativity in the hotel industry. *International Journal of Hospitality Management*, 87(3), 1–9.

De Dreu, C.K.W., Baas, M., Nijstad, B. (2008). Hedonic tone and activation level in the mood-creativity link: Toward a dual pathway to creativity model. *Journal of Personality and Social Psychology*, 94(5), 739–756.

Dybå, T. and Dingsøyr, T. (2008). Empirical studies of agile software development: A systematic review. *Information and Software Technology*, 50(9/10), 833–859.

Ekvall, G. (1996). Organizational climate for creativity and innovation. *European Journal of Work and Organizational Psychology*, 5(1), 105–123.

Feiereisen, S., Wong, V., Broderick, A.J. (2008). Analogies and mental simulations in learning for really new products: The role of visual attention. *Journal of Product Innovation Management*, 25(6), 593–607.

Ford, C.M. (1996). A theory of individual creative action in multiple social domains. *The Academy of Management Review*, 21(4), 1112–1142.

Frost, J. (2019). *Regression Analysis: An Intuitive Guide for Using and Interpreting Linear Models.* Statistics by Jim Publishing [Online]. Available at: https://statisticsbyjim.com.

Glass, R.L. (2006). *Software Creativity 2.0.* Developer Books, New York.

Guilford, J.P. (1950). Creativity. *American Psychologist*, 5(9), 444–454.

Hanssen, G.K. and Fægri, T.E. (2008). Process fusion: An industrial case study on agile software product line engineering. *Journal of Software and Systems*, 81(3), 843–854.

Hart, E.W. and Jacoby, J. (1973). Novelty, recency, and scarcity as predictors of perceived newness. *Proceedings of the Annual Convention of the American Psychological Association.*

Hayes, A.F. (2013). *Introduction to Mediation, Moderation, and Conditional Process Analysis: A Regression-Based Approach.* Guilford Press, New York.

Highsmith, J. (2009). *Agile Project Management: Creating Innovative Products.* Addison-Wesley, Boston.

Higuchi, M.M. and Nakano, D.N. (2017). Agile design: A combined model based on design thinking and agile methodologies for digital games projects. *Revista de Gestão e Projetos*, 8(2), 109–126.

Hoda, R., Noble, J., Marshall, S. (2013). Self-organizing roles on agile software development teams. *IEEE Transactions on Software Engineering*, 39(3), 422–444.

Hoever, I.J., Zhou, J., Knippenberg, D.VA.N. (2018). Different strokes for different teams: The contingent effects of positive and negative feedback on the creativity of informationally homogeneous and diverse teams. *Academy of Management Journal*, 61(6), 2159–2181.

Isaksen, S.G., Lauer, K.J., Ekvall, G., Britz, A. (2001). Perceptions of the best and worst climates for creativity: Preliminary validation evidence for the situational outlook questionnaire. *Creativity Research Journal*, 13(2), 171–184.

Joo, B.K.B., Yang, B., McLean, G.N. (2014). Employee creativity: The effects of perceived learning culture, leader-member exchange quality, job autonomy, and proactivity. *Human Resource Development International*, 17(3), 297–317.

Kakar, A.K. (2017). Assessing self-organization in agile software development teams. *Journal of Computer Information Systems*, 57(3), 208–217.

Keith, C. (2010). *Agile Game Development with Scrum*. Addison-Wesley, Boston.

Koutonen, J. and Leppänen, M. (2013). How are agile methods and practices deployed in video game development? A survey into Finnish game studios. In *Agile Processes in Software Engineering and Extreme Programming*, Baumeister, H. and Weber, B. (eds). Springer, Berlin, Heidelberg.

Lee, G. and Xia, W. (2010). Toward agile: An integrated analysis of quantitative and qualitative field data on software development agility. *MIS Quarterly*, 35(4), 831–858.

Lee, S., Lee, D., Kim, S., Lee, G. (2017). The role of agility in the relationship between use of management control systems and organizational performance: Evidence from Korea and Japan. *The Journal of Applied Business Research*, 33(3), 521–538.

Levene, H. (1960). Robust tests for equality of variances. In *Contributions to Probability and Statistics*, Olkin, I. (ed.). Stanford University Press, Palo Alto, 278–292.

Lindkvist, L., Bengtsson, M., Svensson, D.M., Wahlstedt, L. (2017). Replacing old routines: How Ericsson software developers and managers learned to become agile. *Industrial and Corporate Change*, 26(4), 571–591.

Liu, J., Chen, J., Tao, Y. (2015). Innovation performance in new product development teams in China's technology ventures: The role of behavioral integration dimensions and collective efficacy. *Journal of Product Innovation Management*, 32(1), 29–44.

Lubart, T.I. (2001). Models of the creative process: Past, present and future. *Creativity Research Journal*, 133(4), 295–308.

Mangalaraj, G., Nerur, S., Mahapatra, R., Price, K.H.P. (2014). Distributed cognition in software design: An experimental investigation of the role of design patterns and collaboration. *Pharmacogenomics*, 3(4), 781–791.

Maruping, L. and Magni, M. (2012). What's the weather like? The effect of team learning climate, empowerment climate, and gender on individuals' technology exploration and use. *Journal of Management Information Systems*, 29(1), 79–114.

McAvoy, J. and Butler, T. (2009). The role of project management in ineffective decision making within agile software development projects. *European Journal of Information Systems*, 18(4), 372–383.

Melnik, G. and Maurer, F. (2002). Perceptions of agile practices : A student survey. *Conference on Extreme Programming and Agile Methods*.

Morris, L., Ma, M., Wu, P.C. (2014). *Agile Innovation: The Revolutionary Approach to Accelerate Success, Inspire Engagement, and Ignite Creativity*. John Wiley & Sons, New York.

Musil, J. (2010a). Improving video game development: Facilitating heterogeneous team collaboration through flexible software processes. *Communications in Computer and Information Science*, 99, 233–244.

Musil, J., Schweda, A., Winkler, D., Bif, S. (2010b). A survey on a state of the practice in video game development. Technical report, 1–12.

Nerur, S., Mahapatra, R.K., Mangalaraj, G. (2005). Challenges of migrating to agile methodologies. *Communications of the ACM*, 48(5), 72–78.

Osborn, A.F. (1953). *Applied Imagination: Principles and Procedures of Creative Thinking*. Read Books, New York.

Paolillo, J.G. and Brown, W.B. (1978). How organizational factors affect R&D innovation. *Research Management*, 21(2), 12–15.

Parmentier, G. and Mangematin, V. (2009). Innovation et création dans le jeu vidéo. Comment concilier exploration et exploitation ? *Revue française de gestion*, 35(191), 71–87.

Parmentier, G. and Picq, T. (2016). Managing creative teams in small ambidextrous organizations: The case of videogames. *International Journal of Arts Management*, 19(1), 16–30.

Perry-Smith, J.E. and Shalley, C.E. (2003). The social side of creativity: A static and dynamic social network perspective. *Academy of Management Review*, 28(1), 89–106.

Petrillo, F. and Pimenta, M. (2010). Is agility out there? Agile practices in game development. SIGDOC 2010. *Proceedings of the 28th ACM International Conference on Design of Communication*, 9–15.

Rasnacis, A. and Berzisa, S. (2016). Method for adaptation and implementation of agile project management methodology. *Procedia Computer Science*, 104, 43–50.

Ryan, R.M. and Deci, E.L. (2000). Self-determination theory and the facilitation of intrinsic motivation, social development, and well-being. *American Psychologist*, 55(1), 68–78.

Rydzewski, R. (2019). Market-to-book ratio and creative industries – Example of Polish video games developers. *Economics and Culture*, 16(1), 137–147.

Salanova, M., Llorens, S., Cifre, E., Martínez, I.M., Schaufeli, W. (2003). Perceived collective efficacy, subjective well-being and task performance among electronic work groups. *Small Group Research*, 34(1).

Salanova, M., Rodríguez-Sánchez, A.M., Schaufeli, W.B., Cifre, E. (2014). Flowing together: A longitudinal study of collective efficacy and collective flow among workgroups. *The Journal of Psychology*, 148(4), 435–455.

Sethi, R., Smith, D.C., Park, C.W. (2001). Cross-functional product development teams, creativity, and the innovativeness of new consumer products. *Journal of Marketing Research*, 38(1), 73–85.

Shin, S.J., Kim, T.Y., Lee, J.Y., Bian, L.I.N. (2012). Cognitive team diversity and individual team member creativity: A cross-level interaction. *Academy of Management Journal*, 55(1), 197–212.

Soukhoroukova, A., Spann, M., Skiera, B. (2012). Sourcing, filtering, and evaluating new product ideas: An empirical exploration of the performance of idea markets. *Journal of Product Innovation Management*, 29(1), 100–112.

Stacey, P. and Nandhakumar, J. (2008). Opening up to agile games development. *Communications of the ACM*, 51(12), 143–146.

Sun, L.Y., Zhang, Z., Qi, J., Chen, Z.X. (2012). Empowerment and creativity: A cross-level investigation. *Leadership Quarterly*, 23(1), 55–65.

Tessem, B. (2003). Experiences in learning XP practices: A qualitative study. In *Extreme Programming and Agile Processes in Software Engineering*, Marchesi, M. and Succi, G. (eds). Springer, Berlin, Heidelberg.

Tessem, B. (2014). Individual empowerment of agile and non-agile software developers in small teams. *Information and Software Technology*, 56(8), 873–889.

Tierney, P. and Farmer, S.M. (2002). Creative self-efficacy: Its potential antecedents and relationship to creative performance. *Academy of Management Journal*, 45(6), 1137–1148.

Tierney, P. and Farmer, S.M. (2011). Creative self-efficacy development and creative performance over time. *Journal of Applied Psychology*, 96(2), 277–293.

Torrance, E.P. (1974). *Torrance Tests of Creative Thinking: Norms-Technical Manual*. Ginn and Co, Lexington.

Treffinger, D.J. and Isaksen, S.G. (2005). Creative problem solving: The history, development, and implications for gifted education and talent development. *Gifted Child Quarterly*, 49(4), 342–353.

Tschang, F.T. (2007). Balancing the tensions between rationalization and creativity in the video games industry. *Organization Science*, 18(6), 989–1005.

Tu, C. (2009). A multilevel investigation of factors influencing creativity in NPD teams. *Industrial Marketing Management*, 38(1), 119–126.

Vidgen, R. and Wang, X. (2009). Coevolving systems and the organization of agile software development. *Information Systems Research*, 20(3), 355–376.

Wang, X.H., Kim, T.Y., Lee, D.R. (2016). Cognitive diversity and team creativity: Effects of team intrinsic motivation and transformational leadership. *Journal of Business Research*, 69(9), 3231–3239.

Wood, R. and Bandura, A. (1989). Impact of conceptions of ability on self-regulatory mechanisms and complex decision making. *Journal of Personality and Social Psychology*, 56(3), 407–415.

Woodman, R.W., Sawyer, J.E., Griffin, R.W. (1993). Toward a theory of organizational creativity. *Academy of Management Review*, 18(2), 293–321.

Zackariasson, P., Styhre, A., Wilson, T.L. (2006). Phronesis and creativity: Knowledge work in video game development. *Creativity and Innovation Management*, 15(4), 419–429.

Zhan, X. and Bartol, K.M. (2015). Empowerment and employee creativity: A cross-level integrative model. In *The Oxford Handbook of Creativity, Innovation, and Entrepreneurship*, Zhou, M.A (ed.). Oxford University Press, Oxford.

Zhao, M., Hoeffler, S., Dahl, D.W. (2012). Imagination difficulty and new product evaluation. *Journal of Product Innovation Management*, 29(1), 76–90.

6

Idea Management and Idea Socialization in Organizations

Having ideas and being capable of using them are central for organizations, economists and management researchers. Concerning sources of value and renewal, scholars in economic and management sciences state that ideas become the driving force behind organizational growth and resilience (Phelps 2013; Cohendet et al. 2017). However, despite this commonly adopted statement, the notion of ideas holds only a modest role in the management science literature. Thus, idea management has recently emerged as a discipline. This can be explained by the fact that the literature has tended, for a very long time, to represent the generation of ideas by a creator or a small informal group of individuals, as a particular moment (a "spark" or a "moment of grace") that plays a marginal role at the beginning of an innovation project.

However, in recent years, the literature has begun to delve deeper into the notion of the idea (Harvey et al. 2013; Cohendet et al. 2017; Perry-Smith and Mannucci 2017). Garud et al. (2013) were the first to put ideas back at the center of innovation processes by considering them to cover the phases of invention (the emergence of an idea), development (the elaboration of the idea) and implementation (the widespread acceptance of the idea). Perry-Smith and Mannucci (2017) also argued that a new idea should not be confined at a particular time or attributed to a particular individual, but rather should be interpreted as an evolving, open-ended and collective "idea journey" that can

---

Chapter written by Guy PARMENTIER, Séverine LE LOARNE-LEMAIRE and Romain RAMPA.

be decomposed into four main stages: generation, development, promotion and implementation.

In this chapter, we will introduce a model of idea management that is based on this four-stage process of idea generation. For each stage, we will discuss the key issues that are associated with idea flow, before addressing the question of formal and informal approaches to managing these idea flows in the organization. Finally, we will open a discussion on the outputs that are generated by this recent discipline of idea management, and the limits of the practices and processes aimed at managing ideas.

6.1. The path of ideas

The term "idea" comes from the Latin *eidos*, which means "to see" or "to represent", i.e. what presents itself to the mind. It would take a long time to go back over the different meanings that the notion of idea has taken, especially in philosophy, where it has played a central role throughout the ages. For our purposes, we can use the definition in Cohendet et al. (2017) of the notion of ideas. The authors specify that an idea is composed of three main elements:

– an intention of action that can be latent or conscious, but which gives a direction and which directs the action;

– a set of knowledge and practices that are mobilized for serving the idea, which represents the conditions and the means of satisfaction of the intention;

– a network of members, who represent all of the actors (allies, sponsors, critics, champions, connectors, etc.) set in motion to support and realize the idea, and also to define, validate, refine and revise its value.

The advantage of this definition is that it takes both the cognitive and the social aspects into account. These will be at the center of the evolutionary and iterative dynamics that surround the generation, development, promotion and implementation of ideas. This triptych also makes it possible to better understand the different dimensions that are led to evolve, to be enriched, to be refined or even to be transformed in the path of an idea.

To better understand the dynamics and the journey of an idea, we will, in the next sections, come back to each of the four main stages that in turn affect the progressive development of an idea.

6.1.1. *Idea generation*

Idea generation is the first step of the journey. At this stage, the idea is only a vague intuition that has crossed the mind of an individual or a very small group of people, the *ideators*. Hargadon and Bechky (2006) show, for example, that the creative processes leading to the generation of new ideas very often involve collective activities, where individuals help each other and engage in reflective processes to find solutions or reframe problems. Beyond the expression of a new intention, the new idea aims to foster a shared vision, a commitment and a desire to act on the world (Cohendet et al. 2014). In this idea generation phase, then, *ideators* primarily convey a desired reality that does not yet exist and is not yet fully defined at this stage (Amabile 1983), which actually represents an intention to act.

It is equally important to recognize that ideas do not come out of nowhere. They result from the interaction between the specific cognitive skills of individuals and their environment (Agogué et al. 2014b). What the neurosciences and the psychology of creativity demonstrate, moreover, is that creative ideas particularly mobilize in the prefrontal cortex through several executive functions such as: working memory, abstract thinking, as well as attention and mental flexibility (Dietrich 2004; Thompson-Schill et al. 2009; Chrysikou et al. 2014; De Souza et al. 2014). Ideas also come from exposure to a variety of *stimuli* in the individual's context (Berg 2014). Individuals then combine these *stimuli* within their existing mental models and cognitive schemas to produce a new intuition (Amabile 1983). As such, the neuropsychology of creativity shows that inhibitory control plays a large role in blocking the early generation of old ideas in order to produce new ones, thus limiting fixation effects and creativity blocks (Agogué et al. 2014a; Cassotti et al. 2016).

Ideators subsequently apply different skills, degrees of implication and interpretive schemes to ideas due to their background, experiences and activities (Garud et al. 2013). The cognitive mechanisms of association, bisociation (Koestler 1964), synthesis and analogy then allow new ideas to emerge. The identification, formulation and reformulation of problems, needs and opportunities are also central to this stage preceding the emergence of new ideas (Getzels and Csikszentmihalyi 1976; Runco and Pritzker 1999; Cohendet et al. 2017). The work of Hatchuel et al. finally reminds us that the process preceding the emergence of new ideas is strongly dependent on the knowledge that *ideators* develop, maintain and activate, whether they are individuals alone or collectives of actors (Agogué 2013; Agogué et al. 2014b; Masson et al. 2014).

6.1.2. *Idea development*

After the generation stage, the idea development phase is a crucial part of the process. The goal is to nurture the idea with knowledge so that it becomes a concept that is sufficiently understandable by the same members of the organization or ecosystem that will carry it. *Ideators* typically spend time and energy orchestrating interactions with specialized knowledge holders, in order to reinforce the initial idea with complementary forms of knowledge so that it gradually becomes viable. These efforts are then often made by a small group of individuals gathered around the idea (Gerlach and Brem 2017), in order to gradually build and demonstrate its value. Far from being established in advance, the value of the idea thus develops through a mosaic of perspectives, contributions and revisions that help create a complex set of interrelated options (Garud et al. 2013). As a result of repeated interactions, nested decisions eventually tighten this circle of possibilities and gradually stabilize assumptions about deliverables and patterns of value creation from the idea (Maniak et al. 2014).

The idea development phase can be long and tortuous, because the knowledge necessary to make the idea progress can be difficult to obtain and develop, and also because as the process continues, the *ideators* can be inclined to review the initial intention in order to transform the idea. It is thus by iteration and successive progression that the idea develops quietly. At the end of this phase, after having been supported and nourished by the knowledge emitted by a generally small group, we can then consider that the idea has reached a state of maturity.

6.1.3. *Idea promotion*

An idea also requires a certain level of social acceptance, in addition to its internal coherence and validity. This is required in order to be developed and implemented one day. Consequently, the idea must be disseminated to a wider audience rather than purely to the *ideator*(s). Hence, in parallel and subsequent to the development phase, there is a phase called promotion of the idea. It is here that the ideas are subjected to a first confrontation with reality. The intention must be linked to relevant forms of knowledge and must gain support. Notably, the idea must validate its assumptions, demonstrate its feasibility and refine its value (Ries 2011). Thus, it is both the individuals, who develop, support, react to and modify ideas, and the socio-political process and controversies surrounding them that allow ideas to emerge, build and gradually stabilize (Akrich et al. 1988).

This perspective is in line with Callon's concept of the "actor–network theory", and the art of "interest", i.e. the capacity to interest a growing number of allies and a series of arrangements that make it acceptable for human (the social world) and non-human (the material world) actors (Akrich et al. 2002). The article by Bakker et al. (2006) also demonstrates with great finesse the social and political aspect of this work of construction, translation and progressive legitimization of the idea:

> [...] the management of creative expression within an organization is a matter of political strategies. Actors not only have to come up with innovative ideas based upon research in the research department (or elsewhere), but they have to "sell" these ideas to their colleagues, peers and managers. In the end, this is a difficult process of justification in which the *ideators* have to translate their ideas (Bakker et al. 2006, p. 300).

This is what they call a "creative-political" process. Through sharing, interaction, debate and argumentation, the *ideator*(s) develop both the idea and the network that carries and supports it. The creative-political act marks this double process of construction and refinement of the idea, and also of seduction and legitimization to find allies, sponsors and actors allowing its development. This legitimization stage then marks the numerous efforts made by the first circle of actors restricted to the idea, to progressively build the value of the idea. From negotiation to negotiation, interlocking decisions eventually tighten this circle of possibilities and stabilize the hypotheses on the deliverables, the models for creating value from the idea and can even enhance the learning expected from the exploration.

The risk is that an idea becomes insufficiently contextually appropriate, understandable or does not adequately demonstrate that its value will be rejected, transformed or set aside until a more favorable context emerges (Grimes 2018), if the organization's slack is sufficiently developed for the idea to be stored and retrieved. In addition, if *ideators* are unable to find enough allies, sponsors, or the appropriate network to implement the associated knowledge, they may lack the resources or motivation to move the idea forward.

6.1.4. *Idea deployment*

If the course of an idea is strongly linked to this social and political dimension, it is no less linked to the knowledge and resources that must be acquired and put into action to make the innovation possible. The implementation of a new idea, as well as the phase that precedes its generation, require the acquisition and even the development of new knowledge and skills (Le Masson et al. 2006).

At an organizational level, the new idea can mobilize relatively stabilized skills and competences and then become part of a dominant design (Utterback 1994) without affecting the main attributes or architecture of a product, service, process or organizational model. But it can also reconfigure and transform them, which is particularly the case when the innovation is architectural (Henderson and Clark 1990). Or, it can create new ones and require a much greater expansion of knowledge (Masson et al. 2014) if the idea is particularly in division with the existing (Ritala and Hurmelinna-Laukkanen 2013; Forés and Camisón 2016).

The absorptive capacity of the organization's collectives is then key to scan, identify, understand, translate and integrate new or distant knowledge (Cohen and Levinthal 1990). In all cases, "the initial idea must snowball into a set of assets, resources, and capabilities that combine to make, nurture, and sustain the innovation" (Garud et al. 2013).

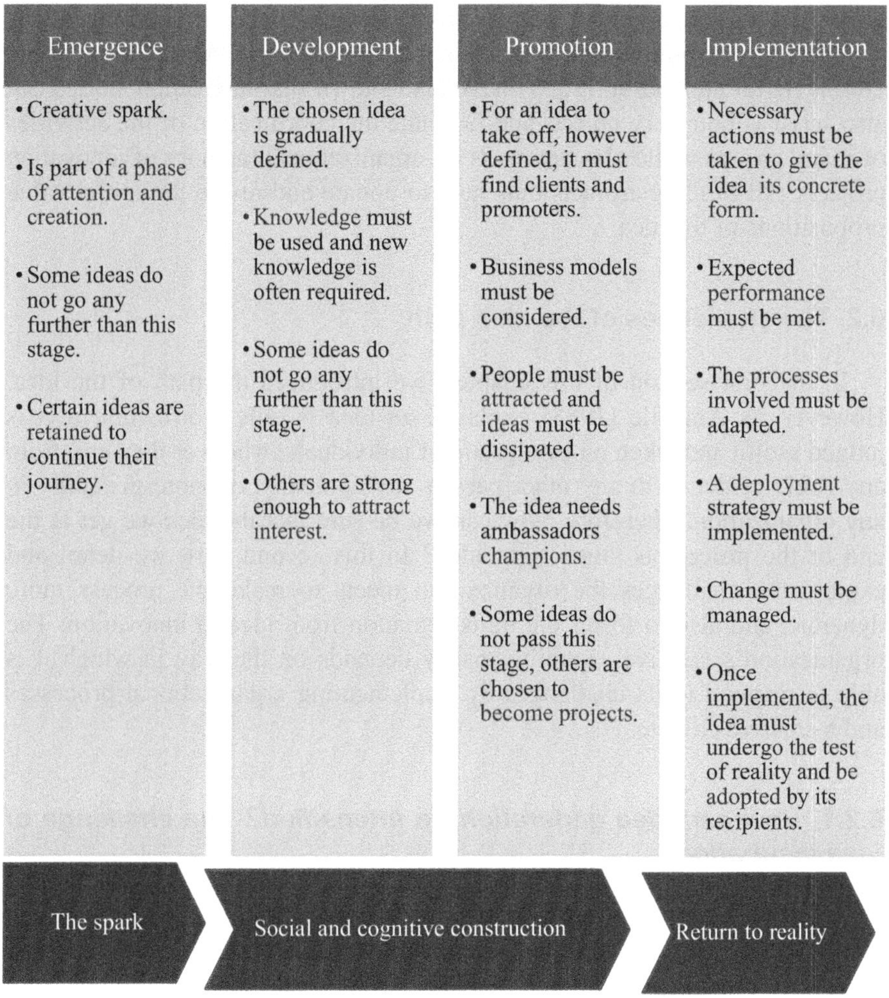

Figure 6.1. *Illustration of the path of an idea. For a color version of this figure, see www.iste.co.uk/parmentier/organizational.zip*

In addition to the knowledge and skills to implement it, an idea must prove its feasibility, and also its value for being implemented. Prototypes and experiments (Thomke 1998) play a significant role in these two aspects. By proving the feasibility of the idea, they also test its desirability and uses (von Hippel 1994; von Hippel et al. 1999; von Hippel and Katz 2002). They can also serve as boundary objects, i.e. the objects that are flexible enough in terms of interpretation to create links between different heterogeneous groups whose commitment is key for the innovation to take place (Carlile 2002). Bartel and Garud (2009) have also shown that innovation stories can also serve as boundary objects and facilitate the coordination of the activities of many groups while also acting as an organizational memory of innovation projects. All of these artifacts thus help to update and revise the initial value propositions of the idea.

6.2. The challenges of the idea path

In the first section of this chapter, we introduced the path of the idea. However, as Amabile (1988) explains, an idea is only worthwhile if it is judged useful and taken on by a group of individuals, whoever they are, from any R&D center or in any other part of any company, or more generally in any organization. Therefore, how can we be sure that the idea we get at the end of the process is "the" right idea? In this second part, we detail and explain the challenges the organization meets to make the process more dynamic, and also to foster the transformation from idea to innovation. The organization's creative capability partly depends on the way in which it is able to respond to its challenges by implementing organizational processes and a creative climate.

6.2.1. *How can idea generation be intensified? The challenge of idea incubation*

The first issue assumes that the organization has the choice between ideas. Choice presupposes both a greater or lesser quantity of ideas and variability among ideas. The research highlights that idea incubation is an imperative for generating quality ideas. Behind this concept of incubation are two key principles.

Firstly, an employee, or a small team of employees, is capable of coming up with creative ideas, but not continuously, and especially when the organization they work for needs them (Unsworth 2001). This employee may know the field, they may practice generating ideas, they may even be motivated to enter into the ideation process; in other words, they may fulfill the three conditions that act on individual creativity (Amabile 1988), but this is not enough. The incubation of ideas therefore offers a temporal *break*

(Ellwood et al. 2009) allowing the originators of these ideas to recharge their batteries in order to be able to formulate others.

The second principle that lays at the heart of idea incubation is that incubation always deserves enrichment and maturation. Just as the business incubator allows the startup to flourish and become viable in an enclosed and protected space, the idea incubator fosters the enrichment of ideas with benevolent people, who will protect, test and enrich them with the senders (O'Reilly and Binns 2019). Following an initial generation of ideas and discussion of those ideas with others, incubation continues. Even unconsciously, the spirit of the idea never dies. Even before the idea is implemented, the individual who originated it, as well as those who discuss it, connect it with existing knowledge and knowledge gained through discussion. This process is vital to sustain the most creative ideas.

6.2.2. *How can ideas be enriched? The stocking issue*

Also, this enrichment of ideas that we observe in the incubator or elsewhere is a combination of the initial idea with other ideas. Let us imagine a writer who has an idea for a character. This character rarely emerges as: the writer is inspired by a character trait they picked up while reading another novel or watching a movie. The idea for the character may also come from observing someone close to him. The final idea of the character that the writer will describe in his book is the combination of ideas that he has had beforehand or that he has captured elsewhere.

But how is this combination possible? In part through the constitution of a stock of ideas and through a process of "bricolage" (An et al. 2018). This stock may be specific to the sender, but it may also be shared by different members of the same organization, of the same network. For example, the idea of the oil-free fryer that took shape in SEB's Actifry product was the result of a long process of maturation and pooling of knowledge among several people. A product manager wanted to develop a solution to obtain low-fat French fries in response to the strong trend among French people to lose weight. A former employee of the group's R&D department remembered a patent developed by SEB for a process that made it possible to cook fries without fat. The stock of knowledge and the meeting of these two people favored the emergence of the idea for this new product (Le Loarne-Lemaire and Blanco 2012).

Bricolage is a metaphor used by anthropologist Claude Lévi-Strauss (1908–2009) in the book *La Pensée sauvage* (1962). He explains how South American Tribes built their religion by using objects "within reach", diverting their purpose and giving them another meaning. Thus, a wild animal observed in their territory may inspire them, the purpose of the animal, which may be food or security, for example, is diverted and takes on a new purpose: that of an incarnated god to be worshipped. Combined with another object gleaned from the same territory, the idea of the of the god is enriched little by little. This metaphor is widely used in information systems, but to express a creative process in a context of improvisation. It is this conception of bricolage that will be taken up initially by entrepreneurship theorists (Baker and Nelson 2005) and then will gradually designate a practice or behavior when the entrepreneur is faced with a lack of resources (Fisher 2012; Le Loarne-Lemaire and Maalaoui 2015). In an organizational context, bricolage can be either familiar or a convention (Duymedjian and Rüling 2010). In both cases, it is based on the principle of borrowing and diverting ideas from a stock, which could be similar to the knowledge stock (Maalaoui et al. 2020) developed by the individual or shared by the organization. In a creative process, the bricolage is not the idea, but the mediating effect that allows the passage of a problem, of a first idea to a more accomplished idea.

Box 6.1. *Bricolage: the mediating effect of creativity?*

6.2.3. *How can the idea be enriched? The challenge of its socialization*

The examples of the ideas of the writer's characters, as well as those of the oil-free fryer, illustrate this: having an idea implies a link with the outside world, an observation of the other, an exchange with the other. Socialization is therefore important to have a valuable idea that meets the intention of action. These examples also show the importance of this socialization to enrich ideas. Scientific research confirms the primordial role of the social network in which the *ideator* evolves, during the phases of generation, enrichment and selection of the idea. Perry-Smith and Mannucci (2017) argue that the knowledge fabric of the originator does not play the same role during the different phases of the idea's trajectory:

– During the idea generation phase, this network is passive. Only the one who emits it acts and is inspired by it. Also, the more the creative is present in different social networks and the more diversified these same networks are, the stronger the stock of inspiration will be. What Perry-Smith and Mannucci (2017) call the strength of weak ties.

– During the idea development phase, the network is invited to be more participatory, but it will remain benevolent. Note that the network of the organization in which the sender evolves starts to be solicited in a largely formal way. If there is an idea incubator or an innovation department in charge of collecting ideas, the participating or invited members are benevolent and seek to enrich the idea with the sender.

– During the promotion and selection phase of the idea, the organization's network plays a promotional and legitimizing role (Ford et al. 2000) and completes the picture by reminding us that the idea is adopted because "it makes sense" for all stakeholders. The sender's network, whether it is a hierarchical superior or an expert in the organization, can help to provide evidence of the "good sense" of the idea. The *ideators* are led here to mobilize their close network, with whom they have strong links, to increase their chances of making the idea succeed.

– During the phase of adoption of the idea by the organization, the social network that constitutes the organization is very active, since it takes hold of the idea, appropriates it and puts it into practice.

6.2.4. *How to select the best idea*

As we have just explained, an idea is selected by the organization when all stakeholders agree that it makes sense. But how is this agreement achieved? We distinguish two more or less complementary approaches (Ininou and Loilier 2021).

The calculatory approach: being formal, this approach consists of evaluating an idea with pre-established criteria, generally originality, feasibility and relevance to a given problem, and possibly its cost of implementation. Each of the stakeholders is asked to evaluate the idea and score it for each of these criteria on a scale that can go from 1 to 5 or from 1 to 3 (on this subject, see the work of Amabile and Mueller (2008)). In the end, each of the ideas is evaluated quantitatively and the idea selected will be the one that has obtained the highest score among the stakeholders. This approach is mainly used in internal or external creativity competitions.

For example, the *La Poste* Group assesses business startup ideas as follows: the managers of the entrepreneurial ideas competition invite juries whose members are experts in entrepreneurship, often accustomed to evaluating business startup ideas. The ideas are submitted in the form of a video in which the submitter presents their business idea. Each of the experts evaluates each idea individually. A computer system collects all the scores and calculates an average score per project. This approach provides a basis for discussion among experts to decide, in the end, which idea will be selected and awarded during the competition.

A more flexible example of quantitative evaluation of business ideas is the one used during *Startup Weekend*: each participant who wants to work on his project has 1 minute to present their project orally. The other participants vote by "investing" all or part of a fictitious 3,000 euros on one or several proposed ideas.

The argumentative approach: being more informal, the approach is based on an exchange between experts or stakeholders, who choose the creative ideas not in a quantitative way, but by looking for the idea that makes the most sense to answer a problem that the organization is facing. This less formal approach is often used in companies in the decision-making process. The objectivity of the computational approach then gives way to a more subjective analysis, in which the attention of the decision-makers must be captured (Ocasio and Joseph 2005). The power relations and the network of the *ideators* are then very useful to find support relays, and also to place themselves in the right platforms, in order to be listened to. In practice, the selection thus often relies not only on the decision-makers but also on the promotion strategies that are put in place by the *ideators*.

6.2.5. *What impact does the transporter of the idea and the form of the presentation have on selection?*

The last issue related to the management of the ideation process is the recognition that nothing in the process is neutral and that an idea is never selected for itself in an intrinsic way. In various previous research works, we have shown that the idea certainly needs to be intrinsically judged as relevant in terms of originality, technical feasibility with respect to deadlines and costs and relevance for it to be selected. However, the composition of the team that carries the idea has an impact. Based on an innovation idea competition that involves more than 600 students, who have only known each other for a few hours, and who are divided into groups of five to six students to develop and then issue their innovation idea, we show that the composition of the team, particularly in terms of gender, has an impact on the way in which the idea is perceived and, in fine, evaluated in particular by the other students (Parmentier et al. 2017). More specifically, near-perfectly mixed groups put forth ideas that are less well evaluated and, in fine, less selected.

In the same way, and beyond the characteristics of those who carry it, our work on the selections of entrepreneurial project pitches during *Startup Weekend* tends to show that the manner in which the idea is presented, and in particular the manner in which the idea is stated, is an indispensable condition for its good evaluation (Parmentier et al. 2021).

6.3. Global idea management

The challenges of the idea journey underline the interest in managing ideas, in order to stimulate, promote and facilitate their emergence, development, promotion and implementation to nurture organizational creative capability. From this point of view, managing ideas means setting up management systems to orient, collect, evaluate, implement and store ideas based on the creativity of employees, and also of other stakeholders of the organization, customers, users and suppliers.

Idea management is not new; organizations for a long time have been using idea boxes and continuous improvement methods, such as Kaizen, which are based on employees' ideas to improve daily work. Yet, since the 2010s, computerized idea management systems have appeared and the idea is increasingly considered as a valuable asset. Idea management has thus become more complex and takes many forms. We can distinguish two main modes of idea management that will mobilize different management systems: informal idea management and formal management.

6.3.1. *Informal idea management*

Informal management consists of creating a context that is favorable to the development of ideas without direct intervention on the ideas themselves. It is based on interactions between members of a group, a collective or an organization in the form of discussions and feedback to encourage the emergence, development and promotion of ideas. Indeed, when an individual develops a large number of social relationships, they are all the more likely to generate quality innovation ideas (Björk and Magnusson 2009). Strong ties of a dyadic nature also facilitate idea generation (Sosa 2011). Just as a central position in an organization's networks with few external ties is positively associated with an individual's creativity (Perry-Smith 2006). Within these networks, it is advisory, acquaintance and friend relationships in which creative interactions develop that are the most successful in idea generation (Lee and Lee 2015). During these interactions, feedback on ideas also acts strongly on idea generation by promoting the reformulation of the solution space and the connection of ideas with other, older ideas (Harrison and Rouse 2015). Ultimately, all of the systems that promote connection, discussion and feedback are susceptible to affect individuals' creativity and the quality of final ideas.

These devices take the form of open physical spaces, such as co-working and OpenLab spaces, communities of practice, innovation communities or user communities, and virtual spaces in the form of open corporate networks or external forums for the discussion of ideas. For example, Schneider Electric supports the development of communities of practice, so that employees share their problems, knowledge and ideas to improve productivity, service quality, and accelerate the time to market for new products and services (Guillaume et al. 2017). The arrangement can also be temporal, by giving employees time to develop their ideas (see Chapter 4 on creative slack), such as the 20% of free time that has been developed at 3M and Google. However, while these spaces and timeframes encourage the emergence and elaboration of ideas, their implementation requires an evaluation that requires a minimum formalization. For example, at Google, for an idea to be presented to a manager in order to obtain development resources, it must be approved by at least seven colleagues. This process does not set explicit criteria for evaluation; however, it does define a path to follow for promoting an idea.

Informal idea management does not clearly distinguish the different stages of the idea process. In communities or in a workgroup, ideas emerge, are discussed directly with feedback on their usefulness, relevance and feasibility. During these discussions, they are transformed and enriched by the contribution of other ideas. Thus, beyond the *ideator*, they interest a network of people, which participates in its promotion. This informal mode of idea management needs a climate favorable to creativity to work well. Indeed, as we have seen, a high degree of freedom favors the initiative to generate and develop ideas that seem interesting to the *ideator*. The possibility of taking risks frees the *ideator* from fear of failure. Trust and openness promote the discussion of ideas, and a high level of challenge pushes idea-givers to find creative and innovative solutions (for an explanation of these dimensions see Chapter 1 on *The Foundations of Organizational Creative Capabilities*).

The informal mode offers many advantages. It is inexpensive to set up, except in the case where the management system relies on time left free. The development of community within an organization requires human resources for the overall management; however, it is the participants themselves who manage their time in parallel to their main task. This method of management allows for a great amount of freedom for ideas to mature and develop into an interesting concept for the organization. However, the lack of formalization does not allow for the establishment of monitoring indicators, with the exception of the number of ideas submitted to managers when the selection process is formalized. Moreover, as the selection is partly done in discussions within the working groups and communities, it can be very subjective, as it is based more on the reputation of the emitter and the way the ideas are presented than on the value of the idea itself.

A study on pitching shows, for example, that the way the idea is presented (structure of the discourse, presence of the *ideator*, manner of the statement) can have as much impact as the intrinsic value of the idea (Parmentier et al. 2021). However, another study shows that even without explicit selection criteria, in an intuitive way, experts unconsciously use criteria of originality, value for the user and feasibility, and are sometimes complemented by criteria of profitability and alignment with the organization's strategy (Magnusson et al. 2014). Finally, this mode of informal management relies on the creation of favorable conditions for ideas to emerge and circulate in the collectives that enrich it through interactions of advice, feedback and contribution of new ideas and considerations to enrich the basic idea. It leaves a great deal of freedom to creative individuals and time for the idea to become socialized, and favors serendipity at the level of both the emergence and the development of the idea.

Creaholic, founded by Elmar Mock, the creator of the Swatch, is an innovation factory that has developed hundreds of projects and holds over 150 patents. It designs innovations for other companies in multiple sectors, such as IT, telecoms, medical, automotive and packaging, and also develops its own projects which are then carried by spin-offs of the company. Idea management is therefore at the heart of this company, which has developed an atypical idea management model. According to Elmar Mock, the innovation process goes through three phases: the gas, liquid and solid phase. In the gas phase, ideas emerge, collide and open up new ways of thinking. In the liquid phase, ideas combine and condense into more mature concepts and prototypes. The solid phase corresponds to the final design and industrialization. Creaholic has set up a rather informal idea management system to favor the gaseous and liquid states, while encouraging the transition to the solid state. All Creaholic's collaborators can participate in the generation of ideas which sometimes lead to the creation of spin-offs. If they have an idea for a new product, each employee can devote 20% of their working time for four months to develop an idea that will eventually be presented to a strategic committee. The idea is to encourage an active pool of valuable ideas both to continue to respond to customers who are looking for innovative solutions and to create new activities from Creaholic. An incubation project follows four phases. In the idea phase, the project is completely informal and is carried by one or more collaborators who devote time to it in relation to the workload of the mandates. In the caterpillar phase, the project is identified and Creaholic plays the role of client with internal billing for the time spent on the project. In the chrysalis phase, a commercial and business model study is undertaken. In the final butterfly phase, the incubation project is entrusted to an affiliate company with a license agreement. All ideas and concepts developed, whether successful or not, are stored in shoeboxes in the center of the company (for a detailed study of innovation at Creaholic, see the case study by Asquin and Picq (2015)).

Box 6.2. *Idea management at Creaholic*

6.3.2. *Formal idea management*

The other major mode of formal idea management is based on formalized processes and routines with direct action on ideas. In this type of management, which is called "idea management system", the different process steps of idea management and the types and roles of key stakeholders are often clearly identified. Gerlach and Brem (2017) identify a generic model found in many idea management systems with six phases (preparation, idea generation, improvement, evaluation, implementation, and deployment) and four key players (idea manager, *ideators*, idea selectors and idea discussion groups). Unlike the informal management mode, in these idea management systems, the idea journey is thus well segmented and the stages of emergence, development, promotion, and even the first implementation of the idea, are clearly separated.

Idea management systems often mobilize artifacts, such as Internet-based idea management platforms (Elerud-Tryde and Hooge 2014; Gerlach and Brem 2017), and also rely on events such as idea competitions (Nicolajsen et al. 2019). Online idea management platforms in organizations, moreover, encourage employee idea generation and facilitate an involvement of all employees in creativity campaigns (Elerud-Tryde and Hooge 2014). In these systems, platform managers play a crucial role in the effectiveness of this type of idea management to design and facilitate the program (phase, participants, rewards, selection process and criteria). They must select and implement the idea management IT platform and manage the system on a day-to-day basis (Gerlach and Brem 2017; Ininou 2020).

To continuously feed the idea management platforms, the organization must also, as we have already shown, develop a creative climate that is conducive to ideation. Among the conditions for the development of creative climates, we find a strategic vision that puts forward innovation objectives, as well as organizational incentives that have a strong effect on the motivation of employees to formalize their ideas and discuss them with their colleagues. Amabile (1993) highlighted the central role of intrinsic and extrinsic motivation as a driver of individual creativity. In a system of idea management, the question of reward arises, which can take tangible forms (money, gifts, vouchers, etc.) or intangible forms (trips, training, promotion in the organization's internal and external communication supports). The literature does not settle the question of the effectiveness of particular rewards, but it does stress the need to offer a wide range of rewards (Fairbank and Williams 2001) and to establish an equitable reward structure (Gerlach and Brem 2017).

> Bosch MoP is a manufacturer of electronic components for the automotive industry. To face the strong competition from low-cost country OEMs in the automotive industry, management is implementing a new strategic direction to be a leader in the production of connected objects. The goal is to increase revenues to 30% outside the automotive sector and to preserve the 500 jobs at the site. To achieve this, the company is mobilizing all of its employees in a participatory innovation process that draws on their knowledge and creativity. Bosch has set up a global idea management system which has managed 1,350 ideas over 4 years, 378 of which have been implemented. These ideas have led to the implementation of new processes using digital technologies and have made it possible to win new markets for connected objects. The idea management system, called "suggestion spark", allows employees to submit their ideas via an intranet site. All ideas are processed through this system according to a formalized process and with the support of the platform manager. This manager manages more than 300 ideas per year, verifies that the idea is well documented in the system, and analyzes the idea to direct the evaluation to the right departments and experts. They actually provide the link between the idea owner and the subject specialists to enrich the idea and to ensure a good evaluation. The evaluation is first done on the basis of a multi-criteria system (logical–mathematical evaluation) before leading to a selection committee if the idea has a score higher than 1 (according to a complex formula based on 6 criteria), in which the evaluation is done in the argumentative mode, in the form of discussion. This formal system is supported by an active recognition of the company towards the carriers of the ideas: award ceremonies, and bonuses to the carrier for the ideas ranging from 15 euros for non-selected ideas to 150,000 euros for ideas with high added value for the company (Ininou 2020).

Box 6.3. *The Bosh MoP idea management system of Bosh MoP*

Idea management systems also use formal criteria to evaluate and select ideas such as novelty (degree of differentiation from the existing), originality (degree of rarity and ingenuity), usefulness (the value provided to the user), feasibility (technical and acceptability), completeness (clarity and degree of development of an idea) and business potential (see Gerlach and Brem (2017, p. 153) for a complete list). These systems mix a logical–mathematical approach based on a set of formal criteria and an argumentative approach based on complex and dynamic collective decision-making (Ininou and Loilier 2021). At Bosh Mop, for example, the idea is first evaluated in the computerized idea management system before being submitted to a selection committee, which discusses more qualitative elements and makes the final decision on whether to accept the idea and on the resources to be mobilized to deploy the selected ideas (Ininou and Loilier 2021). Evaluation also takes different forms depending on whether it is an incremental or disruptive idea (Sandstrom and Bjork 2010; Ininou and Loilier 2021). The evaluation of a disruptive idea mobilizes more actors at the strategic, tactical and operational levels and experts external to the company (Ininou and Loilier 2021).

A formal system of idea management can also take the form of a series of creative sessions based on creativity methods with a formal process for collecting and selecting ideas (see Chapter 3).

Rexroth, part of the Bosch Group, is a manufacturer of hydraulic systems for construction equipment. In 2014, to improve productivity and explore the potential of using digital technologies within its plant, management set a goal for the IT manager to introduce these technologies in less than 18 months. Faced with the magnitude of the task, the manager set up a global strategy to gather ideas and support the digital transformation. He started with a one-day workshop with participants from all departments. The workshop used creative techniques with a morning on the theme of "for you, what is the factory of the future?" and an afternoon on "what is our factory of the future?". At the end of this day, participants selected about 10 ideas. These ideas were then discussed, enriched, developed among teams of potential users held during incubation meetings facilitated by participants of the launch workshop. At the end of 23 meetings of 8–10 people, involving a total of 400 people, three projects were selected with 10 potential applications and funding to develop them. The project resulted, for example, in a quality control application using augmented reality glasses or the installation of RFID chips on joysticks to better locate them in the production chain and make their technical information elements more easily accessible to manufacturers.

Box 6.4. *Idea management for digital transformation at Rexroth*

Dimension	Indicators
Process performance measurement	– Number of participants
	– Diversity of participating departments
	– Number of ideas submitted
	– Completeness of ideas
	– Number of ideas selected
	– Rate of implementation of the ideas selected
	– Percentage of participant satisfaction
	– Rate of external
	– Utilization rate of ideas stored
Measuring the quality of ideas	– Average score of ideas
	– Variance of idea score
	– Variety of ideas
	– Rate of radical ideas
	– Distribution of ideas between departments/areas of expertise
	– Idea conversion rate
Outcome measures	– Number of new products and services resulting from the ideas implemented
	– Revenues generated by products and services resulting from the ideas implemented
	– Number of new customers captured by the products and services resulting from the ideas implemented
	– Expenses saved through improved production processes
	– Indicators for improving well-being at work

Table 6.1. *Examples of measurement indicators for idea management*

The formal mode of ideas contains many advantages. It allows for monitoring indicators to be set up to measure the performance of the system, to inform system performance, inform management and detect malfunctions in order to take corrective action to improve the idea management system (see Table 6.1). Indicators can measure the performance of the system itself, the quantity and quality of ideas, or the results related to the implementation of ideas from the system (Gerlach and Brem 2017). However, these indicators can give a false sense of control by giving the idea management system manager the impression that they have a panoptic view of all ideas. Many phenomena are not expressed in quantitative indicators. For example, a framework that is too restrictive in the form of a compulsory framework to follow in order to submit an idea can lead *ideators* to abandon their approach or to fill in the framework incorrectly. Finally, the idea is presented in the wrong form, which can harm the perception of its value potential.

Idea managers must therefore complement their indicators with qualitative surveys of users and non-users of the idea management system. This is to highlight the negative effects of an overly constrained process and too much formalization. Formalizing the idea process also has the advantage of making it easier to align idea generation with the organization's innovation strategy. However, if the alignment is too strong, the system may not collect radically new ideas that could eventually inspire a new strategy for the organization.

6.3.3. *Synthesis*

Each of the two ways of managing ideas, formal and informal, has its advantages and disadvantages. Nevertheless, in practice, an organization can completely mix these two management methods. For example, the establishment of communities of practice at Schneider Electric is not a purely informal management of ideas. This company has also set up a comprehensive community management program that connects community facilitators, provides tools and measures the performance of the value produced by communities. The measurement of the value produced is an indirect measurement of the quality and quantity of the ideas generated in these communities, which provides an estimate of the impact of these ideas on the company's activity. This program therefore adds a formal layer to the informal and poorly controlled management of the ideas circulating in this type of community. Similarly, an "ideas" competition within an informal mode of idea management, communities, dedicated time or collaboration space, adds a layer of organization that makes it possible to direct ideation towards strategic priorities and evaluate the performance of current ideas management methods in an organization.

And if organizations can favor a rather formal or rather informal management mode, idea management is ultimately based on informal activities, formal activities and tangible tools. Informal activities organize ideation spaces that activate social mechanisms for sharing ideas and knowledge. They are privileged places for obtaining opinions, advice and benevolent feedback on these ideas. The actors, who provide this advice, are able to give more or less personal opinions and come from backgrounds outside of that of the ecosystem that is supposed to carry the idea. They are also the basis of future formal collaborations, future coalitions that will be very useful to defend the ideas when necessary.

Formal activities, on the contrary, constrain the action of ideation and the formalization of ideas in processes and frameworks. They facilitate the institutionalization of the idea within the ecosystem by imposing a place of socialization, communication, promotion and implementation stages. Finally, the tangible tools support the ideation, collaboration and formalization of ideas in a form that can be used by the organization. They contribute to a better understanding of the idea, and therefore to its adoption by the ecosystem.

Each of these three elements is essential and complementary to the others: without informal activity, the cross-fertilization of the idea will not take place and will be potentially less creative and original for the ecosystem in which it is supposed to develop. Without formal activity, the idea may not be institutionalized. Finally, without tangible tools, the idea may not really take shape and remain less understandable by the rest of the ecosystem, which will therefore not appropriate it. On the contrary, with these three devices, the idea benefits from a breeding ground, but also from a format and a vehicle allowing it to develop, and also to be stored, in a way that is conducive to its use.

6.4. Conclusion

Idea management is based on activities, artifacts and processes that are increasingly central in organizations to enable new ideas to emerge, develop and be implemented. Managing ideas well is therefore one of the main levers managers can use to ensure that the creative spark can one day lead to the creation of value.

And if the idea's journey does not succeed and eventually stops, formal and informal idea management systems still allow for keeping a trace of the intended action and knowledge associated with the idea, which can be useful in a more favorable context or for other ideas. It is around this dynamic that idea management is partly linked to the creative *slack*, which can be rather formal if systems and idea repositories are set up by the organization, or rather informal if it is the communities that manage and, between them, hold this corpus of knowledge and past ideas.

Finally, beyond the simple potential outlets in terms of the value of ideas at the end of the road for the organization, idea management also plays a central role today in the processes of attracting and retaining talent in organizations. Indeed, the new generations entering the job market are increasingly demanding in order to make their voices heard, and to have the opportunity to propose and even develop their ideas in organizations. Companies that are able to offer mechanisms to support the development, promotion and implementation of ideas will have a competitive advantage in attracting and retaining creative staff. This aspect, which is not emphasized in this chapter, is also an essential element of idea management and should be the subject of future research.

6.5. References

Agogué, M. (2013). *L'innovation orpheline. Lutter contre les biais cognitifs dans les dynamiques industrielles.* Transvalor Presses des Mines, Paris.

Agogué, M., Kazakçi, A., Hatchuel, A., Le Masson, P., Weil, B., Poirel, N., Cassotti, M. (2014a). The impact of type of examples on originality: Explaining fixation and stimulation effects. *The Journal of Creative Behavior*, 48(1), 1–12.

Agogué, M., Poirel, N., Pineau, A., Houdé, O., Cassotti, M. (2014b). The impact of age and training on creativity: A design-theory approach to study fixation effects. *Thinking Skills and Creativity*, 11, 33–41.

Akrich, M., Callon, M., Latour, B. (2002). The key to success in innovation part I: The art of interessement. *International Journal of Innovation Management*, 6(2), 187.

Amabile, T.M. (1983). *The Social Psychology of Creativity*. Springer-Verlag, New York.

Amabile, T.M. (1988). A model of creativity and innovation in organizations. *Research in Organizational Behavior*, 10, 123–167.

Amabile, T.M. (1993). Motivational synergy: Toward new conceptualizations of intrinsic and extrinsic motivation in the workplace. *Human Resource Management Review*, 3(3), 185.

Amabile, T.M. and Mueller, J.S. (2008). Studying creativity, its processes, and its antecedents: An exploration of the componential theory of creativity. In *Handbook of Organizational Creativity*, Zhou, J. and Shalley, C.E. (eds). Taylor & Francis Group, New York, 33–63.

An, W., Zhang, J., You, C., Guo, Z. (2018). Entrepreneur's creativity and firm-level innovation performance: Bricolage as a mediator. *Technology Analysis & Strategic Management*, 30(7), 838–851.

Asquin, A. and Picq, T. (2015). Créaholic : quand les saltimbanques de l'innovation s'inventent une organisation par projet. In *Cas en management de projet*, Boudès, T. and Guédon, J. (eds). Éditions EMS, Cormelles-le-Royal [Online]. Available at: www.cas-store.fr.

Baker, T. and Nelson, R.E. (2005). Creating something from nothing: Resource construction through entrepreneurial bricolage. *Administrative Science Quarterly*, 50(3), 329–366.

Bakker, H., Boersma, K., Oreel, S. (2006). Creativity (ideas) management in industrial R&D organizations: A crea-political process model and an empirical illustration of corus RD&T. *Creativity & Innovation Management*, 15(3), 296–309.

Bartel, C.A. and Garud, R. (2009). The role of narratives in sustaining organizational innovation. *Organization Science*, 20(1), 107–117.

Berg, J.M. (2014). The primal mark: How the beginning shapes the end in the development of creative ideas. *Organizational Behavior and Human Decision Processes*, 125(1), 1–17.

Björk, J. and Magnusson, M. (2009). Where do good innovation ideas come from? exploring the influence of network connectivity on innovation idea quality. *Journal of Product Innovation Management*, 26(6), 662–670.

Carlile, P.R. (2002). A pragmatic view of knowledge and boundaries: Boundary objects in new product development. *Organization Science: A Journal of the Institute of Management Sciences*, 13(4), 442.

Cassotti, M., Agogué, M., Camarda, A., Houdé, O., Borst, G. (2016). Inhibitory control as a core process of creative problem solving and idea generation from childhood to adulthood. *New Directions for Child and Adolescent Development*, 151, 61–72.

Chrysikou, E.G., Weber, M.J., Thompson-Schill, S.L. (2014). A matched filter hypothesis for cognitive control. *Neuropsychologia*, 62, 341–355.

Cohendet, P., Grandadam, D., Simon, L., Capdevila, I. (2014). Epistemic communities, localization and the dynamics of knowledge creation. *Journal of Economic Geography*, 14(5), 929–954.

Cohendet, P., Parmentier, G., Simon, L. (eds) (2017). Managing knowledge, creativity and innovation. In *The Elgar Companion to Innovation and Knowledge Creation*. Edward Elgar, Cheltenham, 197–214.

De Souza, L.C., Guimarães, H.C., Teixeira, A.L., Caramelli, P., Levy, R., Dubois, B., Volle, E. (2014). Frontal lobe neurology and the creative mind. *Frontiers in Psychology*, 5, 761.

Dietrich, A. (2004). The cognitive neuroscience of creativity. *Psychonomic Bulletin & Review*, 11(6), 1011–1026.

Duymedjian, R. and Rüling, C.C. (2010). Towards a foundation of bricolage in organization and management theory. *Organization Studies*, 31(2), 133–151.

Elerud-Tryde, A. and Hooge, S. (2014). Beyond the generation of ideas: Virtual idea campaigns to spur creativity and innovation. *Creativity & Innovation Management*, 23(3), 290–302.

Ellwood, S., Pallier, G., Snyder, A., Gallate, J. (2009). The incubation effect: Hatching a solution? *Creativity Research Journal*, 21(1), 6–14.

Fairbank, J.F. and Williams, S.D. (2001). Motivating creativity and enhancing innovation through employee suggestion system technology. *Creativity & Innovation Management*, 10(2), 68.

Fisher, G. (2012). Effectuation, causation, and bricolage: A behavioral comparison of emerging theories in entrepreneurship research. *Entrepreneurship: Theory & Practice*, 36(5), 1019–1051.

Ford, C.M., Drazin, R., Glynn, M.A., Kazanjian, R. (2000). Dialogue: Creative developments in creativity theory. *Academy of Management Review*, 25(2), 284–287.

Forés, B. and Camisón, C. (2016). Does incremental and radical innovation performance depend on different types of knowledge accumulation capabilities and organizational size? *Journal of Business Research*, 69(2), 831–848.

Garud, R., Tuertscher, P., Van de Ven, A.H. (2013). Perspectives on innovation processes. *Academy of Management Annals*, 7(1), 775–819.

Gerlach, S. and Brem, A. (2017). Idea management revisited: A review of the literature and guide for implementation. *International Journal of Innovation Studies*, 1(2), 14–161.

Getzels, J. and Csikszentmihalyi, M. (1976). *The Creative Vision: A Longitudinal Study of Problem Finding in Art*. Wiley, New York.

Grimes, M.G. (2018). The pivot: How founders respond to feedback through idea and identity work. *Academy of Management Journal*, 61(5), 1692–1717.

Guillaume, L.P., Delmas, C., Goglio-Primard, K. (eds) (2017). Schneider Electric pilote les communautés de pratique avec le programme Communities@Work. In *Les communuatés d'innovation : de la liberté créatrice à l'innovation organisée*. Éditions EMS, Caen.

Hargadon, A.B. and Bechky, B.A. (2006). When collections of creatives become creative collectives: A field study of problem solving at work. *Organization Science*, 17(4), 484–500.

Harrison, S.H. and Rouse, E.D. (2015). An inductive study of feedback interactions over the course of creative projects. *Academy of Management Journal*, 58(2), 375–404.

Harvey, J.F., Naggar, R., Cohendet, P., Simon, L. (2013). Gérer les idées pour mieux innover. *Gestion*, 38(3), 2–34.

Henderson, R.M. and Clark, K.B. (1990). Architectural innovation: The reconfiguration of existing product technologies and the failure of established firms. *Administrative Science Quarterly*, 35(1), 9–30.

Ininou, Y. (2020). La sélection des idées : processus mixte. PhD Thesis, Université de Caen Normandie, Caen.

Ininou, Y. and Loilier, T. (2021). La sélection des idées incrémentales et radicales : les enseignements d'une étude de cas. *Innovations, Prépublication*, 116–136.

Koestler, A. (1964). *The Act of Creation*. Macmillan, New York.

Le Loarne-Lemaire, S.L. and Blanco, S. (2012). *Management de l'innovation*. Pearson Education, London.

Le Loarne-Lemaire, S.L. and Maalaoui, A. (2015). How high-tech entrepreneurs bricole the evolution of business process management for their activities. *Business Process Management Journal*, 21(1), 152–171.

Le Masson, P., Weil, B., Hatchuel, A. (2006). *Les processus d'innovation : conception innovante et croissance des entreprises*. Hermes-Lavoisier, Paris.

Le Masson, P., Weil, B., Hatchuel, A. (2014). *Théorie, méthodes et organisations de la conception*. Presses des Mines Transvalor, Paris.

Lee, S. and Lee, C. (2015). Creative interaction and multiplexity in intraorganizational networks. *Management Communication Quarterly*, 29(1), 56–83.

Maalaoui, A., Le Loarne-Lemaire, S.L., Razgallah, M. (2020). Does knowledge management explain the poor growth of social enterprises? Key insights from a systematic literature review on knowledge management and social entrepreneurship. *Journal of Knowledge Management*, 24(7), 1513–1532.

Magnusson, P.R., Netz, J., Wästlund, E. (2014). Exploring holistic intuitive idea screening in the light of formal criteria. *Technovation*, 34(5/6), 315–326.

Maniak, R., Midler, C., Beaume, R., Pechmann, F. (2014). Featuring capability: How carmakers organize to deploy innovative features across products. *Journal of Product Innovation Management*, 31(1), 114–127.

Nicolajsen, H.W., Mathiassen, L., Scupola, A. (2019). IT-enabled idea competitions for organizational innovation: An inquiry into breakdowns in adaptation. *Creativity & Innovation Management*, 28(4), 436–449.

Ocasio, W. and Joseph, J. (2005). An attention-based theory of strategy formulation: Linking micro- and macroperspectives in strategy processes. *Strategy Process*, 22, 39–41.

O'Reilly, C. and Binns, A.J.M. (2019). The three stages of disruptive innovation: Idea generation, incubation, and scaling. *California Management Review*, 61(3), 49–71.

Parmentier, G., Le Loarne-Lemaire, S.L., Belkhouja, M. (2017). Female creativity in organizations: What is the impact of team composition in terms of gender during ideation processes? *Management International*, 22(1), 33–43.

Parmentier, G., Le Loarne-Lemaire, S.L., Mellard, M. (2021). Do we really judge the book by its cover? Idea selection during start-up weekends. In *Organizing Creativity in the Innovation Journey*, Schuessler, E., Cohendet, P., Svejenova, S. (eds). Emerald Publishing Limited, Bingley, 231–247.

Perry-Smith, J.E. (2006). Social yet creative: The role of social relationships in facilitating individual creativity. *Academy of Management Journal*, 49(1), 85–101.

Perry-Smith, J.E. and Mannucci, P.V. (2017). From creativity to innovation: The social network drivers of the four phases of the idea journey. *Academy of Management Review*, 42(1), 53–79.

Phelps, E.S. (2013). *Mass Flourishing: How Grassroots Innovation Created Jobs, Challenge, and Change*. Princeton University Press, Princeton.

Ries, E. (2011). *The Lean Startup: How Today's Entrepreneurs Use Continuous Innovation to Create Radically Successful Businesses*. Currency, New York.

Ritala, P. and Hurmelinna-Laukkanen, P. (2013). Incremental and radical innovation in coopetition – The role of absorptive capacity and appropriability. *Journal of Product Innovation Management*, 30(1), 154–169.

Runco, M.A. and Pritzker, S.R. (1999). *Encyclopedia of Creativity*. Academic Press, Cambridge.

Sandstrom, C. and Bjork, J. (2010). Idea management systems for a changing innovation landscape. *International Journal of Product Development*, 11(3), 310–324.

Sosa, M.E. (2011). Where do creative interactions come from? The role of tie content and social networks. *Organization Science*, 22(1), 1–21.

Thomke, S.H. (1998). Managing experimentation in the design of new products. *Management Science*, 44(6), 743–762.

Unsworth, K. (2001). Unpacking creativity. *Academy of Management Review*, 26(2), 289–297.

Utterback, J.M. (1994). *Mastering the Dynamics of Innovation: How Companies Can Seize Opportunities in the Face of Technological Change*. Harvard Business School, Boston.

Von Hippel, E. (1994). "Sticky information" and the locus of problem solving: Implications for innovation. *Management Science*, 40(4), 429.

Von Hippel, E. and Katz, R. (2002). Shifting innovation to users via toolkits. *Management Science*, 48(7), 821–833.

Von Hippel, E., Thomke, S., Sonnack, M. (1999). Creating Breakthroughs at 3M. *Harvard Business Review*, 77(5), 47.

Zhou, J. and George, J.M. (2001). When job dissatisfaction leads to creativity: Encouraging the expression of voice. *Academy of Management Journal*, 44(4), 682–696.

7

Measuring Organizational Creative Capabilities

In a recent article, Dutraive and Szostak (2021) referred to the creative economy paradigm to describe the new economic regime of growth, employment and innovation in today's organizations, which is increasingly based on creativity, culture and technology. In this regime, characterized by rapid technological change and a much more unstable environment, creativity and new ideas play a central role in the success of organizations. The mastery of skills and organizational capabilities to stimulate, enrich, select and retain creative ideas is strategic and essential for organizations (Parmentier et al. 2017). Organizations are thus led to develop creative capabilities, i.e. a set of organizational routines in order to achieve creative results.

Managing these creative capabilities is a strategic activity, and as Drucker (2001) writes, we cannot manage what we do not measure. We therefore aim, based on this work, to build a scale for measuring organizational creative capability (OCC), because measuring OCC contributes to building (1) an internal tool, as well as (2) a best practice guide for creative organizations to assess and strengthen their creative capability. An OCC scale will also allow us to follow, in a longitudinal perspective, the evolution of the creative capability of different companies (French and international), and the diagnosis of potential sources of difficulties in creative production. In this chapter, we present the first steps in the construction of the OCC measurement scale. Firstly, we present these dimensions, adding a construct

Chapter written by Zeinab SHEET, Florence JEANNOT and Guy PARMENTIER.

explained by OCC (creative outcome), as well as control variables that may influence the proposed factorial structure. Secondly, we specify the procedure and the methodology of the construction of the scale. Finally, we present the proposed model for the OCC scale in section 7.3.

7.1. Theoretical framework

7.1.1. *Dimensions of OCC*

OCC is defined by a set of organizational routines that a creative organization implements in order to generate new ideas, change and improve the organization, its creative behavior and its products (Napier and Nilsson 2006; Parmentier and Szostak 2016). A creative organization builds and strengthens its capability to create by generating and selecting new creative ideas (Parmentier and Szostak 2016), and is agile at the organizational level (Hill et al. 2014) and at the project team level (Mellard et al. 2020). These routines, described in the introductory chapter of this book, grouped into six dimensions (socialization of ideas, creative equipment, creation of room to maneuver, idea management, external openness and organizational agility) "are formed" by OCC (see Figure 7.1). Since these organizational routines are supposed to lead to a creative outcome, we place the latter as an output variable of OCC. We describe the different dimensions and the origin of the items identified in the literature in more detail in the following paragraphs.

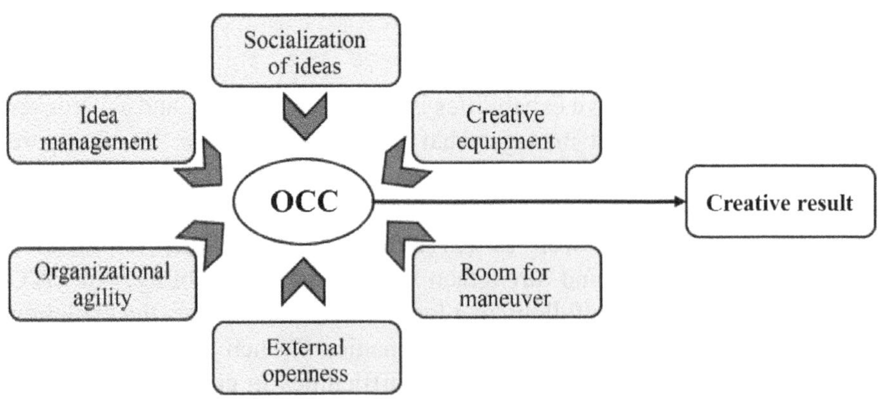

Figure 7.1. *Conceptual model of OCC and its consequence. For a color version of this figure, see www.iste.co.uk/parmentier/organizational.zip*

The internal socialization of ideas. Socialization routines strengthen OCC by involving the organization of relationships among collaborators (Handzic and Chaimungkalanont 2004) to encourage them to share their ideas (Nonaka and Konno 1998) and generate new ones. We measure the socialization of ideas using the Pérez López et al. (2004) scale on collaborative culture and internal knowledge acquisition. The items of this dimension focus on the presence of discussions and exchanges between collaborators, as well as on events and meetings organized for the purpose of exchanging ideas (see Chapter 6).

The creative equipment. In this section, we consider creative equipment as referring to everything that is implemented in an organization in order to provide people and teams with the capabilities, methods, materials and tools that allow creative acts. From several research works on creativity, we identify two aspects, cognitive equipment and material equipment, and we deduce the items of creative equipment. Cognitive equipment includes training and creative methods that stimulate the creativity of employees (Woodman et al. 1993; Wang and Horng 2002). The material equipment includes the organization of the workspace (Amabile 1999; Drake 2003; Mellard and Parmentier 2020) (see Chapter 3).

Room for maneuver. Room to maneuver represents the establishment of reserves in the organization's resources, such as knowledge, time or human resources (Bourgeois 1981; Voss et al. 2008; Penrose 2009). This creation of margins facilitates the emergence, selection and realization of ideas. Creative organizations naturally create these margins, but what interests us in this work is the conscious action of creating them. Building on the work of Bourgeois (1981), Voss et al. (2008) and Penrose (2009), we have produced margin items that focus on the voluntary implementation of margins in resources and processes (see Chapter 4).

Idea management. According to Brem et al. (2016), idea management, internal or external, is the effective and efficient generation, selection and evaluation of ideas. Idea management positively affects OCC, as it allows the organization to innovate and create faster and more often (Harvey et al. 2013). Based on the research of Gerlach and Brem (2017), we produced idea management items focused on the organization of the idea collection and selection process, the use of an idea management system or the presence of an idea selection committee and criteria for selecting and evaluating ideas (see Chapter 6).

External openness. The routines and processes of opening an organization to the outside affect its creative capability. Indeed, openness to the outside world is a source of new knowledge, information and ideas for organizations, which increases their ability to generate new creative ideas (Lewin et al. 2011; Salter et al. 2015). Based on the scale of Rangus et al. (2016), we defined outward-looking items, which focus on implementing outward-looking practices with various external actors to generate new creative ideas (see Chapter 2).

Organizational agility. Organizational agility represents the ability of an organization to quickly identify and respond to changes in its environment (Lee and Lee 2017). The importance of organizational agility to OCC is that the ability to be agile ensures the continued creativity of an organization (Darvishmotevali et al. 2020). Based on the Charbonnier-Voirin (2009) scale, we produced organizational agility items that focus on the ability to track and understand market changes, and the ability to develop responses quickly.

7.1.2. *The consequence of OCC*

The creative outcome. The main objective of a creative organization is to produce creative results. A creative result can be a product, service, creative idea or even a new idea or work process. It is characterized by its novelty, originality, usefulness and relevance (Besemer 1998; Dean et al. 2006). Building on the research of Besemer (1998) and Dean et al. (2006), we developed the Creative Outcome Scale by focusing on the perceived characteristics of the organization's creative outcomes.

7.1.3. *The control variables*

In addition to the dimensions and constructs already discussed in this chapter, we believe it is relevant to consider control variables (or organizational behaviors) that may influence the effects of OCC on the creative outcome, namely psychological safety, project team diversity, work atmosphere and social desirability.

Team psychological safety consists of a sense of trust and respect shared among collaborators, which leads them to believe that interpersonal risk-taking is safe. This feeling encourages collaborators to express themselves and speak up without fear of embarrassment or punishment

(Edmondson 1999). This makes psychological safety one of the control variables that can affect the relationship between OCC and creative outcome. The more psychologically safe a person feels, the more comfortable they are expressing themselves and sharing their ideas. From this perspective, we consider Edmondson's (1999) scale to measure psychological safety in the team.

The diversity of project teams includes the individual characteristics of team members, including age, education, experience, personality and length of service (Egan 2005). This diversity influences the relationship between collaborators and can enrich the generation of creative ideas. Based on the work of Wu et al. (2019), we construct a scale on the composition of the project team.

The creative climate is the set of behaviors and feelings that characterize organizational life (Ekvall 1996). The more comfortable employees feel at work, the more it affects their ability to generate new and creative ideas. We measure this climate with the Sundgren et al. (2005) scale, based on Ekvall's work on creative climate. In the confirmatory phase, we administrate the OCC scale and the creative climate scale in order to determine whether they are two separate constructs. This will test the construct validity of the OCC scale.

Social desirability is an important control variable in statistical analyses, because the projection of socially undesirable sentiment affects respondents' evaluations, as well as their responses to questions (Hays et al. 1989). To this end, we consider the Hays et al. (1989) scale.

Control variables, such as age, gender, sector of work, function of respondents, size and name of organization, and location of business, were also added to the questionnaire.

7.2. Methodology and procedure for generating items

Following Churchill's (1979) methodology, we began by specifying the research area, before moving on to the exploratory phase. The importance of the latter is that it leads to the validation (or invalidation) of the factorial structure of a construct and to the elimination of items that do not correspond to it. During the exploratory phase, we first proceeded to the generation of items, then to the collection of data and the purification of the measure. In this chapter, we will only detail the first part of the exploratory phase, the one devoted to item generation (see Figure 7.2).

As shown in Figure 7.2, there are three steps in generating the items to construct the starting scale. We began by extracting the items that measure the different dimensions of OCC from the literature. To this end, in section 7.1, we have already indicated the existing scales and the research from which we proceeded to develop our scale.

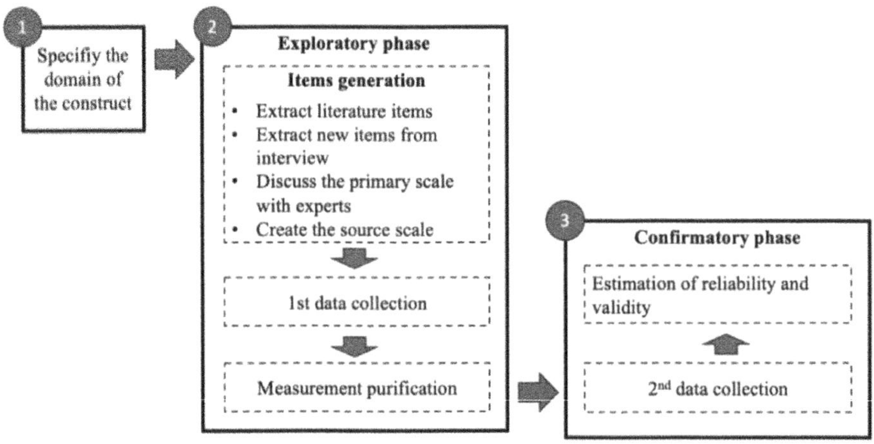

Figure 7.2. *Methodology of Churchill (1979) completed by Diamantopoulos and Winklholfer (2001)*

7.2.1. *The procedure for generating items*

Next, we conducted semi-structured interviews to generate new items. Since creativity is at the heart of creative industries' activity (Caves 2003), we conducted the interviews with executives and experts within three sectors of these industries[1]: video games, architecture and animation.

From these interviews, we first validated the presence and deployment of the dimensions of OCC in the three sectors. However, the analysis also

1 The UK DCMS model classifies the creative industries into several categories: advertising, architecture, art and antiques, crafts, design, fashion, film and video, music, performing arts, publishing, software, television and radio, video games, and computing.

identified new items that did not exist in the literature and that form the OCC routines. We therefore followed an abductive reasoning to achieve our goal.

Activity sector	Size of the organization	Interviewee's role
Video game	10,000 employees	Diversity and Inclusion Project Manager/Author
	10,000 employees	General Delegate of the French Entertainment Software Publishers Union (SELL)/Vice President of Business at a video game studio
	–	General Manager of the French Video Game Union (SFJV)
	–	Director General of the French Agency for Video Games (AFJV)
	23–100 employees	Owner of the studio
	4 developers	Owner of the studio
	–	University professor in video games/expert
	–	Game Development Consultant
Animated film	1,200–5,000 employees	Director of Digital Animation
	100–200 employees	Director and producer
	40–80 employees	Distribution Manager
	20 employees	Owner of the studio
Architecture	31 employees	Owner of an architectural firm
	10 employees	Owner of an architectural firm
	10 employees	Owner of an architectural firm
	–	University professor of architecture/expert

Table 7.1. *The list of interviews conducted by size, sector of the organization and role of the interviewee*

As for the sample, on the one hand, its diversity was ensured by choosing organizations of different sizes to conduct the interviews (see Table 7.1). On the other hand, since we wanted to construct a measurement scale that, at the end of our study, will be generalized to all creative industries, the three sectors were chosen on the basis of the differences in creativity management existing between them[2]. Therefore, our objective with this choice was to define new items based on the sectoral differences in the implementation of organizational routines.The interviews were conducted using an interview guide with questions on the different dimensions of OCC. In addition, these interviews allowed us to extract new items that did not exist in the literature and identify certain aspects that characterize the dimensions of OCC that we will discuss in section 7.3. For this type of study, Baker and Edwards (2012) recommend conducting between 5 and 25 interviews. In this work, the researchers conducted 16 interviews, which seemed sufficient to extract new relevant items.

After conducting the interviews and extracting the new items, we sent our scale to nine creativity experts, who evaluated it and provided feedback. This step is important because the experts suggest improvements and changes to the wording, sequence and content of the questions in our measure (Malhotra et al. 2007). Based on the experts' evaluations, which we discuss in section 7.3, we made some changes to the scale. This step allowed us to achieve face validity[3] of our measure and, subsequently, to produce our baseline scale.

7.3. Results and discussion

7.3.1. *Interview results: qualitative exploration*

The qualitative exploration allowed us to identify new items for our scale, as well as different levels in the deployment of organizational routines, which were integrated into our scale.

At the level of the socialization of ideas, we have identified the existence of two types of socialization: direct when meetings are organized to discuss ideas, and indirect when exchanges, interactions or meetings can be a source of new idea generation. This distinction led us to add items to find out whether the organization consciously put in place organizational routines to generate new ideas.

2 These differences lie in the collective or individual nature of the design, the (de)centralization of the creative process and the degree of reliance on technology to create.

3 Face validity determines whether the construct being studied is well represented by the scale in question. It consists of studying the items of the scale one by one to ensure that they do indeed measure the phenomenon being studied.

Regarding equipment, we have added an item relating to new technologies. During the interviews, we noted that new software technologies used in architecture or in animation, and in video games to design characters, can be a source of inspiration to generate new ideas.

Within external openness, we also noted the presence of two levels of openness: 1) direct openness by directly involving external actors in the design of new products; 2) indirect openness by drawing inspiration from these actors, their opinions, other products, etc., to generate new ideas.

Finally, in terms of organizational agility, we have added an element concerning the testing of ideas with employees. During the interviews, we noted that creative organizations seek to test their ideas with their employees.

7.3.2. *Expert feedback: quantitative exploration*

We developed an initial questionnaire based on the interviews conducted and the literature. This questionnaire was sent to several academic and professional experts. Nine academic experts responded to our initial questionnaire and gave us their comments in order to adjust the questionnaire. Based on their evaluation, some items were reworded and others were added or deleted. For example, we added a question about collaboration methods in the dimension of creative equipment. Finally, taking into account the feedback from the experts, face validity was achieved and we finalized the construction of the initial scale.

7.3.3. *Initial scale*

Once the item generation stage was completed, based on the literature, interviews and feedback from experts, we were able to finalize the initial scale (see the Appendix). Regarding this scale, it is important to note that the formulation of the questions is important (Carricano et al. 2008), and we tried to avoid the contamination effect. The latter occurs when several questions with the same meaning are asked in the same sequence, leading the respondent to give similar answers to these questions.

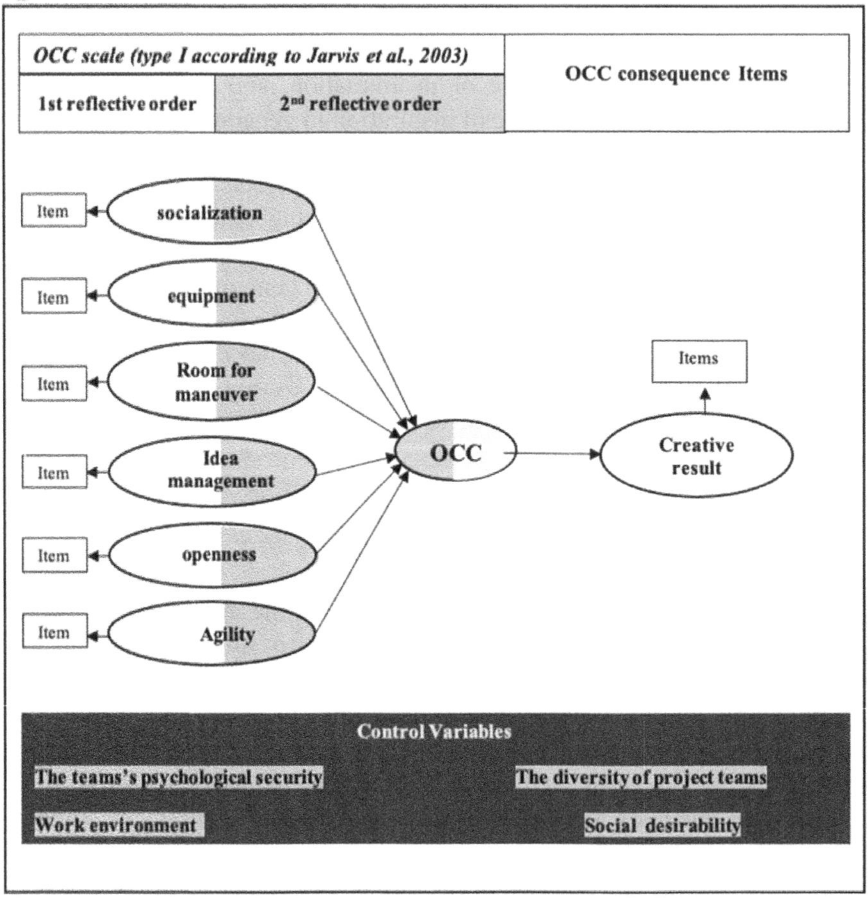

Figure 7.3. *Second-order reflective model of OCC and its consequence*

Various precautions were taken during data collection to limit possible methodological biases (Podsakoff et al. 2003). In the introductory phase of the questionnaire, we specified that the anonymity of the responses would be respected, and that there were no good or bad answers. The order of the questions was counterbalanced, using the "randomization" function available in the Qualtrics interface. We preferred simple, precise and clear wording and used several scale formats. We also conducted a pre-test of the questionnaire, in which we checked that the questions were well understood and estimated the exact time needed to answer them. Finally, we added an attention check question, which is used to check whether respondents read the questions correctly or answered the questionnaire by chance. This type of question cleans up collected responses and emphasizes the credibility of respondents.

In order to judge the type of scale, according to Jarvis et al. (2003), we must assess the causal relationship between the latent variables (the constructs) and the indicators (the measured variables). If the indicators are the cause of a latent variable, then it is a formative scale[4]. If a latent variable is reflected in the measured variables, then it is a reflective scale. Based on the criteria proposed by Jarvis et al. (2003), we envision the OCC scale to consist of first-order reflective measures (the items of the six OCC dimensions) and second-order reflective measures, which correspond to the six explanatory dimensions of OCC. As shown in Figure 7.3, we therefore consider a type I (reflective first-order, reflective second-order) measurement model following the typology of Jarvis et al. (2003).

Finally, using the Creative Outcome Scale, we will be able to assess the predictive validity of OCC. We consider that the creative outcome is positively influenced by OCC. We will also need to ensure that OCC is different from the creative climate construct.

7.4. Conclusion

Our initial OCC scale is the first step towards a valid and reliable measure of organizational creative capability. Such a scale will serve as an internal diagnostic tool for creative organizations to measure their creative capability and provide them with a best practice guide to strengthen their creative capability.

In the rest of our study, we will try to evaluate the importance of each of the dimensions in the definition of OCC, as well as the influence of the latter on the creative result. These results will help managers to understand how to manage their resources and exploit their individual and collective creativity to achieve creative results.

---

4 Recall that for a construct to be formative, four conditions must be met: 1) the indicators are conceived not as manifestations of the construct, but as constituent elements of that construct; 2) they are not interchangeable; 3) they do not necessarily covary; 4) they do not share the same nomological network, i.e. they are not assumed to have the same antecedents and consequences (Jarvis et al. 2003).

From a methodological point of view, a principal component analysis performed on the first data collection (exploratory phase) will allow us to verify whether the OCC dimensions are consistent with the expected factorial structure. Then, a confirmatory factor analysis, carried out on the second data collection (confirmatory phase), will aim to test the reliability, the convergent validity, the discriminant validity and the predictive validity of the OCC scale.

7.5. Appendix: scale items

7.5.1. *Socialization of ideas*

Regarding the social relations in your organization, you would say: in my organization:

– we can easily discuss our ideas with our colleagues;

– we regularly exchange information and ideas;

– we conduct meetings to exchange new ideas;

– we often schedule events to meet new people;

– we have formal processes for sharing best practices across business areas;

– we encourage cooperation between employees.

7.5.2. *Creating room to maneuver*

Regarding how your organization responds to the unexpected, you would say:

– we can easily adapt the creation process to the situation;

– we can easily assign more collaborators to our projects;

– we can easily mobilize new work spaces;

– we have the freedom to adapt our work processes according to the situation;

– we allow extra time to deal with the unexpected events and changes;

– we are planning additional budget to deal with unforeseen events and changes;

– management has little control over compliance with rules and the application of processes.

7.5.3. *Creative equipment*

1) Regarding your organization's equipment, you would say:

- work spaces are designed to stimulate our ability to create new ideas;

- we have work spaces dedicated to the development of new ideas (generation, rapid prototyping);

- we have friendly places for breaks and informal meetings;

- our creativity is stimulated by the introduction of new technologies;

- our creativity is stimulated by the use of collaborative tools;

- the work spaces are open.

2) Regarding the creative methods used in your organization, you would say:

- my organization organizes creative sessions to find new ideas;

- my organization organizes training on creativity methods;

- my organization organizes training on design methods;

- my organization mobilizes dedicated processes that allow us to generate new ideas;

- my organization uses generic methods (design thinking, CPSTRIZ, C-K method, etc.) to generate new ideas.

7.5.4. *Idea management*

Regarding idea management in your organization, you would say in my organization:

– we use an idea management system (idea box, idea files or software);

– we formalize the ideas to be able to share and evaluate them;

– we keep good ideas to use them in other projects;

– we allocate specific resources to develop the best ideas;

– there is a committee dedicated to the evaluation of ideas;

– there are criteria to measure the quality of ideas;

– employees can propose ideas freely to their managers;

– employees receive feedback on the ideas they propose;

– managers are receptive to ideas proposed by employees;

– the originators of ideas receive recognition.

7.5.5. *External openness*

Regarding the openness of your organization, you would say:

– my organization encourages its employees to regularly participate in external events, conferences and exhibitions;

– my organization encourages its employees to join formal or informal networks outside the organization;

– my organization partners with other companies to develop new ideas;

– my organization looks to other industries for inspiration;

– my organization involves external actors (customers, suppliers or researchers) to find new ideas;

– my organization draws inspiration from external actors (customers, suppliers or researchers) to find new ideas;

– my organization partially outsources design to come up with new ideas;

– my organization develops ideas internally from outside ideas;

– my organization draws inspiration from other existing products to come up with new ideas;

– my organization participates in clusters, competitiveness clusters or communities to find new ideas.

7.5.6. *Organizational agility*

Regarding your organization's adaptability, you would say:

– my organization's processes allow me to respond quickly to market needs;

– my organization's processes allow for quick decisions to be made when circumstances change;

– my organization is able to identify new trends to anticipate changes;

– my organization is rapidly making changes to meet the changing environment;

– my organization frequently tests current developments with its customers;

– my organization regularly tests its ideas with its employees.

7.6. References

Amabile, T.M. (1999). How to kill creativity: Keep doing what you're doing. Or, if you want to spark innovation, rethink how to motivate, reward, and assign work to people. *Harvard Business Review*, 13.

Baker, S.E. and Edwards, R. (2012). How many qualitative interviews is enough? Expert voices and early career reflections on sampling and cases in qualitative research. National Centre for Research Methods Review Paper.

Bergendahl, M., Magnusson, M., Björk, J. (2015). Ideation high performers: A study of motivational factors. *Creativity Research Journal*, 27(4), 361–368.

Besemer, S.P. (1998). Creative product analysis matrix: Testing the model structure and a comparison among products—three novel chairs. *Creativity Research Journal*, 11(4), 15.

Bourgeois, L.J. (1981). On the measurement of organizational slack. *Academy of Management Review*, 6(1), 12.

Brem, A., Puente-Diaz, R., Agogué, M. (2016). Creativity and innovation: State of the art and future perspectives for research. *International Journal of Innovation Management*, 20(4).

Carricano, M., Poujol, F., Bertrandias, L. (2008). *Analyse de données avec SPSS*. Pearson Education, Paris.

Caves, R.E. (2003). Contracts between art and commerce. *Journal of Economic Perspectives*, 17(2), 73–83.

Charbonnier-Voirin, A. (2009). Création et validation d'une échelle de mesure de l'agilité organisationnelle : étude exploratoire et confirmatoire. *20ème congrès AGRH*. 24.

Churchill, G. (1979). A paradigm for developing better measures of marketing constructs. *Journal of Marketing Research*, 16, 64–73.

Cohendet, P., Lleren, P., Simon, L. (2012). The routinization of creativity: Lessons from the case of a video-game creative powerhouse. In *Frontiers in Evolutionary Economics,* Cantner, U. and Dosi, G. (eds). De Gruyter, Berlin, 120–141.

Dampérat, M., Jeannot, F., Jongmans, E., Jolibert, A. (2016). Team creativity: Creative self-efficacy, creative collective efficacy and their determinants. *Recherche et Applications en Marketing*, 31(3), 6–25.

Darvishmotevali, M., Altinay, L., Köseoglu, M.A. (2020). The link between environmental uncertainty, organizational agility, and organizational creativity in the hotel industry. *International Journal of Hospitality Management*, 87, 102–499.

Dean, D., Hender, J., Rodgers, T., Santanen, E. (2006). Identifying quality, novel, and creative ideas: Constructs and scales for idea evaluation. *Journal of the Association for Information Systems*, 7(10), 646–699.

Diamantopoulos, A. and Winklhofer, H.M. (2001). Index construction with formative indicators: An alternative to scale development. *Journal of Marketing Research*, 38(2), 269–277.

Dove, R. (1999). Knowledge management, response ability, and the agile enterprise. *Journal of Knowledge Management*, 3(1), 18–35.

Drake, G. (2003). This place gives me space: Place and creativity in the creative industries. *Geoforum*, 34(4), 511–524.

Dutraive, V. and Szostak, B. (2021). Essay on the characteristics and ambivalences of the creative economy paradigm. *Revue d'économie industrielle*, 174, 159–185.

Edmondson, A. (1999). Psychological safety and learning behavior in work teams. *Administrative Science Quarterly*, 44(2), 350.

Egan, T.M. (2005). Creativity in the context of team diversity: Team leader perspectives. *Advances in Developing Human Resources*, 7(2), 207–225.

Ekvall, G. (1996). Organizational climate for creativity and innovation. *European Journal of Work and Organizational Psychology*, 5(1), 105–123.

Gerlach, S. and Brem, A. (2017). Idea management revisited: A review of the literature and guide for implementation. *International Journal of Innovation Studies*, 1(2), 144–161.

Handzic, M. and Chaimungkalanont, M. (2004). Enhancing organisational creativity through socialisation. *The Electronic Journal of Knowledge Management*, 2(1), 8.

Harvey, J.F., Naggar, R., Cohendet, P., Simon, L. (2013). Gérer les idées pour mieux innover. *Gestion*, 38(3), 11.

Hays, R.D., Hayashi, T., Stewart, A.L. (1989). A five-item measure of socially desirable response set. *Educational and Psychological Measurement*, 49(3), 629–636.

Hill, L.A., Brandeau, G., Truelove, E., Lineback, K. (eds). (2014). *Collective Genius: The Art and Practice of Leading Innovation*. Harvard Business Review Press, Cambridge.

Jarvis, C.B., MacKenzie, S.B., Podsakoff, P.M. (2003). A critical review of construct indicators and measurement model misspecification in marketing and consumer research. *Journal of Consumer Research*, 30(2), 199–218.

Kratzer, J., Meissner, D., Roud, V. (2017). Open innovation and company culture: Internal openness makes the difference. *Technological Forecasting and Social Change*, 119, 128–138.

Lee, S. and Lee, D. (2017). The role of agility in the relationship between use of management control systems and organizational performance: Evidence from Korea and Japan. *Journal of Applied Business Research*, 33(3), 521–538.

Lewin, A.Y., Massini, S., Peeters, C. (2011). Microfoundations of internal and external absorptive capacity routines. *Organization Science*, 22(1), 81–98.

Malhotra, N.K., Décaudin, J.M., Shahidi, N., Macé, S. (2007). *Études marketing avec SPSS*. Pearson Education, London.

Mellard, M. and Parmentier, G. (2020). La créativité dans les espaces de coworking : le cas de "La Cordée". *Innovations*, 61(1), 67.

Mellard, M., Parmentier, G., Jeannot, F. (2020). Influence of team agility and creative capabilities on creative outcomes: A moderated mediation model, CINET. *Personnel Review*, 48(1).

Napier, N.K. and Nilsson, M. (2006). The development of creative capabilities in and out of creative organizations: Three case studies. *Creativity & Innovation Management*, 15(3), 268–278.

Nonaka, I. and Konno, N. (1998). The concept of "Ba": Building a foundation for knowledge creation. *California Management Review*, 40(3), 15.

Parmentier, G. and Gandia, R. (2013). Managing sustainable innovation with a user community toolkit: The case of the video game trackmania. *Creativity and Innovation Management*, 22(2), 195–208.

Parmentier, G. and Szostak, B. (2016). How to build the creative capabilities of an organization. *Human Resources Management*, 25.

Parmentier, G., Szostak, B.L., Rüling, C.-C. (2017). Organizational creativity: Challenges for strategic management in globalized world. *Management International*, 22(1), 12–18.

Penrose, E.T. (2009). *The Theory of the Growth of the Firm*. Oxford University Press, Oxford.

Pérez López, S., Manuel Montes Peón, J., José Vázquez Ordás, C. (2004). Managing knowledge: The link between culture and organizational learning. *Journal of Knowledge Management*, 8(6), 93–104.

Podsakoff P.M., MacKenzie S.B., Lee J.-Y., Podsakoff N.P. (2003). Common method biases in behavioral research: A critical review of the literature and recommended remedies. *Journal of Applied Psychology*, 88(5), 879–903.

Rangus, K., Drnovšek, M., Di Minin, A. (2016). Proclivity for open innovation: Construct development and empirical validation. *Innovation*, 18(2), 191–211.

Salter, A., Ter Wal, A.L.J., Criscuolo, P., Alexy, O. (2015). Open for ideation: Individual-level openness and idea generation in R&D: Open for ideation. *Journal of Product Innovation Management*, 32(4), 488–504.

Sundgren, M., Dimenas, E., Gustafsson, J.E., Selart, M. (2005). Drivers of organizational creativity: A path model of creative climate in pharmaceutical R&D. *R&D Management*, 35(4), 359–374.

Tierney, P. (2002). Creative self-efficacy: Its potential antecedents and relationship to creative performance. *Academy of Management Journal*, 45(6), 13.

Voss, G.B., Sirdeshmukh, D., Voss, Z.G. (2008). The effects of slack resources and environmental threat on product exploration and exploitation. *Academy of Management Journal*, 51(1), 147–164.

Wang, C.W. and Horng, R.Y. (2002). The effects of creative problem solving training on creativity, cognitive type and R&D performance. *R&D Management*, 32(1), 35–45.

Woodman, R.W., Sawyer, J.E., Griffin, R.W. (1993). Toward a theory of organizational creativity. *Academy of Management Review*, 18(2), 293–321.

Wu, G., Zhao, X., Zuo, J., Zillante, G. (2019). Effects of team diversity on project performance in construction projects. Engineering. *Construction and Architectural Management*, 26(3), 408–423.

8

The Creative Performance of Organizations

The performance of organizations is a major concept in strategic management. Indeed, an organization is defined as the whole of a community structured around resources and competencies, which it allocates and which in the long-term commit it to achieving its objectives. Then, organizations must regularly assess the extent to which they are accomplishing their goals, plans and objectives. This is done in the specific context of competition, which the term "strategy" recalls precisely if we refer to the etymology of the word *stratos* or "army". It implies, on the one hand, a strategist or a general of an army, and, on the other hand, an enemy to be crushed, eliminated or, on a less war-like level, to be surpassed by the implementation of our plans. Performance is therefore consubstantial with strategic management, knowing that it can be apprehended according to different types. It may be a question of complementary levels of analysis (individual, group, department, organization, project), of varied specialties (financial, commercial, social and societal performance) and of a different temporality (short, medium and long-term). Moreover, whatever the type of performance, it is necessary to question its measurement and control in order to improve it. It can be qualitative via an appreciation, a perception, but it is more often quantitative and mobilizes measurement indicators. For example, financial performance can be measured by sales, EBITDA, growth rate, market share, etc. Commercial performance can be measured by the customer satisfaction rate, and by the brand's reputation, either direct or assisted. Finally, social and societal performance can be measured in terms

---

Chapter written by Bérangère L. SZOSTAK.

of corporate social responsibility (CSR) (Beji et al. 2020). What these illustrations have in common is that the organization's resources and competencies need to be configured so that the anticipated performance is achieved and, as far as possible, exceeded.

These benchmarks are important to keep in mind when considering organizational creativity, i.e. the specialty of the organization whose aim is to create, capture, select and implement new and useful ideas (Carrier and Gélinas 2011; Carrier and Szostak 2014), because this leads the organization to define and consider the creative performance (Szostak 2006; Carrier et al. 2010; Mnisri and Mavoori 2019). In other words, the organization must assess how well it is accomplishing this creative ambition in a competitive environment. To this end, it configures the appropriate resources and competencies to be successful in this regard. These specific configurations refer to creative capabilities. More precisely, the organization builds, integrates and even reconfigures everything that allows it to be able to generate, capture, select and implement new, appropriate and feasible ideas and solutions. The aim is to improve, change and renew both the organizational processes and the organization itself, and thus to achieve the objectives set in terms of creativity vis-à-vis other organizations (Durand 2006; Gay and Szostak 2019).

However, while financial, commercial or social and societal performance is now understood and used by organizations, it must be recognized that this is not fully the case for creative performance, even though researchers and socio-economic actors are increasingly interested in creativity[1]. In our opinion, one of the reasons for this is the weakness of the general framework for understanding what is meant by "creative performance", and also of the instruments and tools for measuring it. Indeed, we must recognize that what cannot be accurately qualified or measured remains an unknown. As Berland et al. (2008) remind us, measurement allows us to represent phenomena, and thus to think about them, decide, act and try to transform them.

The objective of this chapter is to address this weakness. In the first section, we present a general framework for the concept of "creative performance", reviewing what performance means in the case of

1 For example, many organizations, and even territories and countries, are moving towards creativity academic events, and special issues in scientific journals have developed strongly since Amabile's (1988) canonical article.

organizational creativity. In the second section, we propose two tools for managers to help them define their own creative performance: the creativity ladder and KPI creatives (of creative performance).

8.1. Proposal of a general framework for creative performance

Even though some major authors have addressed the notion of creative performance, it is generally at the level of individuals, as Amabile (1988) does. At the level of the organization, it has yet to be described, understood and explained, so that managers can appropriate it. This is all the more important for those belonging to organizations whose core competencies are not linked to a creative activity, because they may consider that this concept is irrelevant for them. This would be a misdiagnosis on their part, given the importance of creativity in today's economy. To give just one example, in the 2010s, two-thirds of CEOs and executives of public companies recognized that managing creativity is the main challenge facing their companies (IBM CEO study 2010). Therefore, it is not only managers working in cultural and creative industries (design agencies, video games, fashion, architecture, music, etc.) who are fully concerned by the subject, even though it is clear that a good number of studies dealing with creative performance at the organizational level focus on this type of structure. This is the case, for example, in design (Szostak 2006), in advertising agencies (Mnisri and Mavoori 2019) or in video games (Mellard 2020). This section thus proposes a conceptual framework for thinking about the creative performance of organizations. We start with what is meant by "performance" (see section 8.1.1), and then we present four essential themes to be investigated by managers (see section 8.1.2).

8.1.1. *Creative performance: definitions and issues*

Performance in itself is an ambiguous concept. Indeed, it can be defined according to a rational or irrational approach. In the first case, the vision is based on a reduced temporality, with a utilitarian search for the achievement of short-term objectives. This is, for example, the case for organizations that want to grow at all costs, in order to satisfy strong shareholder demands. This vision often underestimates, or even ignores, the societal and social costs. It can be the case when organizations engage in heavy restructuring (closing subsidiaries, factories, reducing central positions, etc.);

their objective is to avoid counter-performance, particularly financial counter-performance.

In the second case, the irrational vision brings with it a universe close to artistic creativity, insofar as it values impulse and the spontaneity, leading to the pleasure of acting. An emblematic example is that of art. The performance or "artistic action" goes beyond the work. The artist accomplishes an ephemeral objective, which can be enduring in its effects on the spectators and on the audience in the grip of the action that they witness. Indeed, certain performances are extreme and set the scene of the artist's parts of the body; they often have a critical political and societal dimension regarding our conception of society and interpersonal relations[2]. If this vision appears to be far removed from strategic management in general, it is less so from the world of the arts and culture, and from the creativity of individuals working in the cultural and creative industries. Without adopting it outright, it nevertheless seems useful to bear in mind for the rest of this chapter on creative performance.

In addition, performance leads to the definition of other concepts that are discussed here in relation to creativity. We focus on two essential concepts: effectiveness and efficiency. Concerning the first concept, the question arises for the strategist of the consistency of the result achieved with that which had been set by a source external to the organization (the consumer market, financiers, institutions, competitors). The standard induced to signify whether there is "performance" or not is judged and decided by individuals outside the organization, such as financiers, who, depending on their nature (employee or family shareholders, institutional investors, business angels, the market, bankers, etc.), have different objectives. The organization must thus demonstrate its ability to create acceptable results and actions according to standards; in other words, it must perform well. In this, it is similar to an entrepreneur who successfully applies creativity in their project and seizes opportunities (Lerch et al. 2015): it is performing. While these can be defined

2 For example, Michel Journiac proposed *Messe pour un corps* in 1969, in Paris; he officiates in Latin and ends his homily with a black texture and a host made of blood sausage with his own blood. His objective is to show what the act of creation is from the energizing food that the artist proposes to men. In 1978, Marina Abramović and Ulay, a couple both on and off stage, gave life to the performance called *AAA-AAA*: face to face, they vocalize an "A", first in tune, then out of tune, to the point where they are screaming into each other's mouths. Their objective is to show the limits of the couple, where solidarity is not always required.

relatively easily in a specific sector, at the financial, business or societal[3] level, this is less the case at the level of creativity, which, in turn, makes it difficult to define creative performance[4]. Indeed, these standards include an element of irrationality due to the perception, the feeling and the closeness of each individual in the face of a new and useful idea. Despite the inability to control this irrational element, it must be recognized that organizations are nowadays increasingly assessed on creativity and must understand what creative performance means for them.

To convince us of this, let us cite two types of arguments: one empirical and the other academic. First, let us consider what the European Commission did in 2009 when it designated that year as the "European Year of Creativity and Innovation". The Commission's objective was formulated with reference to the Lisbon Strategy, to make the Union the most dynamic knowledge-based economy in the world. In short, the decision aimed to "promote creativity and innovation as key competences for all through lifelong learning". The policy objective was to foster "an environment conducive to all forms of creativity and innovation, whether artistic, cultural, social or technological, and to promote the practical use of knowledge and ideas"[5].

In France, on October 5, 2015, from Tokyo, the French Prime Minister at the time officially launched the label "Creative France" to promote the numerous initiatives and important French know-how in creativity and innovation and to support the international development of French companies that create jobs and wealth through their creativity. In short, we can say that the government was pushing French companies to be successful in terms of creativity.

Second, and this is the academic argument, we are seeing an increasingly significant body of work on creativity in organizations. For example, work on

---

3 For example, trade unions or funders are able to characterize to some extent an organization that is more or less successful because of their overall view of a sector – provided that organizations have reported a certain amount of financial, business, social, etc. data.

4. The Community Innovation Survey, CIS, or the "Capacity to Innovate and Strategy", seeks to fill this gap by asking companies questions that can be used in the analysis of performance. This was particularly the case in 2010 when INSEE included the module "Skills and creativity".

5 Decision no. 1350/2008/EC – see: http://europa.eu/legislation_summaries/culture/l29020 fr.htm.

the creative landscape shows what contribution the different existing strata (upper, middle and underground) make to the economy and to the agents present in this territory in developing new ideas and their creativity (Florida 2005; Cohendet et al. 2018; Muller et al. 2020). The question of performance is understood differently in different environments, however. The music industry expects a level of new releases, which is reflected, for example, in the number of album releases, the number of artist signings, etc. In the automotive sector, it could be the number of concept cars. In the academic world, it would be the number of articles published. In summary, the effectiveness of an organization at the level of creativity implies having, as accurately as possible, a global vision of what is happening, in order to know the standards expected (or imposed by a regulatory institution[6]) in the market or in a specific environment.

The second concept that seems essential to discuss in order to frame what we mean by creative performance is that of efficiency, which is the performance, i.e. evaluating whether the means implemented have produced what they could best produce. Efficiency is an internal standard controlled by the members of the organization, which must show its ability to create processes to do things better, with less effort or at lower cost. This is what quality control and other internal self-assessment processes propose to do. Minvielle and Cam (2011) illustrate this point with the TED (*ticket d'entrée du design* or design entry ticket), created by and for the Renault company. The carmaker monitors four dimensions to determine whether the investment in design is efficient: 1) the brand's image with consumers; 2) the press's production and evaluation of the brand's products; 3) the customers' appreciation of the products and 4) the president of the group's appreciation. This tool enables the manufacturer to assess whether the resources it has committed to design enable it to achieve its objectives. This assumes that it has determined internal standards for what is "good" and "bad".

While in the automotive sector, creativity is important, hence the significant investments in design, it must be emphasized that efficiency will not be evaluated in a similar way in all sectors and organizations, because it depends on the place allocated to creativity internally and de facto on the means implemented. In other words, if this place is major, as in the

6 In the case of research in France, researchers are generally considered to be active if they produce, over a relatively short period of time (four years, for example), a fixed number of articles (two, for example) in journals present in lists recognized by their reference authorities.

organizations of the cultural and creative industries, there will certainly be many internal standards relating to creativity, because the investments will be significant. Otherwise, organizational creativity is likely to be a speciality that is not well included in the organization. The centrality of creativity in the definition of the organization's mission is emphasized here. The stronger it is, the more it will be present in the indicators measuring the organization's overall performance.

This can be seen, for example, in the case of design agencies that cannot survive in their competitive environment if they are not creative and do not offer their clients original and new products, packaging, graphics, environment, etc., to the point of being recognized by their peers, experts and the market through awards (Janus of the Industry in France, Best Product of the Year, etc.) (Borja de Mozota 2002; Szostak 2006). Without this recognition they are not considered competitive, as they are unable to offer products of higher value at equal costs or of equal value to what competitors offer. These agencies are therefore driven to define their goals and standards based on creativity, then measure their achievement against what they had envisioned and, if necessary, implement corrective measures. This control is obviously necessary even when it comes to organizational creativity, which includes an element of irrationality, because it potentially entails a reconfiguration of resources and competencies that allow it to generate, capture and implement new, appropriate and feasible ideas and solutions. In short, it can evolve organizational creative capabilities.

8.1.2. *Performance and management of organizational creativity*

The creative capabilities of the organizations at the origin of the envisaged performance are understood as an echo of the management of organizational creativity. Thus, the framework described below aims to structure the manager's work of defining creative performance based on four themes that form the general framework of creativity (see Figure 8.1) (Gay and Szostak 2019). Each echoes a classic management process (finalization, organization, animation, control).

The first theme concerns the finalization process found in "the creativity strategy". This is to determine the existence of a clearly formulated conception by the organization of its activities from the angle of creativity, with regard to its competitive space and, more broadly, its environment. This translates into the formulation of decision-making criteria that guide the activities and structures of the organization decisively and over the long-term. For example, a video game studio will have an art director integrated into the management committee, or a car manufacturer will have a design director. Their mission is to guide the products and the brand towards a specific style and creative universe.

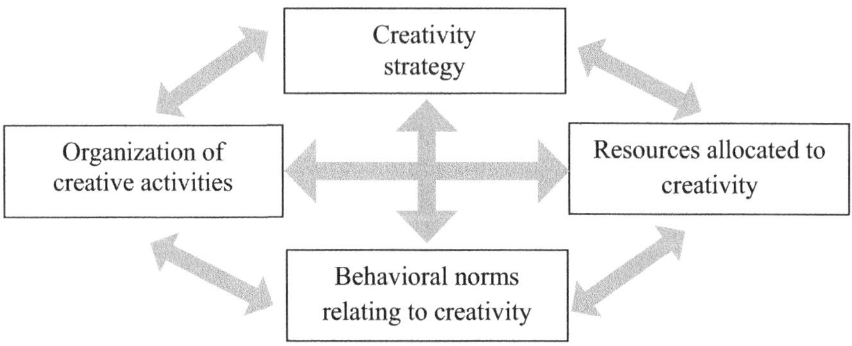

Figure 8.1. *General framework of creativity (Gay and Szostak 2019)*

The other three themes can be seen at first glance as induced by the first one, even though, later on, interactions between the four themes are unquestionably possible. The first of these three concerns the process of animating the collective involved in the creativity strategy, which implies "resources allocated to creativity". If there is a director or a person in charge of the creativity strategy, this means a clear allocation of human resources to creativity – resources that can include, in addition, marketers, engineers, designers and researchers. It also means material resources, such as square meters allocated to spaces dedicated to creativity (a brainstorming room, an internal FabLab), or materials, machines, tools (3D printer, foam or cardboard for mock-up) and methods (Carrier et al. 2010; Ben Mahmoud-Jouini et al. 2016). Finally, these resources can be temporal: the working time left for employees to participate in creativity workshops, visit museums, exhibitions and trade fairs and establish interorganizational relationships with partners (competitors, customers, suppliers, research laboratories, etc.). For example, a consulting firm based in Lyon and Paris invested in an internal FabLab and invested heavily in both machines (a 3D printer, a laser cutter and a vinyl cutter) and personnel (recruitment, free time to explore new ideas), even though its business was not yet fully operational. This is despite the fact that its activity is not inherently focused on creativity (Fagbohoun 2021). All of this is a financial commitment for the organization and is supposed to represent, not a cost, but an investment for the manager.

The second theme induced by the creativity strategy focuses on the norms of behavior related to creativity. If the originality of an individual with unusual ideas or surprising experiments is praised by the organization, and even encouraged to the point, for example, that it is a criterion for evaluating the professional activity of a “good employee” and a characteristic of the organizational climate, this reflects a strong centrality of creativity. These behavioral norms are supported, moreover, by the emotional competencies of leaders, as Chader and Ovono Beyeme (2019) point out. Indeed, since failures in creativity are inevitably numerous, it is important that employees are not demotivated in their efforts and that they feel supported by their manager (Amabile 1988; Zhou and George 2003).

The third theme of this general framework of creativity is about the organization of creative activities, their layout and hierarchical links. By way of illustration, the activities under the authority of the marketing department will not be managed in a manner equivalent to those which would be under the direction of production, R&D or even directly attached to the general manager. The imperatives of the different directorates will guide the objectives of these activities. Chaptal de Chanteloup (2011) shows in the case of design that, if it is placed under R&D, it is the functional performance of the product that is mainly considered. If it is marketing, it is consumer satisfaction and profitability. If it is the strategy, the design is seen according to its ability to generate concepts over the long-term. Finally, if it is under production, the design vision is centered on the perfection achieved by the final product and material. In other words, creative performance is not defined in exactly the same way depending on the organization of creative activities.

These four themes are, moreover, in interaction. Developments in one of them affect the content of the others. But the whole forms a framework for thinking about creativity in companies and, as a result, makes it possible to specify the creative performance, which is the responsibility of the person in charge of the creativity strategy. The effectiveness and efficiency of this strategy call upon the resources mobilized for creativity and are based on the creative behaviors of the employees, according to a specific organization, in a particular competitive environment. Creative performance will then consist of assessing the extent to which the organization has achieved, or even exceeded, the plans, objectives and goals set out in the strategy. The result of the investigation of these four themes will help the manager to better measure the creative performance in their own organization.

8.2. Measuring performance creativity

Berland et al. (2008) show how essential the measurement of a phenomenon is for appropriating it, or at least for trying to understand it better; measurement thus echoes evaluation (see Box 8.1). For this reason, in this second part, we propose a first tool, the creativity ladder, to specify the degree of integration of creativity in an organization, and consequently, the importance of creative performance as an input to the development of the organization's corporate strategy (see section 8.2.1). We then suggest key creative performance indicators or creative KPI to reflect this degree of integration of creativity (see section 8.2.2).

Etymologically, the word *evaluate* means "to determine the value, the price of something". It includes the word *value*, and therefore the meaning of "value, price", or the word *valor* in Latin, to specify, for example, that someone or something has value, that it is "the equivalent of". From the etymological meaning, three aspects seem important to deduce.

Firstly, value is not only financial; it can be social, human, moral. It depends on the criteria used to define the said value. In the case of creative performance, value is defined in terms of creativity, which, as mentioned at the beginning of this chapter, is the organization's specialty, which aims to create, capture, select and implement new and useful ideas.

Secondly, evaluation involves the evaluator and the evaluated, which should be specified. Echoing the way in which effectiveness and efficiency, which are concepts related to that of performance, are approached, for creativity, it can be an external evaluator (the consumer market, finance, institutions, competition) or an internal evaluator (quality department, management control department) (Ford 1996). The object of evaluation may differ, depending, among other things, on the hierarchical attachment of the specialty dedicated to creativity (the product, customer satisfaction, profitability, etc.).

Thirdly, evaluation is conducted at a given moment; the spatio-temporal context guides the action of evaluating. The originality of an idea may be proven in one sector, but not in another because of cross-fertilization between the two sectors, for example. The usefulness of an idea may be strong in one country when it is not (yet) so in another; this was the case with GE Healthcare's portable scanner, which was initially developed for caregivers who, in difficult-to-reach areas, had to carry with them equipment that was generally very cumbersome without being able to transfer patients easily to hospitals.

Thus, we retain that the manager must consider the three aspects set out here when proposing a measure of creative performance: 1) the nature of the criteria used; 2) the identity of the evaluator and the evaluated; 3) the spatio-temporal context of the evaluation of creative performance.

Box 8.1. *A look at the etymology of the word "evaluation"*

8.2.1. *The creativity ladder*

This tool takes its inspiration from the one used in the field of design, which is an emblematic discipline of creativity: design ladder. This was developed by the Danish Design Center (DDC) in 2001, and then disseminated in a report in 2003, to evaluate the economic effects of design (Volkova and Jākobsone 2016; Borja de Mozota 2018). The objective is simple and forms an answer to a classic question when it comes to design, a question that can be found in the case of creativity: what is design (and creativity) for? What does it bring to an organization? The DDC's answer is that it depends on the level of integration of design in the organization. It is therefore not possible to propose a univocal answer. Depending on the degree of integration, of which there are four in the case of the design ladder, the evaluation of the creative performance is different.

The creativity ladder developed below (see Table 8.1) helps the manager in this sense. To better understand it, here are the four levels of the design ladder. The first level is that of organizations with little commitment to design, which translates into the absence of designers in the design process. The second level is design as an expert in final form, whether in 3D or 2D. This is "styling". The professionals involved can be designers by training and background, and also people from other profiles, such as engineering or marketing. The result is obtained by the involvement of the participants on the subjects related to functionality and aesthetics. The users are not well or not at all present. The third level is design as a process; it is integrated early in the development of the idea, the product and the service. Users are strongly solicited to share their experience and discuss the desirability and functionality of the object to be designed. The professionals come from very broad and complementary specialties (technical, marketing, administration, design) and use different ideation methods (Carrier et al. 2010; Wrigley et al.

2020). The fourth level of design integration is strategic: the entire managerial structure rethinks the business in part or in whole, in order to support the development of design at every level of the organization, including the value chain (Verganti 2009). This is the most mature level of design integration.

In the case of the creativity ladder, we retain the four levels of the design ladder, which we adapt to the organizational creativity. The first level is the absence of creativity or it may be so little present that it is not significant. The second level is "creativity as a fad", or what we may call creative washing. In other words, the organization has understood that creativity corresponds to an expectation of the market, of its partners and even of its employees, but it is more in the discourse than in the concrete work of taking creativity into account in its practices. This is why there will be creativity projects, but they will remain one-offs and the result of opportunities for the organization without there being a strong commitment to developing creativity. The third level is "creativity as a process". The organization integrates creativity into its activities; it is a specialty that is recognized and desired by all stakeholders, from management, hence a real investment in creativity. It sets up a context conducive to the development of creativity (Amabile 1988; Brion and Mothe 2017; Fagbohoun 2021). The fourth level is "creativity as strategy" (Gay and Szostak 2019): the organization considers creativity as a fundamental element of its professional activity and even of the definition of its identity. Creativity even defines its corporate culture. Table 8.1 details each of these levels and presents typical examples of companies at each level.

Level	Definition	Typical examples
No creativity	The search for creative ideas is not part of the organization's activities. If there is creativity, it is by accident. It plays no role in itself. The creativity strategy is non-existent; no or few resources are allocated specifically to creativity and there is no dedicated department.	Company aiming for the standardization of products/services. Company managed exclusively according to a cost strategy and a financial logic.
Creativity as a fashion	The organization shows a willingness to look for creative ideas. This is reflected in its speech, advertising or communication. But it is hollow. It may be a case of creativity washing. The formulation of the creativity strategy	A company that uses the word creativity and the tools of creativity in its differentiation strategy. A company that engages in competitions and

	is superficial. People may be dedicated to it, but on an ad hoc basis (such as a doctoral student under contract, or personnel involved in a partnership with a research laboratory); they are integrated into departments such as marketing, production or R&D. They are more involved in the execution of a task requested by a superior. Creativity is a project to be carried out, which is entrusted for a time to people in the organization.	occasionally solicits creative people, such as design or innovation master students, for minor projects. A company that develops dedicated spaces (coworking space), but where few concrete things happen and impact the organization.
Creativity as a process	The organization integrates the search for creative ideas in its central functions (R&D, marketing, design office, integrated design, etc.). It develops creativity methods. It recruits creative individuals (researchers, designers, etc.).	A company that creates a dedicated service and allocates resources (human, material and financial). A budget line exists.
Level	**Definition**	**Typical examples**
Creativity as a process	The creativity strategy is clearly formulated and known to all thanks to the existence of a service or department displayed in the organization chart. The person in charge of this strategy is called upon to make major decisions. Creativity makes “sense”; it is carried out with a precise objective in relation to the mission of the organization.	The company is committed to long-term partnerships with design agencies and research laboratories.
Creativity as a strategy	The organization positions creativity as central to its strategy, even the core of its identity. Creativity brings a vision to all stakeholders. The creativity strategy is integrated into the corporate strategy, which means a strong and sustainable allocation of resources. Creative individuals are valued and sought after. A department is dedicated to creativity and its manager is part of the management committee.	A company whose Top Management Team includes a creative person or even a company run by a creative person, such as a design agency, an advertising agency or an architecture firm. A company that recruits creative individuals and/or individuals with an awareness of creativity.

Table 8.1. *The creativity ladder*

The creativity ladder allows managers to position their organization and question the level at which it is positioned. However, we do not believe that it is vital for all organizations to be at the highest level, because the first-level positions (absence of creativity and creativity as a mode) are not necessarily to be considered "bad", because creativity is now becoming crucial in the economy. Indeed, it depends on the space-time context. If an organization in the fashion sector tends, a priori, to reach the highest level, this should be less the case for the only bakery in a village; it would be different, however, if several bakeries adjoined each other and sought to differentiate themselves in ways other than the price of the baguette.

The position of the organization on the creativity ladder will also influence the number and nature of the indicators used to assess creative performance. In other words, the more the organization positions creativity as a core strategy, the greater the number of indicators and the more varied they will be in nature in order to cover all of the organization's specialties, while taking into account the identity of the evaluator.

8.2.2. *Proposal of creative performance indicators: creative KPIs*

KPIs or key performance indicators are defined as the critical indicators of progress towards the desired outcome; KPIs focus management on strategic and operational improvement of the organization, create an analytical basis for decision-making and help focus attention on what matters most. Four attributes define KPIs: 1) the measure itself (e.g. number of products sold, percentage share of market sales, percentage growth in those sales); 2) the target to be achieved (100,000 consumers, 45% of the market, +10% sales growth); 3) the source of the data or information for the measurement; and 4) the frequency of the measurement (daily, monthly, semi-annually, annually). KPIs can either be used to assess the current state of affairs, to specify the progress to be made or to reflect the change to be made.

In the case of creativity, there is no formal KPI list, as creative performance is still discrete for many organizations. However, indicators are used to assess the extent to which the organization's creative capabilities allow new and useful ideas to emerge, and be captured, selected and implemented. For example, a marketing agency can count the number of ideas that come out of a creative workshop to imagine an advertising campaign; a car manufacturer can look at the number of concept cars imagined by its creatives (see also the TED case in Minvielle and Cam (2011)); a design agency can consider the number of awards and prizes obtained in a year (Szostak 2006); a research laboratory can evaluate the number of productions of its researchers over four years; an indie music label can consider the number of new artists signed (Muller et al. 2021). These examples show, firstly, the variety of possible measures that remain generalist, and also specific to the organization's sector, and, secondly, the fact that these measures potentially echo one of the dimensions of creative capabilities (emergence, capture, selection and implementation).

Dimensions retained	Examples of KPIs
Marketing dimension	– Number of new customers gained by a new idea
	– Number of new distribution channels for the organization
	– Increase in market share, opening of new markets (new business, new geographical areas)
	– Improvement of the brand image on the criteria of originality, novelty, creativity
	– Degree of adherence to brand values
	– Rate of/improvement in customer satisfaction with ideas proposed
	– Rate of/decrease in customer complaints
	– Degree of recognition of the original shape of a product
Strategic dimension	– Number of hires of creative individuals/workforce of creative individuals
	– Degree to which creativity skills of individuals are taken into account during recruitment, promotion, personal evaluation
	– Number of training sessions on creativity tools (design thinking, KCP, *personae*, exploration matrices, etc.)
	– Number of partnerships with structures known for their creativity
	– Degree of motivation of employees to express their creative potential
	– Strategic intelligence on the development of creativity
	– Degree of employee satisfaction with the management of their creativity

Process dimension	– Improvement of creativity processes (number of projects in creativity, number of ideas, acceleration of idea exchanges, use of digital technology)
	– Implementation of creativity management in the organization
	– Degree of openness of the organization's boundaries with external stakeholders (open-innovation, crowdsourcing, coopetition)
	– Integration of digital technology in creativity management (use of idea platforms, idea sharing tools, etc.)
	– Improved agility, flexibility and dialogue of creative teams
Financial dimension	– Share/increase of turnover obtained by new ideas on the local, national and international market
	– Share of the cost of creative activities in the overall cost
	– Share of brand value for its creativity
	– Number and value of patents, designs and models
	– Improved ROI of creative activities compared to investments made in creativity
	– Number of awards for creativity

Table 8.2. *Ideas of creative KPIs (inspired by Borja de Mozota (2006), Szostak (2006) and Szostak and Lenfant (2015))*

If the literature on the management of organizational creativity does not currently propose KPIs, design researchers do (Borja de Mozota 2006; Szostak 2006; Szostak and Lenfant 2015). To the extent that design remains one of the emblematic disciplines of creativity, it seems reasonable to exploit these KPIs and draw on them for creativity. Table 8.2 therefore details some creative KPIs.

These creative KPIs are to be adapted by managers hoping to evaluate the performance of creative capabilities of their organization. Indeed, if the activity guides the type of indicators, it should be remembered that their calculation assumes that the data exists and is accessible. Moreover, echoing the creativity ladder, it seems fair to think that the lower the level of integration of creativity, the lower the number of KPIs retained, or even none at all in the first level. This will also have an impact on the frequency with which these KPI's are assessed. Finally, the experience of managers in using these KPIs will enable them to refine these KPIs and adjust them to their activity.

8.3. Conclusion

While the creative performance of organizations is a concept that can be understood by professionals in creative organizations, this chapter emphasizes that it is essential to disseminate this concept to all managers, whether they are in organizations in which creativity is central or not. Indeed, given the major changes in society (economic, ecological, digital), organizations need to develop their creative capabilities to renew the ideas the basis of the innovations that emerge on the market. To ensure their success, they need to assess whether their capabilities allow them to achieve their objectives, in their particular context and in an efficient manner. Even though creativity has an irrational element, it must be evaluated like any other specialty of the organization. This is one way to make it fully legitimate in the eyes of all stakeholders. The creativity ladder and the creative KPIs can therefore help managers to concretely measure the creative performance of creative capabilities, and consider modifying them to better achieve the envisaged results.

8.4. References

Amabile, T.M. (1988). A model of creativity and innovation in organizations. *Research in Organizational Behavior*, 10, 123–167.

Beji, R., Yousfi, O., Loukil, N., Omri, A. (2020). Board diversity and corporate social responsibility: Empirical evidence from France. *Journal of Business Ethics*, 173, 1–23.

Ben Mahmoud-Jouini, S., Midler, C., Silberzahn, P. (2016). Contributions of design thinking to project management in an innovation context. *Project Management Journal*, 47(2), 144–156.

Berland, N., Chevalier-Kuszla, C. Sponem, S. (2008). On ne gère bien que ce que l'on mesure. In *Petit bréviaire des idées reçues en management*, CriM, Pezet, A., Sponem, S. (eds). La Découverte, Paris, 157–168.

Borja de Mozota, B., (2002). *Design Management*. Allworth Press, New York and Paris.

Borja de Mozota, B. (2006). The four powers of design: A value model in design management. *Design Management Review*, 17(2), 44–53.

Borja de Mozota, B. (2018). Quarante ans de recherche en design management : une revue de littérature et des pistes pour l'avenir. *Sciences du Design*, 7, 28–45.

Brion, S. and Mothe, C. (2017). Le contexte organisationnel favorable à l'innovation ambidextre : la créativité comme chaînon manquant ? *Revue française de gestion*, 264, 101–115.

Carrier, C. and Gélinas, S. (2011). *Créativité et gestion. Les idées au service de l'innovation*. Presses de l'Université du Québec, Québec.

Carrier, C. and Szostak, B. (2014). Créativité, PME et entrepreneuriat : des zones d'ombre et de lumière. *Revue Internationale PME*, 27(1), 13–34.

Carrier, C., Cadieux, L., Tremblay, M. (2010). Créativité et génération collective d'opportunités : quelles techniques pour supporter l'idéation ? *Revue française de gestion*, 206, 113–127.

Chader, A. and Ovono Beyeme, D. (2019). Les compétences émotionnelles des dirigeants au service de la créativité organisationnelle. Une étude dans les startups de la Région Occitanie. *RIMHE: Revue Interdisciplinaire Management, Homme & Entreprise*, 37(8), 53–78.

Chaptal de Chanteloup, C. (2011). *Le design, management stratégique et opérationnel*. Vuibert, Paris.

Cohendet, P., Grandadam, D., Mehouachi, C., Simon, L. (2018). The local, the global and the industry common: The case of the video game industry. *Journal of Economic Geography*, 18(5), 1045–1068.

Durand, R. (2006). Créativité organisationnelle. *Revue française de gestion*, 161(2), 91–94.

Fagbohoun, S. (2021). Fablab interne : quels effets sur le contexte organisationnel ? Le cas d'un cabinet de conseil. *Innovations*, 66(3), 79–107.

Florida, R. (2005). *The Flight of the Creative Class: The New Global Competition for Talent*. Harper Business, New York.

Gay, G. and Szostak, B.L. (2019). *Innovation and Creativity in SMEs*. ISTE Ltd, London, and John Wiley & Sons, New York.

Lerch, C., Thi Thanh Thai, M., Puhakka, V., Burger-Helmchen, T. (2015). La créativité entrepreneuriale : le sens pratique pour concrétiser les idées originales. *Innovations*, 48(3), 5–11.

Mellard, M. (2020). L'identification d'antécédents de la créativité organisationnelle : une approche configurationnelle appliquée aux industries créatives. PhD Thesis, Université Grenoble Alpes, Grenoble.

Minvielle, N. and Cam, C. (2011). Du design, mais à quel coût ? In *Design en entreprises. Les pratiques de gestion du design*, Minvielle, N. and Cam, C. (eds). De Boeck Supérieur, Louvain-la-Neuve, 141–172.

Mnisri, K. and Mavoori, H. (2019). Créativité et pratiques managériales au sein des agences conseil en communication. *Recherches en Sciences de Gestion*, 131, 29–59.

Muller, P., Szostak, B.L., Burger-Helmchen, T. (2020). Le rôle d'intermédiation des activités entrepreneuriales du middleground dans la circulation des idées créatives. Le cas du Krautrock. *Revue Internationale PME*, 33(3/4), 139–168.

Szostak, B. (2006). Liens interorganisationnels et performance créative des agences de design en France. *Revue française de gestion*, 164, 55–76.

Szostak, B. and Lenfant, F. (2015). *La boîte à outils du design management*. Dunod, Paris.

Verganti, R. (2009). *Design-Driven Innovation: Changing the Rules of Competition by Radically Innovating What Things Mean*. Harvard Business Press, Boston.

Volkova, T. and Jākobsone, I. (2016). Design thinking as a business tool to ensure continuous value generation. *Intellectual Economics*, 10, 63–69.

Wrigley, C., Nusem, E., Straker, K. (2020). Implementing design thinking: Understanding organizational conditions. *California Management Review*, 62(2), 125–143.

Zhou, J. and George, J. (2003). Awakening employee creativity: The role of leader emotional intelligence. *The Leadership Quarterly*, 14, 545–568.

Conclusion

Considering organizational creativity as a strategic capability is not only a scientific approach to better understand the phenomena of creativity in organizations, it is also an approach to identify organizational structures capable of addressing the challenges of the 21st century. Since Amabile's 1988 article, which emphasized collective and organizational-level creativity, there has been a growing body of work on creativity in organizations within management sciences. However, as we discussed in the introduction, many approaches to organizational creativity lack links to strategic management. They often focus on creativity within organizations, overlooking the organization as a whole with its structure, processes, and routines. The capabilities approach, which advocates that competitive advantage depends on the ability to deploy and coordinate these resources, (Amit and Schoemaker 1993) places organizational creativity as a strategic issue. Moreover, in an increasingly rapid and uncertain VUCA[1] conditions, organizations confront complex issues related to global warming, de-globalization, and technological revolutions. Addressing these challenges require thinking outside the box, generating new ideas, developing new knowledge and, most importantly, developing new ways of thinking, and, finally, to develop new forms of collectives, production processes, solutions, products and services. In this context, mobilizing intelligences and all forms of creativity at all organizational levels becomes increasingly vital. This challenge is far from simple, as two centuries of organizational development have primarily emphasized financial performance and hierarchical control.

Conclusion written by Florence JEANNOT, Séverinne LE LOARNE-LEMAIRE, Maxime MELLARD, Guy PARMENTIER, Romain RAMPA, Émilie RUIZ, Zeinab SHEET and Bérangère L. SZOSTAK.

1. VUCA: volatility, uncertainty, complexity, ambiguity.

In this book, we have tried, by adopting an approach to organizational creativity dealing with capabilities, to provide some modest answers.

Chapter 1 presents a comprehensive model of creative capabilities, outlining the foundational organizational routines and the factors that facilitate their effective execution.. Organizational capabilities are rooted on organizational routines that are stable configurations of activities. As described in the following chapters, these configurations of activities are organized with formal processes, management devices and physical and cognitive equipment. The intent of this book was not an exhaustive examination of the devices underpinning, but rather to identify the driving force behind the organizational routines that constitute creative capabilities.

Depending on the type of organization, its history, and its environment, the implementation of routines may assume diverse forms. For instance, the process of organizing resources, like in the case of BNP Cardif, varies significantly between a video game studio and a bank. BNP Cardif has embraced the concept by establishing a dedicated creativity room, offering specialized training, and equipping its employees with methods to enhance their creativity. In contrast, in a video game studio, there is no need for a creativity room; ideation is a recurring activity for a large part of the employees. In such a context, it's more a matter of equipping the team with tools and methods to guide, or even curb, the creativity that is sometimes too present and prevents projects from meeting design and production deadlines. Nonetheless, the fundamental purpose and impact of the equipment remains the same: to provide individuals with tools and methods that develop and maintain their creativity in the long-term in the service of a common cause.

Openness, which plays an increasingly important role in innovation processes to bring knowledge, ideas, technologies that are difficult, if not impossible, to develop only within the borders of an organization. Chapter 2 shows that openness is an organizational routine that renews employee creative capability and work groups, and therefore a pillar of organizational creative capabilities. The chapter highlights the complexity of openness due to the variety of types of borders to be managed (efficiency, power, knowledge, identity, digital), the strategic issues, and the multiple devices from which - possible greenness (community, connection to creative cities, crowdsourcing, platform, collaborative space). Furthermore, openness relies on another capability to be truly effective: absorption. Openness is therefore probably one of the most complex organizational routines of creative abilities. The question then arises of its links with other organizational routines: should we develop creative equipment, the management of ideas, organizational agility, slack before developing the opening? Or is the contribution of external ideas likely to facilitate or reinforce other organizational routines?

As Chapter 3 shows, equipment has a special place in the model of creative capabilities. First, it is one of the variables over which managers have the most direct control, by providing access to training, tools, or by transforming the organization's workspace. Most importantly, equipment, by providing cognitive and material resources cognitive and material resources for creativity, plays the role of a kind of foundation for the other dimensions of the model. By working to increase the creative skills of individuals and teams, or to extend the possibilities of spaces by giving access to prototyping spaces, for example, the equipment opens up possibilities for creative action within the organization and outside of it. And like any foundation, it can be interesting for the organization to start with the equipment to initiate and commence the emergence of creative capabilities.

Within the creative abilities, the slack is surely the most protean concept. Chapter 4 elucidates two primary perspectives that have emerged concerning slack: it serves as a reservoir of creative resources and as a margin of maneuver for creativity. The creative resource pool provides access to a myriad of past ideas and knowledge that can be used to by the organization to generate new creative ideas or expedite decision-making. Consequently, it is one of the powerful levers to increase another creative capability, which is organizational agility. A margin for creativity is necessary to give enough freedom and resources to individuals and teams to exercise their creativity.

While slack has always been crucial, its nature has evolved, particularly due to the digital transformation. Once mostly informal, organizations tend to frame and drive it in digital idea management platforms. And with digital, for organizations that also have the ability to be open, slack is no longer just confined to internal creative ideas. It can also be harnessed through crowdsourcing mechanisms, external competitions or even calls for ideas to form new partnerships. The potential of slack for organizations is thus multiplied tenfold if they manage to access the collective intelligence available. However, to really benefit from it, they will probably have to develop new analysis and synthesis tools, and above all have the capacity to translate and absorb the available knowledge and ideas.

Surprisingly, few studies have linked agility and creativity at the organizational level. Agile methods were originally created to develop team creativity, however, Chapter 5's literature review reveals a scarcity of studies confirming this impact on creativity. Agility is one of the organizational routines that is expected to have the broadest effect on organizational creativity. Indeed, we show that agile methods have a direct effect on organizational creative capability and on the creative outcome, and an indirect effect on the creative outcome via creative capability. Although this study was conducted in the context of the video game industry, in which creativity plays a major strategic role, it provides interesting insights into the role of agility in creative capabilities. It's possible that organizational agility extends its influence to other routines, including slack, openness, and idea management. An agile organization should find it easier to implement these organizational routines, and to evolve them to overcome difficulties encountered. This organizational routine was not part of the initial model of the foundations of creative capabilities. It emerged from the discussions and work carried out within the framework of the ANR CCO research project. It was therefore taken into account in Chapter 1 and the development of the creative capability measurement scale outlined in Chapter 7.

Idea management described in Chapter 6, which includes the routines for collecting, socializing, and evaluating ideas. The idea management described in Chapter 6, which combines the routines of collecting, socializing and evaluating ideas, appears to be the most important organizational routine for developing creative capabilities. Chapter 6 builds on the modeling of the idea flow to describe the issues and to describe the challenges and possible responses. It introduces two complementary idea management methods: informal and formal management of ideas. Developing the creativity of individuals and teams without managing ideas would be a considerable waste. Indeed, the path of ideas reveals that, after inception in an individual's mind, it undergoes a gradual process of consumption and socialization before realization. Processes, tools and devices are vital to support ideas along this path and to pinpoint the ideas that are the most relevant for organizations. Maxime Mellard's thesis on the organizational configurations of organizational creativity in video games in the video game demonstrates that this is the only condition necessary for a video game studio to produce creative games (Mellard 2020). He also identifies two sufficient organizational configurations that combine idea management, agile method, openness of the creative process, open workspace, project-based organization, and a relaxed work atmosphere. These configurations encompass a significant portion of the organizational routines constituting creative capabilities. Nevertheless, both Chapter 6 and Maxime Mellard's thesis describe multiple forms of management. Idea management does not necessarily involve a highly formalized process. The management of ideas is very different at Bosch MOP and Créhaolic; and yet, these two modes of management participate strongly in the development of the creative capabilities of these organizations. In the end, it is a question of finding the most appropriate management method for each organization, depending on its structure, culture and objectives of the organization. Additionally, it's plausible that organizational climate factors have the most significant moderating impact on these organizational routines. Future research is needed to determine the moderating role of organizational climate on idea management.

Chapter 7 introduces a measurement scale for assessing organizational creative capability. The model presented in Chapter 1 provides an understanding of what creative capability is, and Chapters 2-6 have described in detail the routines, processes and devices for managing creative capability, but it is still necessary to be able to measure it. This measurement scale is an indispensable tool for verifying its existence in organizations and diagnosing potential sources of difficulties in creative output. Creative capability was measured in a holistic way in Chapter 5 on agility by constructing a measure based on the concept of creative self-efficacy (Tierney and Farmer 2002). However, in this chapter, the aim was to introduce a scale directly derived from the Chapter 1 model, in order to obtain a measurement tool that allows for a detailed analysis of organizational creative capability. To enhance operationality, the scale combines the collection and evaluation of ideas into idea management. Constructing such a scale relies on a rigorous and very demanding methodology in terms of data collection, with a qualitative exploratory phase to refine the items from the literature review, a first quantitative data collection to purify the measurement scale, and a second and sometimes a third quantitative data collection to estimate the validity and reliability of the scale (Churchill 1979).

It is therefore essential to determine an optimum number of dimensions and items to ensure the feasibility of this collection and to maximize the validity and reliability of the measurement tool. The scale presented in this chapter is the first version of the scale before purification and verification of its validity and reliability. At the time of writing, the data collection has been completed and the analysis is still in progress. The preliminary findings are highly promising, largely affirming the model of an organization's creative capabilities, demonstrating a significant direct impact on the creative outcome. Moreover, the creative capabilities construct is quite different from the creative climate. The measurement scale is a 2nd order reflective scale, indicating that creative capability is reflected in the dimensions of the scale. Further analysis is possible from the quantitative data collected, including clustering, to determine whether there is a typology of creative firms, which will allow for a description not just of creative capability, but of the different types of creative capability that exist in organizations.

Defining and understanding the outlines of organizational creative capabilities requires any strategist to question the performance of these capabilities. The Creative Capabilities Scale predicts a significant direct effect on an organization's creative output. However, an organization's creative performance encompasses more than just the creative outcome. In Chapter 8, we initially highlighted that this performance should be comprehended through the lens of creativity management, involving a cohesive framework encompassing (1) the creativity strategy, (2) the resources allocated to creativity, (3) the norms of behavior related to creativity and (4) the organization of creative activities. Next, two tools for measuring creative performance were proposed. The first is the creativity ladder, which is inspired by Borja de Mozota's (2018) design ladder, and aims to specify the level of integration of creativity within the organization. The second tool is composed of typical KPIs, which echo the creativity ladder. Empowered by this framework and these tools, strategists should be able to assess the extent to which the resources and skills they bring to the table enable their organization to be creative.

However, this approach to the organizational creative capabilities assumes that not only the strategists are made aware of them, but also all the employees, including those occupying low-level positions in the hierarchy (Gay and Szostak 2019). Indeed, how can we consider a reflection on decision-making criteria or on behavioral norms, for example, without explaining the importance of creativity management to everyone? Communication is therefore essential, both explicitly (speeches, letters, company journals, welcome booklets, websites, etc.) and implicitly (via mimicry, among other things, companionship). Nevertheless, this communication is not a simple activity due to the existence of two poles from the sender to the receiver, the retroactivity possible from the receiver to the sender, and the disturbances of the environment leading to distortions of the message. This requires the organization to think about the organizational devices to be implemented to achieve this.

The current work environment, which has been significantly influenced by recent health crises, requires us to consider the integration of digital technology into daily professional life. How then can we make them aware of the importance of creativity? How can it be integrated into professional practices and decision-making when the actors are far from each other, for reasons such as new work organizations (telecommuting, desire to get back to nature, etc.)? What tools can be used to achieve this? A high-performing organization must also contemplate the configuration of resources and competencies that foster creativity in today's digital world and in the emerging metaverse. Consequently, evaluating its performance in this new space becomes imperative. This book on organizational creative capabilities therefore provides the first answers to better understand organizational creativity and how to develop creativity in a continuous and sustainable way in an organization. However, the research carried out in the ANR CCO project raises new questions that encourage further research on creative capabilities.

The first group of questions concerns the different types of creative capabilities. In fact, both the term creative capability in the singular and creative capabilities in the plural have been used. Both are possible, but the organizational routines approach and its measurement leads us to use the singular to characterize organizational creative capability. However, it is possible that these routines reflect the creative capability to a greater or lesser extent, thus drawing a typology of creative capabilities according to the relative weight of the routines. Finally, depending on the type of company and industry, there would be different creative capabilities.

The second group of questions revolves around potential connections between organizational routines. Even if each group of routines reflects the creative capability at a particular moment, it is not impossible that, from a dynamic point of view, we can see effects between these groups. For example, does idea management reinforce the slack? Or does organizational agility have an effect on idea management or vice versa? Modeling a temporal relational pattern between capabilities will require longitudinal studies in organizations that have acquired creative capability.

These inquiries lead to a third group of questions: is there a sequence that is more favorable than others to the construction of a creative capability?

Indeed, we understand that, given the complexity of the organizational routines to be organizational routines to be put in place, a creative capability cannot be built in one day. Which routine, or group of routines, should we start with? What would be the order of implementation to have the maximum chance of success in building a creative capability?

The Creative Capability Scale, a distinct construct from the creative climate, was originally positioned as a moderator of creative ability in our model from Chapter 1 However, this effect needs to be verified. What impacts do creative climate dimensions have on creative ability, and how does creative climate moderate the connections between organizational routines and creative outcomes? We conclude this book by announcing that it is the first part of a new collection at ISTE on organizational creativity. Other books are in progress on the dimensions of openness and idea management of creative capabilities. A book is also being written on the imaginary and symbolic productions in organizational creativity. This collection will give us the opportunity to explore new dimensions, probably in a creative way, of this fundamental and strategic component of organizations

References

Amabile T.M. (1988). A model of creativity and innovation in organizations. *Research in Organizational Behavior*, 10, 123–167.

Amit, R. and Schoemaker, P.J.H. (1993). Strategic assets and organizational rent. *Strategic Management Journal*, 14(1), 33–46.

Borja de Mozota, B. (2018). Quarante ans de recherche en design management : une revue de littérature et des pistes pour l'avenir. *Sciences du Design*, 7, 28–45.

Churchill, G. (1979). A paradigm for developing better measures of marketing constructs. *Journal of Marketing Research*, 16, 64–73.

Gay, G. and Szostak, B.L. (2019). *Innovation and Creativity in SMEs*. ISTE Ltd, London, and John Wiley & Sons, New York.

Mellard, M. (2020). L'identification d'antécédents de la créativité organisationnelle : une approche configurationnelle appliquée aux industries créatives. PhD Thesis, Université Grenoble Alpes, Grenoble.

Tierney, P. and Farmer, S.M. (2002). Creative self-efficacy: Its potential antecedents and relationship to creative performance. *Academy of Management Journal*, 45(6), 1137–1148.

List of Authors

Patrick COHENDET
HEC Montréal
Canada

Florence JEANNOT
CERAG
INSEEC
Lyon
France

Séverine LE LOARNE-LEMAIRE
Grenoble École de Management
France

Maxime MELLARD
LUMEN
Université de Lille
France

Guy PARMENTIER
CERAG
Université Grenoble Alpes
Saint-Martin-d'Hères
France

Romain RAMPA
I3-CRG
École polytechnique
Palaiseau
France

Émilie RUIZ
IREGE
Université Savoie Mont Blanc
Annecy
France

Zeinab SHEET
CERAG
Université Grenoble Alpes
Saint-Martin-d'Hères
France

Bérangère L. SZOSTAK
LAREQUOI
Université Paris-Saclay
Gif-sur-Yvette
France

Index

U, V

Other titles from

ISTE

in

Innovation, Entrepreneurship and Management

2023

BOLLINGER Sophie
Management Control and Creativity: Challenges of Managing Innovation Processes
(Smart Innovation Set – Volume 41)

BOUVIER-PATRON Paul
Frugal Innovation and Innovative Creation
(Smart Innovation Set – Volume 40)

BRASSEUR Martine, BARTOLI Annie, CHABAUD Didier, GROUIEZ Pascal, ROUET Gilles
Inclusive Territories 1: Role of Enterprises and Organizations
(Territorial Entrepreneurship and Innovation Set – Volume 1)

CASADELLA Vanessa, UZUNIDIS Dimitri
Agri-Innovations and Development Challenges: Engineering, Value Chains and Socio-economic Models
(Innovation in Engineering and Technology Set – Volume 8)

DARTIGUEPEYROU Carine, SALOFF-COSTE Michel
Futures: The Great Turn
(Innovation and Technology Set – Volume 18)

PEYROUX Élisabeth, RAIMOND Christine, VIEL Vincent, LAVIE Émilie
Development and Territorial Restructuring in an Era of Global Change: Theories, Approaches and Future Research Perspectives

SAULAIS Pierre
Knowledge and Ideation: Inventive Knowledge Analysis for Ideation Stimulation
(Innovation and Technology Set – Volume 17)

2022

AOUINAÏT Camille
Open Innovation Strategies
(Smart Innovation Set – Volume 39)

BOUCHÉ Geneviève
Productive Economy, Contributory Economy: Governance Tools for the Third Millennium
(Innovation and Technology Set – Volume 15)

BRUYÈRE Christelle
Caring Management in Health Organizations: A Lever for Crisis Management
(Health and Innovation Set – Volume 3)

HELLER David
Valuation of the Liability Structure by Real Options
(Modern Finance, Management Innovation and Economic Growth Set – Volume 5)

MATHIEU Valérie
A Customer-oriented Manager for B2B Services: Principles and Implementation

MORALES Lucía, DZEVER Sam, TAYLOR Robert
Asia-Europe Industrial Connectivity in Times of Crisis
(Innovation and Technology Set – Volume 16)

NOËL Florent, SCHMIDT Géraldine
Employability and Industrial Mutations: Between Individual Trajectories and Organizational Strategic Planning
(Technological Changes and Human Resources Set – Volume 4)

DE SAINT JULIEN Odile
The Innovation Ecosystem as a Source of Value Creation: A Value Creation Lever for Open Innovation
(Diverse and Global Perspectives on Value Creation Set – Volume 4)

SALOFF-COSTE Michel
Innovation Ecosystems: The Future of Civilizations and the Civilization of the Future
(Innovation and Technology Set – Volume 14)

VAYRE Emilie
Digitalization of Work: New Spaces and New Working Times
(Technological Changes and Human Resources Set – Volume 5)

ZAFEIRIS Konstantinos N, SKIADIS Christos H, DIMOTIKALIS Yannis, KARAGRIGORIOU Alex, KARAGRIGORIOU-VONTA Christina
Data Analysis and Related Applications 1: Computational, Algorithmic and Applied Economic Data Analysis
(Big Data, Artificial Intelligence and Data Analysis Set – Volume 9)
Data Analysis and Related Applications 2: Multivariate, Health and Demographic Data Analysis
(Big Data, Artificial Intelligence and Data Analysis Set – Volume 10)

2021

ARCADE Jacques
Strategic Engineering
(Innovation and Technology Set – Volume 11)

BÉRANGER Jérôme, RIZOULIÈRES Roland
The Digital Revolution in Health
(Health and Innovation Set – Volume 2)

BOBILLIER CHAUMON Marc-Eric
Digital Transformations in the Challenge of Activity and Work: Understanding and Supporting Technological Changes
(Technological Changes and Human Resources Set – Volume 3)

BUCLET Nicolas
Territorial Ecology and Socio-ecological Transition
(Smart Innovation Set – Volume 34)

DIMOTIKALIS Yannis, KARAGRIGORIOU Alex, PARPOULA Christina, SKIADIS Christos H
Applied Modeling Techniques and Data Analysis 1: Computational Data Analysis Methods and Tools
(Big Data, Artificial Intelligence and Data Analysis Set - Volume 7)
Applied Modeling Techniques and Data Analysis 2: Financial, Demographic, Stochastic and Statistical Models and Methods
(Big Data, Artificial Intelligence and Data Analysis Set – Volume 8)

DISPAS Christophe, KAYANAKIS Georges, SERVEL Nicolas, STRIUKOVA Ludmila
Innovation and Financial Markets
(Innovation between Risk and Reward Set – Volume 7)

ENJOLRAS Manon
Innovation and Export: The Joint Challenge of the Small Company
(Smart Innovation Set – Volume 37)

FLEURY Sylvain, RICHIR Simon
Immersive Technologies to Accelerate Innovation: How Virtual and Augmented Reality Enables the Co-Creation of Concepts
(Smart Innovation Set – Volume 38)

GIORGINI Pierre
The Contributory Revolution
(Innovation and Technology Set – Volume 13)

GOGLIN Christian
Emotions and Values in Equity Crowdfunding Investment Choices 2: Modeling and Empirical Study

GRENIER Corinne, OIRY Ewan
Altering Frontiers: Organizational Innovations in Healthcare (Health and Innovation Set – Volume 1)

GUERRIER Claudine
Security and Its Challenges in the 21st Century (Innovation and Technology Set – Volume 12)

HELLER David
Performance of Valuation Methods in Financial Transactions (Modern Finance, Management Innovation and Economic Growth Set – Volume 4)

LEHMANN Paul-Jacques
Liberalism and Capitalism Today

SOULÉ Bastien, HALLÉ Julie, VIGNAL Bénédicte, BOUTROY Éric, NIER Olivier
Innovation in Sport: Innovation Trajectories and Process Optimization (Smart Innovation Set – Volume 35)

UZUNIDIS Dimitri, KASMI Fedoua, ADATTO Laurent
Innovation Economics, Engineering and Management Handbook 1: Main Themes
Innovation Economics, Engineering and Management Handbook 2: Special Themes

VALLIER Estelle
Innovation in Clusters: Science–Industry Relationships in the Face of Forced Advancement (Smart Innovation Set – Volume 36)

2020

ACH Yves-Alain, RMADI-SAÏD Sandra
Financial Information and Brand Value: Reflections, Challenges and Limitations

ANDREOSSO-O'CALLAGHAN Bernadette, DZEVER Sam, JAUSSAUD Jacques, TAYLOR Robert
Sustainable Development and Energy Transition in Europe and Asia (Innovation and Technology Set – Volume 9)

BEN SLIMANE Sonia, M'HENNI Hatem
Entrepreneurship and Development: Realities and Future Prospects (Smart Innovation Set – Volume 30)

CHOUTEAU Marianne, FOREST Joëlle, NGUYEN Céline
Innovation for Society: The P.S.I. Approach (Smart Innovation Set – Volume 28)

CORON Clotilde
Quantifying Human Resources: Uses and Analysis (Technological Changes and Human Resources Set – Volume 2)

CORON Clotilde, GILBERT Patrick
Technological Change (Technological Changes and Human Resources Set – Volume 1)

CERDIN Jean-Luc, PERETTI Jean-Marie
The Success of Apprenticeships: Views of Stakeholders on Training and Learning (Human Resources Management Set – Volume 3)

DELCHET-COCHET Karen
Circular Economy: From Waste Reduction to Value Creation (Economic Growth Set – Volume 2)

DIDAY Edwin, GUAN Rong, SAPORTA Gilbert, WANG Huiwen
Advances in Data Science (Big Data, Artificial Intelligence and Data Analysis Set – Volume 4)

DOS SANTOS PAULINO Victor
Innovation Trends in the Space Industry
(Smart Innovation Set – Volume 25)

GASMI Nacer
Corporate Innovation Strategies: Corporate Social Responsibility and Shared Value Creation
(Smart Innovation Set – Volume 33)

GOGLIN Christian
Emotions and Values in Equity Crowdfunding Investment Choices 1: Transdisciplinary Theoretical Approach

GUILHON Bernard
Venture Capital and the Financing of Innovation
(Innovation Between Risk and Reward Set – Volume 6)

LATOUCHE Pascal
Open Innovation: Human Set-up
(Innovation and Technology Set – Volume 10)

LIMA Marcos
Entrepreneurship and Innovation Education: Frameworks and Tools
(Smart Innovation Set – Volume 32)

MACHADO Carolina, DAVIM J. Paulo
Sustainable Management for Managers and Engineers

MAKRIDES Andreas, KARAGRIGORIOU Alex, SKIADAS Christos H.
Data Analysis and Applications 3: Computational, Classification, Financial, Statistical and Stochastic Methods
(Big Data, Artificial Intelligence and Data Analysis Set – Volume 5)
Data Analysis and Applications 4: Financial Data Analysis and Methods
(Big Data, Artificial Intelligence and Data Analysis Set – Volume 6)

MASSOTTE Pierre, CORSI Patrick
Complex Decision-Making in Economy and Finance

MEUNIER François-Xavier
Dual Innovation Systems: Concepts, Tools and Methods
(Smart Innovation Set – Volume 31)

MICHAUD Thomas
Science Fiction and Innovation Design
(Innovation in Engineering and Technology Set – Volume 6)

MONINO Jean-Louis
Data Control: Major Challenge for the Digital Society
(Smart Innovation Set – Volume 29)

MORLAT Clément
Sustainable Productive System: Eco-development versus Sustainable Development (Smart Innovation Set – Volume 26)

SAULAIS Pierre, ERMINE Jean-Louis
Knowledge Management in Innovative Companies 2: Understanding and Deploying a KM Plan within a Learning Organization
(Smart Innovation Set – Volume 27)

2019

AMENDOLA Mario, GAFFARD Jean-Luc
Disorder and Public Concern Around Globalization

BARBAROUX Pierre
Disruptive Technology and Defence Innovation Ecosystems
(Innovation in Engineering and Technology Set – Volume 5)

DOU Henri, JUILLET Alain, CLERC Philippe
Strategic Intelligence for the Future 1: A New Strategic and Operational Approach
Strategic Intelligence for the Future 2: A New Information Function Approach

FRIKHA Azza
Measurement in Marketing: Operationalization of Latent Constructs

FRIMOUSSE Soufyane
Innovation and Agility in the Digital Age
(Human Resources Management Set – Volume 2)

GAY Claudine, SZOSTAK Bérangère L.
Innovation and Creativity in SMEs: Challenges, Evolutions and Prospects (Smart Innovation Set – Volume 21)

GORIA Stéphane, HUMBERT Pierre, ROUSSEL Benoît
Information, Knowledge and Agile Creativity (Smart Innovation Set – Volume 22)

HELLER David
Investment Decision-making Using Optional Models (Economic Growth Set – Volume 2)

HELLER David, DE CHADIRAC Sylvain, HALAOUI Lana, JOUVET Camille
The Emergence of Start-ups (Economic Growth Set – Volume 1)

HÉRAUD Jean-Alain, KERR Fiona, BURGER-HELMCHEN Thierry
Creative Management of Complex Systems (Smart Innovation Set – Volume 19)

LATOUCHE Pascal
Open Innovation: Corporate Incubator (Innovation and Technology Set – Volume 7)

LEHMANN Paul-Jacques
The Future of the Euro Currency

LEIGNEL Jean-Louis, MENAGER Emmanuel, YABLONSKY Serge
Sustainable Enterprise Performance: A Comprehensive Evaluation Method

LIÈVRE Pascal, AUBRY Monique, GAREL Gilles
Management of Extreme Situations: From Polar Expeditions to Exploration-Oriented Organizations

MILLOT Michel
Embarrassment of Product Choices 2: Towards a Society of Well-being

N'GOALA Gilles, PEZ-PÉRARD Virginie, PRIM-ALLAZ Isabelle
Augmented Customer Strategy: CRM in the Digital Age

NIKOLOVA Blagovesta
The RRI Challenge: Responsibilization in a State of Tension with Market Regulation
(Innovation and Responsibility Set – Volume 3)

PELLEGRIN-BOUCHER Estelle, ROY Pierre
Innovation in the Cultural and Creative Industries
(Innovation and Technology Set – Volume 8)

PRIOLON Joël
Financial Markets for Commodities

QUINIOU Matthieu
Blockchain: The Advent of Disintermediation

RAVIX Joël-Thomas, DESCHAMPS Marc
Innovation and Industrial Policies
(Innovation between Risk and Reward Set – Volume 5)

ROGER Alain, VINOT Didier
Skills Management: New Applications, New Questions
(Human Resources Management Set – Volume 1)

SAULAIS Pierre, ERMINE Jean-Louis
Knowledge Management in Innovative Companies 1: Understanding and Deploying a KM Plan within a Learning Organization
(Smart Innovation Set – Volume 23)

SERVAJEAN-HILST Romaric
Co-innovation Dynamics: The Management of Client-Supplier Interactions for Open Innovation
(Smart Innovation Set – Volume 20)

SKIADAS Christos H., BOZEMAN James R.
Data Analysis and Applications 1: Clustering and Regression, Modeling-estimating, Forecasting and Data Mining
(Big Data, Artificial Intelligence and Data Analysis Set – Volume 2)
Data Analysis and Applications 2: Utilization of Results in Europe and Other Topics
(Big Data, Artificial Intelligence and Data Analysis Set – Volume 3)

UZUNIDIS Dimitri
Systemic Innovation: Entrepreneurial Strategies and Market Dynamics

VIGEZZI Michel
World Industrialization: Shared Inventions, Competitive Innovations and Social Dynamics
(Smart Innovation Set – Volume 24)

2018

BURKHARDT Kirsten
Private Equity Firms: Their Role in the Formation of Strategic Alliances

CALLENS Stéphane
Creative Globalization
(Smart Innovation Set – Volume 16)

CASADELLA Vanessa
Innovation Systems in Emerging Economies: MINT – Mexico, Indonesia, Nigeria, Turkey
(Smart Innovation Set – Volume 18)

CHOUTEAU Marianne, FOREST Joëlle, NGUYEN Céline
Science, Technology and Innovation Culture
(Innovation in Engineering and Technology Set – Volume 3)

CORLOSQUET-HABART Marine, JANSSEN Jacques
Big Data for Insurance Companies
(Big Data, Artificial Intelligence and Data Analysis Set – Volume 1)

CROS Françoise
Innovation and Society
(Smart Innovation Set – Volume 15)

DEBREF Romain
Environmental Innovation and Ecodesign: Certainties and Controversies
(Smart Innovation Set – Volume 17)

DOMINGUEZ Noémie
SME Internationalization Strategies: Innovation to Conquer New Markets

ERMINE Jean-Louis
Knowledge Management: The Creative Loop
(Innovation and Technology Set – Volume 5)

GILBERT Patrick, BOBADILLA Natalia, GASTALDI Lise,
LE BOULAIRE Martine, LELEBINA Olga
Innovation, Research and Development Management

IBRAHIMI Mohammed
Mergers & Acquisitions: Theory, Strategy, Finance

LEMAÎTRE Denis
Training Engineers for Innovation

LÉVY Aldo, BEN BOUHENI Faten, AMMI Chantal
Financial Management: USGAAP and IFRS Standards
(Innovation and Technology Set – Volume 6)

MILLOT Michel
Embarrassment of Product Choices 1: How to Consume Differently

PANSERA Mario, OWEN Richard
Innovation and Development: The Politics at the Bottom of the Pyramid
(Innovation and Responsibility Set – Volume 2)

RICHEZ Yves
Corporate Talent Detection and Development

SACHETTI Philippe, ZUPPINGER Thibaud
New Technologies and Branding
(Innovation and Technology Set – Volume 4)

SAMIER Henri
Intuition, Creativity, Innovation

TEMPLE Ludovic, COMPAORÉ SAWADOGO Eveline M.F.W.
Innovation Processes in Agro-Ecological Transitions in Developing Countries
(Innovation in Engineering and Technology Set – Volume 2)

UZUNIDIS Dimitri
Collective Innovation Processes: Principles and Practices
(Innovation in Engineering and Technology Set – Volume 4)

VAN HOOREBEKE Delphine
The Management of Living Beings or Emo-management

2017

AÏT-EL-HADJ Smaïl
The Ongoing Technological System
(Smart Innovation Set – Volume 11)

BAUDRY Marc, DUMONT Béatrice
Patents: Prompting or Restricting Innovation?
(Smart Innovation Set – Volume 12)

BÉRARD Céline, TEYSSIER Christine
Risk Management: Lever for SME Development and Stakeholder Value Creation

CHALENÇON Ludivine
Location Strategies and Value Creation of International Mergers and Acquisitions

CHAUVEL Danièle, BORZILLO Stefano
The Innovative Company: An Ill-defined Object
(Innovation between Risk and Reward Set – Volume 1)

CORSI Patrick
Going Past Limits To Growth

D'ANDRIA Aude, GABARRET Inés
Building 21st Century Entrepreneurship
(Innovation and Technology Set – Volume 2)

DAIDJ Nabyla
Cooperation, Coopetition and Innovation
(Innovation and Technology Set – Volume 3)

FERNEZ-WALCH Sandrine
The Multiple Facets of Innovation Project Management
(Innovation between Risk and Reward Set – Volume 4)

FOREST Joëlle
Creative Rationality and Innovation
(Smart Innovation Set – Volume 14)

GUILHON Bernard
Innovation and Production Ecosystems
(Innovation between Risk and Reward Set – Volume 2)

HAMMOUDI Abdelhakim, DAIDJ Nabyla
Game Theory Approach to Managerial Strategies and Value Creation
(Diverse and Global Perspectives on Value Creation Set – Volume 3)

LALLEMENT Rémi
Intellectual Property and Innovation Protection: New Practices and New Policy Issues
(Innovation between Risk and Reward Set – Volume 3)

LAPERCHE Blandine
Enterprise Knowledge Capital
(Smart Innovation Set – Volume 13)

LEBERT Didier, EL YOUNSI Hafida
International Specialization Dynamics
(Smart Innovation Set – Volume 9)

MAESSCHALCK Marc
Reflexive Governance for Research and Innovative Knowledge
(Responsible Research and Innovation Set – Volume 6)

MASSOTTE Pierre
Ethics in Social Networking and Business 1: Theory, Practice and Current Recommendations
Ethics in Social Networking and Business 2: The Future and Changing Paradigms

MASSOTTE Pierre, CORSI Patrick
Smart Decisions in Complex Systems

MEDINA Mercedes, HERRERO Mónica, URGELLÉS Alicia
Current and Emerging Issues in the Audiovisual Industry
(Diverse and Global Perspectives on Value Creation Set – Volume 1)

MICHAUD Thomas
Innovation, Between Science and Science Fiction
(Smart Innovation Set – Volume 10)

PELLÉ Sophie
Business, Innovation and Responsibility
(Responsible Research and Innovation Set – Volume 7)

SAVIGNAC Emmanuelle
The Gamification of Work: The Use of Games in the Workplace

SUGAHARA Satoshi, DAIDJ Nabyla, USHIO Sumitaka
Value Creation in Management Accounting and Strategic Management: An Integrated Approach
(Diverse and Global Perspectives on Value Creation Set –Volume 2)

UZUNIDIS Dimitri, SAULAIS Pierre
Innovation Engines: Entrepreneurs and Enterprises in a Turbulent World
(Innovation in Engineering and Technology Set – Volume 1)

2016

BARBAROUX Pierre, ATTOUR Amel, SCHENK Eric
Knowledge Management and Innovation
(Smart Innovation Set – Volume 6)

BEN BOUHENI Faten, AMMI Chantal, LEVY Aldo
Banking Governance, Performance And Risk-Taking: Conventional Banks Vs Islamic Banks

BOUTILLIER Sophie, CARRÉ Denis, LEVRATTO Nadine
Entrepreneurial Ecosystems
(Smart Innovation Set – Volume 2)

BOUTILLIER Sophie, UZUNIDIS Dimitri
The Entrepreneur
(Smart Innovation Set – Volume 8)

BOUVARD Patricia, SUZANNE Hervé
Collective Intelligence Development in Business

GALLAUD Delphine, LAPERCHE Blandine
Circular Economy, Industrial Ecology and Short Supply Chains
(Smart Innovation Set – Volume 4)

GUERRIER Claudine
Security and Privacy in the Digital Era
(Innovation and Technology Set – Volume 1)

MEGHOUAR Hicham
Corporate Takeover Targets

MONINO Jean-Louis, SEDKAOUI Soraya
Big Data, Open Data and Data Development
(Smart Innovation Set – Volume 3)

MOREL Laure, LE ROUX Serge
Fab Labs: Innovative User
(Smart Innovation Set – Volume 5)

PICARD Fabienne, TANGUY Corinne
Innovations and Techno-ecological Transition
(Smart Innovation Set – Volume 7)

2015

CASADELLA Vanessa, LIU Zeting, DIMITRI Uzunidis
Innovation Capabilities and Economic Development in Open Economies
(Smart Innovation Set – Volume 1)

CORSI Patrick, MORIN Dominique
Sequencing Apple's DNA

CORSI Patrick, NEAU Erwan
Innovation Capability Maturity Model

FAIVRE-TAVIGNOT Bénédicte
Social Business and Base of the Pyramid

GODÉ Cécile
Team Coordination in Extreme Environments

MAILLARD Pierre
Competitive Quality and Innovation

MASSOTTE Pierre, CORSI Patrick
Operationalizing Sustainability

MASSOTTE Pierre, CORSI Patrick
Sustainability Calling

2014

DUBÉ Jean, LEGROS Diègo
Spatial Econometrics Using Microdata

LESCA Humbert, LESCA Nicolas
Strategic Decisions and Weak Signals

2013

HABART-CORLOSQUET Marine, JANSSEN Jacques, MANCA Raimondo
VaR Methodology for Non-Gaussian Finance

2012

DAL PONT Jean-Pierre
Process Engineering and Industrial Management

MAILLARD Pierre
Competitive Quality Strategies

POMEROL Jean-Charles
Decision-Making and Action

SZYLAR Christian
UCITS Handbook

2011

LESCA Nicolas
Environmental Scanning and Sustainable Development

LESCA Nicolas, LESCA Humbert
Weak Signals for Strategic Intelligence: Anticipation Tool for Managers

MERCIER-LAURENT Eunika
Innovation Ecosystems

2010

SZYLAR Christian
Risk Management under UCITS III/IV

2009

COHEN Corine
Business Intelligence

ZANINETTI Jean-Marc
Sustainable Development in the USA

2008

CORSI Patrick, DULIEU Mike
The Marketing of Technology Intensive Products and Services

DZEVER Sam, JAUSSAUD Jacques, ANDREOSSO Bernadette
Evolving Corporate Structures and Cultures in Asia: Impact of Globalization

2007

AMMI Chantal
Global Consumer Behavior

2006

BOUGHZALA Imed, ERMINE Jean-Louis
Trends in Enterprise Knowledge Management

CORSI Patrick, CHRISTOFOL Hervé, RICHIR Simon, SAMIER Henri
Innovation Engineering: the power of intangible networks

Printed and bound by CPI Group (UK) Ltd, Croydon, CR0 4YY

28/07/2026

14931340-0002